TROUBLEMA~~~~

The construction c
families' as a soci~

Stephen Crossley

C000102726

P

First published in Great Britain in 2018 by

Policy Press
University of Bristol
1-9 Old Park Hill
Bristol
BS2 8BB
UK
t: +44 (0)117 954 5940
pp-info@bristol.ac.uk
www.policypress.co.uk

North America office:
Policy Press
c/o The University of Chicago Press
1427 East 60th Street
Chicago, IL 60637, USA
t: +1 773 702 7700
f: +1 773-702-9756
sales@press.uchicago.edu
www.press.uchicago.edu

© Policy Press 2018

British Library Cataloguing in Publication Data
A catalogue record for this book is available from the British Library

Library of Congress Cataloging-in-Publication Data
A catalog record for this book has been requested

ISBN 978-1-4473-3474-3 paperback
ISBN 978-1-4473-3472-9 hardcover
ISBN 978-1-4473-3475-0 ePub
ISBN 978-1-4473-3476-7 Mobi
ISBN 978-1-4473-3473-6 ePdf

The right of Stephen Crossley to be identified as author of this work has been asserted by him in accordance with the Copyright, Designs and Patents Act 1988.

The statements and opinions contained within this publication are solely those of the author and not of the University of Bristol or Policy Press. The University of Bristol and Policy Press disclaim responsibility for any injury to persons or property resulting from any material published in this publication.

Policy Press works to counter discrimination on grounds of gender, race, disability, age and sexuality.

Cover design by Liron Gilenberg
Front cover image: Getty
Printed and bound in Great Britain by CMP, Poole
Policy Press uses environmentally responsible print partners

For Harriet, Daisy and Sam

Contents

List of acronyms

ASB	anti-social behaviour
ASBO	Anti-Social Behaviour Order
ASBU	Anti-Social Behaviour Unit
COS	Charity Organisation Society
CSM	Children's Services Manager
DCC	Dundee City Council
DCLG	Department for Communities and Local Government
DFP	Dundee Families Project
DWP	Department for Work and Pensions
ESA	Employment Support Allowance
FIP	Family Intervention Project
FW	Family Worker
IEA	Institute for Economic Affairs
IFSP	Intensive Family Support Project
IPPR	Institute for Public Policy Research
JSA	Jobseeker's Allowance
PAC	Public Accounts Committee
PbR	Payment by Results
RTF	Respect Task Force
SETF	Social Exclusion Task Force
SEU	Social Exclusion Unit
TFP	Troubled Families Programme
WFE	Working Families Everywhere

Acknowledgements

Much of the research undertaken for this book was carried out while I was studying for a PhD, in the School of Applied Social Sciences at Durham University. The PhD research was funded by an Economic and Social Research Council PhD Studentship. I would like to thank the Economic and Social Research Council (ESRC) for their support and I trust that they approve of the approach I have taken in pursuit of 'impact'. During the four years that I was doing my PhD I received support and advice from so many people, and I hope I can thank many of them here. The list below is not exhaustive and there are many people who I have not thanked by name here, but who have provided me with support, encouragement and inspiration. I hope I can return these gifts one day.

The first person I spoke to at Durham University about applying for funding was Maggie O'Neill, who provided me with immediate encouragement and support. Colleagues in the School of Applied Social Sciences (SASS) have continued and augmented that support. Kate O'Brien and Ian Greener were helpful reviewers, reminding me it was 'only a PhD', and urging me to clarify and remember whose side I was on. Helen Charnley calmly steered me through my ethical approval process. Fiona Bonar was, and probably still is, the best Postgraduate Secretary a student could wish for. Many other colleagues in SASS, staff and students alike, provided support, encouragement and opportunities to discuss issues and explore challenges over the course of the thesis. Thank you to all of you.

I could not have wished for better PhD supervisors than Roger Smith and Lena Dominelli. I cannot speak highly enough of Roger, who has provided me with brilliant support, guidance and wisdom ever since he agreed to be my primary supervisor. I owe him a lot and when I eventually grow up, I would like to be like him. At my first meeting, Lena encouraged me to write something for a publication, and suggested reading to me that would prove pivotal in shaping my thoughts and approach to the thesis. This level of support was maintained throughout my period of study and has continued since I graduated.

Outside of Durham, I have been incredibly lucky enough to have received the support and interest of many colleagues. Viv Cree, Brid Featherstone, Liam Foster, Val Gillies, Deb Harrison, Tracey Jensen, Majella Kilkey, Linda McKie, Kate Morris, Ted Schrecker, Anna Tarrant, Jenny Thatcher, Jane Tunstill, Aniela Wenham and Rob

Wilson invited me to speak at events at various stages of my studies and supported my work in many other ways as well. In addition, Anne Brunton, Danny Dorling, Brid Featherstone, Jo Finch, John Hudson, Jadwiga Leigh, David McKendrick, Sadie Parr and Charlotte Pell all encouraged or invited me to write various pieces, chapters or articles relating to 'troubled families'. Will McMahon and his colleagues at the Centre for Crime and Justice Studies deserve special mention for encouraging me to write a report about the Troubled Families Programme for a non-academic audience and subsequently organising a conference on the programme. Kim Allen, Vic Armstrong, Matt Barnes, Michaela Benson, Sue Bond-Taylor, Jonathan Bradshaw, Jacqui Close, Ros Edwards, Kayleigh Garthwaite, David Greig, Kathryn Hollingsworth, Steph Lawler, Ruth Levitas, Rob Macdonald, John Macnicol, Lisa McKenzie, Gerry Mooney, Kirsty Morrin, Aoife Nolan, Ruth Patrick, Jonathan Portes, Tracy Shildrick, Adrian Sinfield, Tom Slater, Imogen Tyler, John Veit-Wilson and John Welshman have all provided exceptional moral and/or intellectual support in different ways. Michael Lambert, the future of history, has been immense throughout and was the ideal PhD partner. Dan Silver has been supportive in numerous ways, not least in providing the inspiration for the cover of the book. Again, I thank you all.

My family haven't been bad either. I owe my mam and dad, and my sister and Paul more than could ever be articulated here, but acknowledging all your help and support during the last four years is a good place to start. Angus, Anna, George and Dominic and Ian and Maggie provided food and shelter during periods of fieldwork, and much more besides. Charlie and Sally also put me up and put up with me on my way to work. Gill Crozier was a wonderful Bourdieusian host and discussant as well. Most importantly, and aside from all the specific help during my study and work, spending time and having discussions with family and friends helped to keep personal challenges in perspective, while reinforcing the importance of some of the work I try to contribute to and be part of. Harriet, Daisy and Sam, quite simply I could not have done this without you. You are the most amazing source of inspiration and support to me. I have enjoyed, and benefitted immensely from, our many family discussions on Bourdieu. I know you have too ... Harriet in particular deserves thanks for not only tolerating me spending too much time with French sociologists, but also listening to me, and correcting me, when I attempted to discuss them with her. Harriet also does a good line in choosing book names and book covers.

Alison Shaw, Rebecca Tomlinson and Jessica Miles at Policy Press have been supportive, patient and helpful throughout the process of writing the book. I'd like to thank them, and their colleagues, for their interest in my work, and for the opportunity to share it with a wider audience.

Finally, and most importantly, I would like to acknowledge and thank the individuals who agreed to participate in research, and those who agreed to provide institutional support for the study. In addition to those who participated formally through interviews in three local authority areas, referred to here as Northton, Southborough and Westingham, I was contacted by many people working on the Troubled Families Programme who shared information and interesting leads with me because of their concerns. The research could not have taken place, or developed in the way it has, without the goodwill and support of these people. I do not doubt that some of my research participants may disagree with my interpretation and theorising of the discussions we had, and with my wider critical perspective on the implementation of the programme. Where this is the case, I hope that I have not misrepresented their views, and that they can at least appreciate the positions I have taken.

ONE

Introduction:
'Looking for trouble'

> Politics is the art of looking for trouble, finding it
> everywhere, diagnosing it wrongly, and applying unsuitable
> remedies. (Sir Ernest Benn)

In August 2011, riots took place in towns and cities across England,
sparked by the police shooting and killing of Mark Duggan on 4
August. An already tense situation erupted when members of a peaceful
protest march on 6 August, involving Duggan's friends and family,
became disillusioned with police responses to their requests for senior
officers to provide them with information about what happened during
the shooting. Those requests fell on deaf ears. Rioting and looting
took place in Tottenham that evening and then spread to other parts
of London in the following days and other towns and cities after that.
By 15 August, more than 3000 people had been arrested, with more
than 1000 criminal charges issued in relation to the riots.

Many prominent politicians and media commentators were quick
to highlight that structural causes such as poverty, unemployment and
racism were not to blame in any way for the riots. The then Home
Secretary Theresa May highlighted the 'violent gang culture [that]
exists in so many of our towns and cities' and argued that 'the only
cause of a crime is a criminal' (May, 2011). The Justice Secretary Ken
Clarke (2011) stated in a column for the *Guardian* that what he 'found
most disturbing was the sense that the hardcore of rioters came from
a feral underclass, cut off from the mainstream in everything but its
materialism'. The *Daily Mail* columnist Melanie Phillips (2011) argued
that not only were the children feral, but so were their parents. The
prime minister at the time, David Cameron (2011a), in a 'fightback
speech' following the end of the riots, pre-empted the findings of any
future inquiries, stating:

> So as we begin the necessary processes of inquiry,
> investigation, listening and learning: let's be clear. These
> riots were not about race: the perpetrators and the victims
> were white, black and Asian. These riots were not about

government cuts: they were directed at high street stores, not Parliament. And these riots were not about poverty: that insults the millions of people who, whatever the hardship, would never dream of making others suffer like this.

No, this was about behaviour, people showing indifference to right and wrong, people with a twisted moral code, people with a complete absence of self-restraint. They were about people with a twisted moral code.

Cameron argued that the 'broken society' agenda was 'back at the top of my agenda', thus re-invigorating a favoured trope of the Conservatives in opposition, one that had been marginalised by the focus on austerity once they entered government in 2010. The idea of a broken society – a policy focus on the alleged behavioural failings of the poorest and most disadvantaged members of society – had been promulgated by the Centre for Social Justice (CSJ), a right-wing thinktank established by Iain Duncan Smith following his 'Easterhouse epiphany'. Aided by supportive sections of the media and Conservative politicians, it popularised the idea of five, largely behavioural, 'pathways to poverty': family breakdown, educational failure, worklessness and economic dependence, addictions, and indebtedness – which focus on individual behaviours and conveniently ignore structural issues (CSJ, 2007).

The issues of family breakdown and 'worklessness' were central to the government's analysis of the causes of the riots. In his fightback speech, Cameron (2011a) said he did not doubt that 'many of the rioters out last week have no father at home', suggesting that:

> Perhaps they come from one of the neighbourhoods where it's standard for children to have a mum and not a dad, where it's normal for young men to grow up without a male role model, looking to the streets for their father figures, filled up with rage and anger.

He went on to say that 'if we want to have any hope of mending our broken society, family and parenting is where we've got to start.' Making good on this commitment, Cameron stated that a previous 'light-touch', volunteer-led *Big Society* approach to working with the country's 'most troubled families' – 'the ones that everyone in their neighbourhood knows and often avoids' – would be speeded up.

In December 2011, Cameron (2011b) launched a new Troubled Families Programme (TFP), a single central government programme that aimed to meet his ambition of 'turning around' the lives of 120,000 'troubled families' before the end of the parliament in May 2015. With the launch of the programme, Cameron – and his government – effectively created a new and *official* social problem, and he wanted people to know what he meant when he talked about 'troubled families':

> Let me be clear what I mean by this phrase. Officialdom might call them 'families with multiple disadvantages'. Some in the press might call them 'neighbours from hell'. Whatever you call them, we've known for years that a relatively small number of families are the source of a large proportion of the problems in society. Drug addiction. Alcohol abuse. Crime. A culture of disruption and irresponsibility that cascades through generations.

The prime minister not only conflated poor families experiencing disadvantage with poorly behaved families in popularising the term 'troubled families', his government also published criteria for what a 'troubled family' looked like, how many of them could be found in each local authority area in England, and what it would take to consider their lives to be 'turned around'. The fact that these families could be 'counted' and could be identified on the basis of meeting at least two out of three national criteria (crime and/or anti-social behaviour, truancy or school exclusion, and 'worklessness'), and one locally decided indicator, brought them to life in the eyes of the public and the media. The government used existing research carried out on families experiencing multiple structural disadvantages such as poverty, material deprivation, low skills and poor quality housing to 'prove' the existence of troubled families characterised by crime, anti-social behaviour, truancy and worklessness. 'Troubled families' were, in the first phase of the programme alone, also associated with a much wider range of 'problems' including drug and alcohol addiction, domestic violence, child abuse and poor physical and mental health, gang membership, radical extremism and organised crime.

A second phase of the programme, expanding its reach to 400,000 more families and beginning officially in May 2015, was announced in June 2013, barely 12 months after the programme had started in earnest. The detail on these new families was announced over a year later in August 2014. 'Troubled families' in the second phase of the programme would, in addition to the three criteria from Phase 1, also specifically target those families that experienced health problems; where domestic violence was present; that had a child or children in need; and that were experiencing financial exclusion. Despite the new and expanded criteria, the 'troubled families' moniker remained and the newly-found 'troubled families' were presented as evidence of a 'new underclass' by *The Sunday Times* (Hellen, 2014: 1). In April 2017, and with Theresa May prime minister, the 'next phase' of the TFP was announced, which intended to focus on workless families, and the allegedly associated issues of 'parental conflict' and 'problem debt' (DCLG, 2017a).

At the heart of the TFP, throughout these phases, and regardless of the presenting issues of the families involved, has been the emphasis on a whole family approach called 'family intervention'. This model involves a single key worker or 'troubleshooter' working with all family members, purportedly in an intensive way, helping them to address, and take responsibility for, their own issues. There is a strong rhetorical focus on workers who are able to 'get through the front door' and into the family home to work with the family 'from the inside out' (DCLG, 2012a: 4). Much of the putative success of the programme is credited to the 'persistent, assertive and challenging' workers who are prepared to 'walk in the shoes of these families every day' (DCLG, 2012a: 4). Good family intervention workers '"grip" the family, their problems and the surrounding agencies and are seen to be standing alongside the families, their difficulties and the process being put in place' (DCLG, 2012a: 18). Louise Casey, the senior civil servant who was placed in charge of the TFP by Cameron prior to its launch, described the approach thus:

> The beauty in this programme is that it starts with what's happening in the families—why they cause the problems they have and why they have the problems they have. We work back from that in how we then tackle the system. (Public Accounts Committee, 2014: 45)

'Tackling the system' has also been central to the 'troubled families' agenda, with the TFP positioned as a response not just to the problem of 'troubled families' themselves, but also to the problem of the state services that had failed to address their problematic behaviours. Following the riots, Cameron (2011a) had spoken at length about the need to fix a broken welfare system that apparently encouraged this bad behaviour and irresponsibility:

> For years we've had a system that encourages the worst in people – that incites laziness, that excuses bad behaviour, that erodes self-discipline, that discourages hard work, above

all that drains responsibility away from people. We talk about moral hazard in our financial system – where banks think they can act recklessly because the state will always bail them out. Well this is moral hazard in our welfare system – people thinking they can be as irresponsible as they like because the state will always bail them out.

Exactly four months later at the official launch of the TFP, this theme continued, with Cameron (2011b) arguing that 'troubled families are already pulled and prodded and poked a dozen times a week by government' and suggesting that 'one of the reasons for their dysfunction is their hatred of "the system" which they experience as faceless, disjointed and intrusive'. Subsequent phases of the programme have played up the 'service transformation' and the better 'integration' of local services that has allegedly occurred under the TFP (see, for example, DCLG, 2016a, 2017a), especially in light of negative findings surrounding the actual impact of the programme on the families concerned.

The programme was to be, and still is, delivered in England alone, and all 152 local authorities across England 'signed up' to deliver the programme in 2012. The then Communities Secretary, Eric Pickles, stated that 'the fast and unanimous level of take-up shows that the Government has got the confidence of local councils that together we can tackle a problem that councils have long grappled with' (DCLG, 2012b). Local authorities receive funding on a Payment by Results (PbR) basis, although, again, the workings of the process have changed over time. In Phase 1, initial 'attachment' funding was paid to councils for each 'troubled family' they started working with and the remainder being paid once certain behavioural change thresholds had been met. The proportion of funding available as an attachment fee was 80 per cent in the first year, reducing to 60 per cent and 40 per cent in the second and third years (DCLG, 2012c: 8), thereby encouraging local authorities to start working with families early in the programme. In order for a local authority to claim funding for a family that they had 'turned around': juvenile crime had to decrease by at least 33 per cent; anti-social behaviour across the family had to decrease by at least 60 per cent; and school attendance for each child in the household had to be above 85 per cent; and adults had to demonstrate 'progress to work' by 'volunteering' for the Work Programme; or an adult in the family had to move off out of work benefits and into continuous employment for over 6 months (DCLG, 2012c: 9). Hence, if an adult entered 'continuous employment' for 6 months, local authorities could claim they had 'turned around' the entire family, no matter what progress, or lack of it, had been made on other issues. Other potential improvements in the family's circumstances, such as reduction of debt, increased household income and/or reduction of poverty, cessation of domestic violence, or improved housing conditions, were not recognised by the PbR process. The evaluation of the first phase of the TFP found that the 'PbR financial framework and targets were contentious in many local areas and were thought to have resulted in certain perverse incentives' (Day et al, 2016: 69).

The second phase of the programme saw the PbR mechanism shift towards rewarding councils where families made 'significant and sustained progress' or achieved 'continuous employment' against issues they presented with on entry to the programme. This was intended to recognise the existence and importance of wider issues that were often present in some families, but a council would still be rewarded if an adult in the family came off out of work benefits for a sustained period, no matter what their progress, or lack of it, against all other indicators. A review of the PbR process was announced as part of the change of focus of the TFP in April 2017. This review was to assess 'alternative funding models against three reform principles: sustainable service reform and integration (beyond the lifetime of the programme); an enhanced focus on parental worklessness; and deliverability by local authorities' (DCLG, 2017a: 23–4).

Progress in the first phase of the programme (December 2011–May 2015) was remarkable, according to the government. By December 2014, over 85,000 'troubled families' had been 'turned around', with almost all of the 117,910 'troubled families' (rounded up to 120,000) identified by local authorities. Incredibly, a number of local authorities had identified, worked with and 'turned around' exactly the number of 'troubled families' identified for them by the government. In March 2015, the number of 'turned around' 'troubled families' was over 105,000 and around one-third of the local authorities involved in delivering the programme had, according to the government's published figures, apparently perfect records in identifying, working with and 'turning around' their 'troubled families'. In June 2015, the government announced that the first phase of the TFP successfully 'turned around' 99% of the 120,000 'troubled families' within the timescale that the prime minister had laid out in December 2011. All of this 'success' occurred at a time of national austerity, with wide ranging cuts to public services and welfare 'reforms' which often made people living in poverty even poorer (see, for example, De Agostini et al, 2014; Beatty and Fothergill, 2016).

These claims received relatively little scrutiny with much of the mainstream press content to re-publish the figures and help to perpetuate the stereotype of poor families as a badly-behaved burden on 'hard-working families' and other 'taxpayers'. A small number of researchers and journalists found these claims hard to believe. Paul Spicker (2013) highlighted that the government figures were not 'official statistics' and were therefore not subject to scrutiny by the UK Statistics Authority. Jonathan Portes (2015) doubted that the 'North Korean Statistical Office would have the cheek' to claim a 99 per cent success rate for a social policy programme. Patrick Butler (2015) and Anna Bawden (2015) wrote articles for the *Guardian* highlighting the 'miraculous success' of the TFP and querying whether or not it was 'too good to be true'. The Centre for Crime and Justice Studies published a report mocking the government's implied claim that the TFP was the 'perfect social policy' (Crossley, 2015).

In August 2016, *BBC Newsnight* announced that the official evaluation of the first phase of the TFP had been 'suppressed', claiming that it showed that the programme had '"no discernible" effect on unemployment, truancy or criminality' (Cook, 2016). In September, the Public Accounts Committee (PAC) announced an inquiry into the TFP and, in October 2016, the day before the inquiry was due to hear oral evidence, the official evaluation of the first phase was published. The evaluation comprised a number of different documents examining the programme from different perspectives, including the views of the families, the approach of local authorities to implementing the programme, and characteristics of families. The national impact study report, examining the difference that the programme had made, provided a damning indictment of its proclaimed 'success':

> The key finding is that across a wide range of outcomes, covering the key headline objectives of the programme – employment, benefit receipt, school attendance, safeguarding and child welfare – we were unable to find consistent evidence that the Troubled Families Programme had any significant or systematic impact. That is to say, our analysis found no impact on these outcomes attributable to the programme. The vast majority of impact estimates were statistically insignificant, with a very small number of positive or negative results. These results are consistent with those found by the separate and independent impact analysis using survey data, which also found no significant or systemic impact on outcomes related to employment,

job seeking, school attendance, or anti-social behaviour.
(Bewley et al, 2016: 20)

The government claimed that the lack of evidence of impact was as a result of the timing of the research, the design of the survey and problems with how the data was collected and analysed (Public Accounts Committee, 2016a). However, another stream of the evaluation – a survey of families that had either been involved with the programme for nine months or those that were about to start on the programme – reached largely similar conclusions:

> The survey analysis suggests that – across nearly all the outcome measures collected – the Troubled Families group did not have statistically significantly better outcomes in the three months prior to the interview than the matched comparison group. (Purdon and Bryson, 2016: 9)

Despite the criticisms and concerns that were levelled at the TFP throughout its first phase, and the controversy that that surrounded the publication of the official evaluation, it was announced in February 2017 that the TFP would be 'rebooted' (Savage, 2017) and, in April 2017, details on the 'next phase' of the TFP, which would 'continue the evolution' (DCLG, 2017a: 9) were announced. The remainder of this book traces and critiques the emergence and subsequent evolution of the 'troubled families' story in more detail.

Research approach

An obvious starting point for research examining the TFP would be to, as the government has done, 'start with what's happening in the families' (Public Accounts Committee, 2014: 27) and interview 'troubled families' to gain a better understanding of how they construct and represent their own lives. Making 'troubled families' themselves the subject of the research, however, runs the risk of accepting and endorsing them as 'the problem' to be examined and scrutinised. Such an approach would be in keeping with the government's trope that it is necessary to 'get in through the front door' in order to understand the problems that 'troubled families' face – a clear case of social science doing 'little more than ratify[ing] a social problem produced by the state' (Bourdieu et al, 1994: 2).

Similarly, a narrow focus on the frontline workers involved in the delivery of the programme may appear to support the view that it is individual workers who can make the difference, ignoring the structural conditions and bureaucratic environments in which they operate, and the forces they are subjected to. This approach could 'under-theorise the state and its role in generating and sustaining patterns of "othering"' and support the thesis that the 'resolution of issues' can be almost 'entirely displaced onto micro-encounters' (Garrett, 2013: 182), such as those that take place between the family worker and members of 'troubled families'.

Both of these approaches have merit, but the intention here is to look primarily in a different direction. If the TFP starts with the families and works backwards and looks at the families 'from inside out rather than outside in' (DCLG, 2012a: 26), this book draws on research that 'bends the stick the other way' (Bourdieu, 2014: 167), and starts with the state, working backwards towards the families, thus examining the state 'from the inside out'.

Drawing inspiration from a variety of academics and researchers from different disciplines, this book sets it sights firmly on how the state has constructed 'troubled families' as an *official* social problem. The American anthropologist Laura Nader (1972: 5) argued that anthropologists should be 'studying up' in their own society as well as down and asked:

> What if, in reinventing anthropology, anthropologists were to study the colonizers rather than the colonized, the culture of power rather than the culture of powerlessness, the culture of affluence rather than the culture of poverty?

Nader went on to highlight the potential benefits of understanding the structures and systems shaping life for poor and disadvantaged communities by 'studying up':

> If ... we were principally studying the most powerful strata of urban society our view of the ghetto might be largely in terms of those relationship larger than the ghetto. We would study the banks and the insurance industry that mark out areas of the city to which they will not sell insurance of extend credit. We would study the landlord class that 'pays off' or 'influences' enforcement of municipal officials to that building codes are not enforced. Slums are technically illegal; if building codes and other municipal laws were enforced our slums would not be slums (if enforcement were successful), or they might be called by another name which would indicate that they were results of white collar crime.

The same case can be made when deciding how to 'study' 'troubled families'. As they are an official classification, their lives cannot be understood without taking account of the social and political processes by which that classification was reached. Similarly, governments rarely identify and create a problem unless they are confident that they have a policy answer to hand that can resolve the problem. The problem is usually framed in such a way that the government's desired policy response or intervention appears to be a 'common sense' approach. 'Troubled families' require 'family intervention', and austerity requires new, more efficient, ways of delivering public services.

French sociologist Pierre Bourdieu has argued for a politically engaged, critical sociology, noting that 'State bureaucracies and their representatives are great producers of social problems' (Bourdieu et al, 1994: 2) and that one must 'retrace the history of the emergence of these problems' (Bourdieu and Wacquant, 1992: 238) in order to understand them fully.

Elsewhere, Bourdieu has argued that social scientists cannot hope to understand the true nature of things by looking in the most obvious places, or the places to which we are directed to by creators of social problems, such as the media or the government. Providing a compelling case for not focusing on the relationship between 'troubled families' and family intervention workers, Bourdieu et al (1999: 181) argue that:

> The perfectly commendable wish to go see things in person, close up, sometimes leads people to search for the explanatory principles of observed realities where they are not to be found (not all of them, in any case), namely at the site of observation itself. The truth about what happens in the 'problem suburbs' certainly does not lie in these usually forgotten sites that leap into the headlines from time to time. The true object of analysis, which must be constructed against appearances and against all those who do no more than endorse those appearances, is the social (or more precisely political) construction of reality as it appears, to intuition, and of its journalistic, bureaucratic and political representations, which help to produce effects that are indeed real, beginning with the political world, where they structure discussion.

Similarly, the American sociologists Malcolm Spector and John Kitsuse argued, in their classic work *Constructing Social Problems*, that '[T]he notion that social problems are a kind of condition must be abandoned in favour of a conception of them as a kind of activity' (Spector and

Kitsuse, 1977: 73). They go on to specify that social problems are the 'activities of those who assert the existence of conditions and define them as problems' (1977: 74). Other sociologists of deviance have adopted similar perspectives. For example, in the UK, Stan Cohen's classic work *Folk Devils and Moral Panics* (2002) focused on the *societal response* to battles between mods and rockers than the events themselves. Hall et al's *Policing the Crisis* sought to understand mugging as 'a social phenomenon, rather than as a particular form of street crime' (1978: 1). Across the Atlantic, Howard Becker (1963) highlighted the importance of the roles of 'rule creators' and 'rule enforcers' in understanding what kinds of activities came to be labelled as deviant. In examining the concept of labelling specifically in relation to poor communities identified as an 'underclass' in the US, Gans argues that a 'label formation process' occurs, which requires certain actors to play different roles or carry out different activities, including those of 'label-makers', 'alarmists', 'counters' and 'label users' (Gans, 1995: 11–26). There is, then, a strong sociological and theoretical argument for examining the concept of 'troubled families' while largely, in the nicest possible way, ignoring the families themselves. But there are also practical and ethical arguments for adopting this approach. There is, as Laura Nader and other have pointed out, an abundance of social scientific literature on poor people, marginalised groups and disadvantaged communities. There is even an emerging literature on 'over-researched' communities (see Neal et al, 2016) and some 'troubled families' would potentially fall into a similar category.

There are also issues of deceit to contend with, as we will see, and many of the families involved with the programme are not aware that they have been labelled as 'troubled families' or that their lives have been officially 'turned around' by the TFP. Researchers involved in gaining families' views of the programme have to decide whether to be complicit in this undesirable deceit and not mention the phrase 'troubled families', or to reveal to the families their official classification and risk leaving them feeling stigmatising and deceived. Some researchers have managed to reconcile these ethical issues and have interviewed 'troubled families', but the views and experiences of families are not, for the reasons highlighted above, the primary focus of this book. While this book does not stick rigidly to the 'label formation process' proposed by Gans, it is a book that is concerned with the emergence and subsequent development of the label 'troubled families' and the myriad work of government in sustaining and nourishing that label. It is, then, or at least aims to be, a book on the Troubled Families Programme, and thus the sociology and social policy of 'troubled families', rather than a book on 'troubled families' themselves.

Muckraking sociology

As a discipline, sociology has often taken as good a look at itself as it has done with its more traditional research subjects. Edwin Lemert (1951: 3) accused early sociologists, who 'took their cue from social reformers of the time', of simply 'riding to the sound of the guns'. Howard Becker (1967) famously asked the American Sociology Association conference in 'whose side are we on?' A year later, Martin Nicolaus (1968) gave an impassioned and trenchant critique of what he called 'fat-cat' sociology arguing that 'the eyes of sociologists, with few but honourable (or honourable but few) exceptions, have been turned downward, and their palms upward' and 'the things that are sociologically "interesting," are the things that are interesting to those who stand at the top of the mountain and feel the tremors of an earthquake'. He went on to say that:

> Sociology has risen to its present prosperity and eminence on the blood and bones of the poor and oppressed; it owes its prestige in this society to its putative ability to give information and advice to the ruling class of this society about ways and means to keep the people down …
>
> The honoured sociologist, the big-status sociologist, the jet-set sociologist, the fat-contract sociologist, the book-a-year sociologist, the sociologist who always wears the livery – the suit and tie – of his masters: this is the type of sociologist who sets the tone and the ethic of the profession, and it is this type of sociologist who is nothing, more or less than a house-servant in the corporate establishment …

More recently, Bourdieu railed against 'lackey intellectuals' (Stabile and Morooka, 2010: 329) who put themselves in the service of neoliberal governments and, along with his long-time collaborator Loïc Wacquant, referred to such individuals as 'defector[s] from the academic world entered into the service of the dominant, whose mission is to give an academic veneer to the political projects of the new state and business nobility' (Bourdieu and Wacquant, 2001: 1). Michael Burawoy (2005), the American sociologist, has called in recent times for a 'public sociology', one that is directed outwards from academia and which can engage new audiences in new ways.

He states that 'public sociology brings sociology into a conversation with publics, understood as people who are themselves involved in conversation' (2005: 7). More recently, there have been similar calls from sociologists for DIY sociology (Paton, 2015), punk sociology (Beer, 2014), 'live sociology' (Back and Puwar, 2012) and 'amphibious sociology' (Lury, 2012; Jones, 2015).

This book, then, aims to be a 'public sociology' book, intended to be read by and stimulate discussion among lay people, practitioners, policy makers and many other people who do not identify themselves as 'academics'. This goal can, however, be achieved using different tactics. The approach adopted here, while drawing on a wide range of sociological researchers, is based on a style of research proposed by Gary T. Marx in the early 1970s. Marx argued for a 'muckraking sociology' which, using the tools of social science, could help to unearth 'dirty data'. Marx, like many others, proposed that sociology should not be a 'disinterested calling pursued for purely intellectual and aesthetic reasons' and instead should be 'committed to, and involved in, solving current problems' (1972: 4). Writing in the 1970s, but with continuing relevance, he argued that social scientists studying contemporary social issues could not discharge [their] responsibilities by retreating from the world until more is known' (Marx, 1972: 1). He identifies a number of issues similar to those presented above – the tendency of researchers to go to where they are pointed, and the desire to produce and publish research that is 'useful' to policy makers. These trends often lead researchers to target their research at, or on, disadvantaged groups, but their findings at powerful groups and institutions who have the resources to affect change. Marx, like Nicolaus and Nader, argues that researchers interested in addressing issues of social injustice should be more inclined to do the opposite.

Muckraking research should help to document and publicise 'the gap between values and actual practices and in questioning established orthodoxies' (Marx, 1972: 2), and could be of benefit to those groups seeking change. Such research, Marx argued, could 'give us a clearer picture of our world, stripped of protective verbiage and without the usual selective perceptions (and misperceptions)' (1972: 4–5). Marx highlighted some of the topics addressed by muckraking research, which often sought to link the actions and decision of those at the top with the conditions of life and experiences of those at the bottom (1972: 7). These issues included the ways in which schools failed to meet the needs or different ethnic populations, how employment services often lowered the self-esteem of job applicants, how the courts treated women differently, the exploitation of migrant farm labourers and the ways in which minority groups are excluded from positions of power (1972: 6).In a passage particularly relevant to an examination of the TFP and its emphasis on 'hands-on' practical support for families, while marginalising structural inequalities and poverty, Marx argued that muckraking research 'can expose the fallacies in certain common sense beliefs about social problems and show how certain ideas rationalize an unsatisfactory status quo' (1972: 5). In the face of such 'common sense' approaches to problems with complex structural causes, the labelling and othering of disadvantaged groups, the misrepresentation of research data, claims of near perfect success, and attempts to 'suppress' negative research findings adopting a muckraking approach becomes a legitimate decision for a researcher to take. Marx (1972: 3) suggests that:

> Such research uses the tools of social science to document unintended (or officially unacknowledged) consequences of social action, inequality, poverty, racism, exploitation, opportunism, neglect, denial of dignity, hypocrisy, inconsistency, manipulation, wasted resources and the displacement of an organization's stated goals in favour of self-perpetuation. It may show how, and the extent to which, a dominant or more powerful class, race, group or stratum takes advantage of, misuses, mistreats, or ignores a subordinate group, often in the face of an ideology that claims it does exactly the opposite.

Marx also clarified the concepts of 'muckracking sociology' and 'dirty data'. In the former instance, he insisted that it was not a concept used pejoratively and instead stated that the usage remained close to its origin of muckrake: 'an instrument used to gather dung into a heap' (Marx, 1972: 2). Marx also highlighted that its usage built on the legacy of investigative journalists who engaged in muckraking activities. Marx argued that muckraking came to be defined as 'the searching out and public exposure of misconduct on the part of prominent individuals and the discovery of scandal and incriminating evidence'. He defined 'dirty data' as 'information which is kept secret and whose revelation would be discrediting or costly' to those attempting to keep the data hidden. 'Dirty data' goes beyond incidental or minor inconsistencies, errors of judgement or 'soft-core discrepancies' (Marx, 1984: 79). Instead, Marx argues, it relates to more serious issues such as 'behaviour that is illegal, the failure of an agency or individual to meet responsibilities, cover-ups, and the use of illegal or immoral means'. Dirty data is a combination of information that is generally protected, secret or private and data that is potentially highly discrediting. Dirty data is not just data that is withheld, hidden or kept secret. It also relates to information designed to 'mislead or obscure', or announcements and proclamations that can be labelled as '"misinformation" and "disinformation"' (1984: 80). These are strong words, but they are used here with confidence. This book argues that there is a structural duplicity to the TFP, and that it is based on duplicitous practices and systematic misrepresentations of data at almost every stage of its development and evolution. These misrepresentations are so widespread and so significant to the functioning of the programme that they cannot be explained away as individual errors of judgement or 'soft-core discrepancies'.

As well as highlighting the benefits of muckraking research, Marx also highlights some pitfalls and problems with muckraking research, which should be acknowledged here. If one seeks out a topic because there is potential to find material that may support social criticism, there is the potential to embellish findings or to simply find what one went looking for. The level of indignation that can arise a result of undertaking muckraking research can allow 'civility [to] decline and self-righteousness [to] run rampant' (1972: 19). The desire to unearth material may lead researchers to forego ethical considerations and deviate from established, methodical and reliable research procedures.

There may be occasions where the presentation of the research undertaken may succumb to some of the pitfalls Marx identifies. I am not the best judge of that. The research that underpins the book relies primarily on data produced and published by the government. Policy documents, speeches, interviews, research publications and spreadsheets relating to the TFP have all been examined to understand the coherence between the official presentation of the approach and success of the TFP and the data that lie behind those claims. At times, there are significant gaps between the public presentation of the programme and the evidence that is often mobilised to support it. In contemporary terms, there are 'alternative facts' that do not match the government's preferred discourse. These alternative facts can, however, be found, in the government own documents. The analysis of government publications and other interventions and texts is supported by interviews and conversations with local authority and voluntary sector workers involved with the day-to-day delivery of the TFP. This research was carried out as part of my doctorate studies and was subject to Durham University's ethical guidelines. I am confident that, despite my desire to unearth dirty data that the government may prefer to keep hidden, I behaved ethically at all stages in the carrying out of my research.

I do not expect the book to have an 'impact' on public policy making, which may surprise some readers. There are no 'policy recommendations' to be found within it. Highlighting untruths, misrepresentations, inaccuracies and duplicitous practices among government officials and politicians is not the way to get invited to roundtable discussions or policy briefings. But that is not the intention of the book. I hope that the book will serve as a comprehensive explication of the programme, so that interested readers, now and in the future, are able to find a large amount of the muck surrounding the programme raked into a single heap. Some people may take issue with some of the sociological approaches that underpin the book and the unrelentingly critical approach of the book. Bourdieu (2011: 17), however, argued that the task of sociology was to 'help reveal what is hidden' and 'to tell about the things of the social world and, as far as possible, to tell them the way they are' (Bourdieu, 2000: 5). He also argued that people were 'pernickety about the scientific nature of sociology ... because it's a troublemaker' (Bourdieu, 1993: 8). I hope that the book helps to sustain this tradition.

The structure of the book

The rest of the book attempts to provide an explication of the emergence and development of the 'troubled families' narrative and some of the key concepts and issues associated with it. Following this introduction, the second chapter charts both the long and problematic history of the underclass thesis, and the shorter history of the concept of 'troubled families'. The first half of the chapter draws on comprehensive research from social policy academics and social historians that has traced different reconstructions of the underclass thesis from Victorian times. This history has been extensively documented elsewhere, and the focus here is on highlighting some of the continuities and discontinuities with the 'troubled families' concept. The second half of the chapter concentrates on the shift from a concern about the 'underclass' in more recent years, from a mid-1970s concerns about a 'cycle of deprivation' through Charles Murray's work on the 'underclass' in the 1980s, to the New Labour concern with 'problem families' in the mid-2000s and the Conservatives' interest in an allegedly 'broken society'.

Chapter Three examines the development of the 'troubled families' discourse, starting in the early years of the coalition government that was formed in 2010. The shift from the localist approach of Whole

Place Community Budgets and the Big Society Working Families Everywhere project to the local authority led Troubled Families Programme, is documented here. The role of the riots in England in 2011 in shifting the government discourse and opening a 'policy window' for a more robust interventionist approach is fully explored, with 'compassionate Conservatism' giving way to a more muscular policy programme following the disturbances. The political response to the riots and the launch of the TFP are analysed, along with detail on the establishment of the TFP in its first phase and the role of Louise Casey, the charismatic senior civil servant in charge of the first phase of TFP is also presented here.

The fourth chapter expounds the 'evolution' of the programme as it has been implemented. Shifts and developments in the first phase are discussed, including the problems of some local authorities in finding 'troubled families' and the subsequent relaxation of the criteria for what constituted a 'troubled family' at that stage of the programme. The changes that have resulted as a result of the 'massive expansion' of the programme into its second phase, working with 400,000 more families are then discussed, including new entry criteria for families, new measures of success, and a new PbR framework. Finally, in this chapter, the 'next phase' of the programme, announced in April 2017 and with a stronger focus on supporting 'workless families' into employment is examined, along with some of the evaluation reports examining the early stages of Phase 2 of the TFP.

The fifth chapter examines Cameron's claim, when he launched the TFP, that his mission in politics was 'fixing the responsibility deficit'. Turning this 'mission' on its head, the focus in this chapter turns to the ways in which the coalition and Conservative governments have abdicated their responsibilities to poor, disadvantaged and marginalised families. This chapter locates the TFP as a central plank of attempts to craft a neoliberal state in the UK. Drawing on the work of Loïc Wacquant and his call for neoliberalism to be understood sociologically rather than economically, the ways in which the TFP has been expanded at the same time that traditional welfare services have been rolled back are examined. Wide ranging welfare reforms and cuts to public services are discussed as the chapter highlights the ways in which a neoliberal state is being crafted in the UK at the current time.

The TFP is predicated on the family intervention model, which relies on a key worker gaining the trust of a family, building a relationship with them and then working intensively with them in a holistic manner, getting them to take responsibility for their actions. Chapter Six explores both the domestic and international history of such approaches, including returning to the 1940s Family Service Unit approach, which was characterised as 'friendship' with a purpose'. The shorter history of the family intervention model is also examined and the journey from a single Scottish voluntary sector project to a nationwide government programme in England is documented, with a number of changes noted, including: the discursive shift from 'support' to 'intervention'; the introduction of the threat of sanctions; the types of families targeted across all projects; and changes to the level of resources allegedly required for effective 'family intervention'. The chapter suggests that what the government calls 'family intervention' now bears very little resemblance to the 'Dundee model' it is putatively based on.

Drawing primarily on interviews and discussions with local authority officers, Chapter Seven focuses on the implementation of the TFP and explores the changes that have been made to the programme at local levels. The chapter highlights deviations from the national rhetoric and the way in which much of the aggressive, muscular rhetoric has been softened to reflect a more supportive approach towards families at both a local authority level and from individual workers. Local authorities have adapted the programme to make it work for them in a number of different ways and 'success' has often been achieved in spite of the programme rather than because of it. The ways in which local authorities have subverted, negotiated and resisted the national rhetoric in order to make the programme work and to achieve the targets set by the government are examined. Ways in which pressure has been applied to local authorities to demonstrate compliance with the aims of the programme are also highlighted.

In an ill-fated, widely publicised speech to senior police officers in her role as head of the Anti-Social Behaviour Unit (ASBU), Casey rhetorically asked the question 'Research: help or hindrance?' before answering 'Hindrance thank you very much.' Chapter Eight examines the engagement of researchers with previous debates about 'the underclass' and notes that a recurring feature of such debates is the involvement of researchers. The research approach within the TFP is then analysed, with the chapter highlighting the use, misuse and abuse of research in a number of key areas. The initial misrepresentation of the research behind the 120,000 figure is presented along with a summary of the critiques of Casey's own 'dipstick' research for her *Listening to Troubled Families* report. Other issues covered include: the misrepresentation of data behind the DCLG *Understanding Troubled Families* report which helped support the case for the expansion of the TFP to 400,000 more families; the invention of a survey that allegedly proved the need for 'radical reform' of services to help 'troubled families'; the use of case studies in the 'troubled families' narrative; and the criticism of researchers involved with the official evaluation of the first phase of the TFP.

The ninth and concluding chapter highlights the structural duplicity of the TFP across a number of areas. From its inception as a policy response to the riots, the TFP has relied on deceit and deception in the day-to-day running of the programme. A brief summary of the 'obfuscation' and 'evasion' that has already been discussed precedes a more detailed examination of three key tenets of the TFP. First, the role of 'extraordinary workers', the bureaucratic heroes who are able to support 'troubled families' no matter what challenges they face, is examined and critiqued. Second, the attention turns to the allegedly special and different relationship that exists between these workers and the 'troubled families' they work with. Drawing on interviews with workers and data from the evaluation of the first phase of the programme, doubt is cast on the quality and importance of these relationships. Thirdly, and finally, the chapter considers the idea that families' lives have been 'turned around' by the TFP, again drawing on data from the evaluation but also by scrutinising the many loopholes in the PbR mechanism for the first phase. The chapter concludes with an argument that it is the behaviours of the most powerful people in our society, rather than the most disadvantaged, that is most troubling, and in most need of an intensive intervention.

TWO

The 'long and undistinguished pedigree'

> Whatever you call them, we've known for years that a relatively small number of families are the source of a large proportion of the problems in society. (Cameron, 2011b)

Introduction

Concepts such as 'troubled families' are, of course, nothing new. The idea of a group of families, or a class of people, cut adrift at the bottom of society, exhibiting different cultural values and representing a threat to the 'mainstream', has 'a long and undistinguished pedigree' (Macnicol, 1987: 315). By way of example, in 1816, the Committee for Investigating the Causes of the Alarming Increase in Juvenile Delinquency in the Metropolis (1816: 10) suggested that the 'principal causes' of the boys' 'dreadful practices' were:

- The improper conduct of parents
- The want of education
- The want of suitable employment
- The violation of the Sabbath, and habits of gambling in the streets.

It has also been claimed that ever since 'the happy sixteenth-century custom of chopping off the ears of vagabonds, rogues and sturdy beggars, the British have had some difficulty in distinguishing poverty from crime' (Golding and Middleton, 1982: 186). Cameron's conflation of 'families with multiple disadvantages' and 'neighbours from hell' highlights the enduring similarities between different reconstructions of the 'underclass' thesis. With his (Cameron, 2011b) announcement at the launch of the Troubled Families Programme that 'troubled families' were characterised by anti-social behaviour (ASB), poor school attendance or educational exclusion and 'worklessness', he revealed the lack of progress that has been made in both analysing the 'problem' and identifying a solution to it. However, while throughout history the 'ragged classes' have often been conflated with 'dangerous classes' (Himmelfarb, 1984: 381; Morris, 1994), there also exists an extensive history of attempts to delineate different types of poor people. Early Poor Laws in England included attempts to distinguish between 'vagrants' and the 'impotent poor' and the Poor Law of 1834 included an official distinction between the 'deserving' and 'undeserving' poor. In 1852, Mary Carpenter argued that there existed 'a very strong line of demarcation which exists between the labouring and the "ragged" class, a line of demarcation not drawn by actual poverty' (in Himmelfarb, 1984: 378). Fast forward over 100 years and Charles Murray, who did so much to advance the concept of an 'underclass' on both sides of the Atlantic in the 1980s and 1990s, provided a contemporary perspective, making it clear that the 'underclass' 'does not refer to degree of poverty, but to a type of poverty' (Murray, 1994: 24):

> It is not a new concept. I grew up knowing what the underclass was; we just didn't call it that in those days. In the small Iowa town where I lived, I was taught by my middle-class parents that there were two kinds of poor people. One class of poor people was never even called 'poor'. I came to understand that they simply lived with low incomes, as my own parents had done when they were young. Then there was another set of poor people, just a handful of them. These poor people didn't lack just money. They were defined by their behaviour. Their homes were littered and unkempt. The men in the family were unable to hold a job for more than a few weeks at a time. Drunkenness was common. The children grew up ill-schooled and ill-behaved and contributed a disproportionate share of the local juvenile delinquents.

The long history of the 'underclass' thesis has been extensively documented elsewhere, primarily by social policy and social history researchers (Jordan, 1974: Macnicol, 1987, 1999; Morris, 1994; Welshman, 2013), and it is not the intention, nor is it possible, to cover similar ground in similar detail here. Instead, this chapter presents a brief history of the genesis of ideas about the differences between the 'deserving' and 'undeserving' poor from 14th century England to the modern day, with a particular focus on the constructs from the past 20 years. The chapter also highlights: the gendered nature of these debates with a frequent focus on the role of mothers; the continuing salience of family in different iterations of the 'underclass'; the tensions between the 'care' and 'control' functions of the state in providing for poor people; the role of social science in these debates; and the political utility of them, particularly in recent times. The focus here is primarily on UK constructions, although international examples are also referred to, where appropriate.

The next section provides a necessarily brief and incomplete summary of the longue durée, from the introduction of the Statute of Labourers in the 14th century, through the Poor Laws and Victorian concerns about a social residuum, to concerns about a 'cycle of deprivation' in the UK in the 1970s (see Welshman, 2013, for the most comprehensive historical account of the 'underclass' over this period). The focus then moves to a more detailed explication of recent constructions: the 'underclass' and the 'dependency culture' debates in the UK in the 1980s and 90s; New Labour's programme to address social exclusion and ASB in the early 2000s; and the 'Broken Britain' discourse most closely associated with the Conservative Party under the leadership of David Cameron. This takes the 'troubled families' backstory up to the formation of a coalition government in the UK, in May 2010, where the next chapter starts. A concluding section analyses some of the continuities and discontinuities through different constructions of the 'underclass' thesis over time, again with the focus remaining primarily on recent developments.

The long history

The emergence of government initiatives to address problems of poverty and disorder can be traced back to the 14th century at least, to the decline of feudalism in the UK (de Schweinitz, 1961). Prior to this date, the feudal system meant that most people should have been protected by their masters from destitution, distress and suffering. The demise of feudalism led to workers enjoying greater freedom from their masters, but this also meant greater insecurity and the lack of a patron when misfortune or ill health occurred. Given their predicament, many people turned to 'mendicancy and theft' (de Schweinitz, 1961: 3). In 1349, amid the collapse of feudalism and the increased freedom of poor people, the Statute of Labourers was enacted, which compelled unemployed people to work for a maximum wage, prevented them from travelling and forbade others to give alms or charitable donations to them. It was this Act of Parliament that arguably paved the way for the systems of social security and the 'welfare states' that now exist in most countries with capitalist economies.

Prior to these interventions, poor relief was seen as the preserve of the church and private, locally organised philanthropic endeavours (Piven and Cloward, 1971: 12). The development of government initiatives towards the poor continued to be heavily influenced by public order issues and 'remained primarily a direct result of the government's concern with public security' (Waxman, 1983: 76). Piven and Cloward (1971: 11) argue that it was 'food riots' and 'mobs of starving peasants' overrunning the town that, in the 1530s 'led the rulers of Lyon to conclude that the giving of charity should no longer be governed by private whim'. They go on to note that:

> Most of the features of modern welfare – from criteria to discriminate the worthy poor from the unworthy to strict procedures for surveillance of recipients and measures for their rehabilitation – were present in Lyons' new relief administration.

Similar arrangements, also with continuing relevance, were put in place in England at around the same time and, in 1531:

> the government, under Henry VIII, for the first time recognized governmental responsibility for the care of the poor, established what may be the first "means test" for determining eligibility for the right to beg and provided areas within which begging was permitted (Waxman, 1983: 78).

This act 'represented the beginning of definite assumption by government of responsibility for the care of persons in economic distress' (de Schweinitz, 1961: 21), but the provisions for the 'impotent poor' also meant that the 'able-bodied unemployed', the 'vagabonds', were dealt with more severely. The punishment for illegal begging was a whipping until the blood ran. In the 1570s, during Elizabethan times, a distinction between 'vagrants' or 'professional beggars' and the 'impotent poor' was established (Waxman, 1983: 78) and in 1601, following riots, food shortages, and economic depression, the Poor Relief Act, popularly known as the Elizabethan Poor Law, came into being. A series of amendments and additions were made to this 'Old Poor Law' before the 'New Poor Law' was introduced in 1834, via the Poor Law Amendment Act. A Poor Law Commission was established to oversee and implement a new national system of poor relief, which represented a shift from localised, parish-based arrangements under the Old Poor Law.

The 1800s saw an increasing distinction between the 'ragged' classes and the 'perishing' and 'dangerous' classes. Himmelfarb (1984: 371) notes that the term 'ragged' had been used to describe the poor for centuries but that '[b]y the early nineteenth century that label was being applied more selectively' to the very poor or to those who were 'conspicuously ragged'. Special 'Ragged schools' were set up to educate the '"substrata", "residuum", "outcasts", the lowest of the poor' (Himmelfarb, 1984: 375). Mary Carpenter (in Himmelfarb, 1984: 378), a founder of a ragged school believed that not only was it easy to distinguish between the working classes and the 'ragged' classes, but that this clear distinction meant that different ways of 'dealing with them' were required:

> There is, and long will be, a very strongly defined line of separation between them, which must and ought to separate them, and which requires perfectly distinct machinery and modes of operation in dealing with them.

A number of social investigations into the plight of the poor took place in Victorian England (Welshman, 2013: 15). Researchers and journalists such as Henry Mayhew took it upon themselves to document the conditions of the lower-classes and 'slumming', the practice of visiting the East End of London to observe first-hand these conditions, became a popular pastime for affluent Londoners (Koven, 2004). Welshman (2013: 15) has argued that the tendency of historians to focus on the empirical investigations of the time, from well-known figures such as Charles Booth and Benjamin Seebohm Rowntree, has neglected the 'wider ideological context' and the 'moral assumptions that often lay behind policy' in Victorian England. Drawing on the work of Stedman Jones (1971), Welshman (2013: 26) argues that Booth was central in 'amplifying' the 'new distinction between the residuum and the respectable working class'. Booth's namesake, General William Booth, the founder of the Salvation Army, drew on his work to propose the idea of a 'submerged tenth', those who were destitute in England (Booth, 1890).

The flurry of media attention and research led to an increase in philanthropic activity in Victorian England and this, in turn, led to the establishment of the Society for Repressing Mendicity and Organizing Charity (better known as the Charity Organization Society, or COS) in 1869. The COS believed that the plethora of local philanthropic initiatives only served to encourage pauperism, rather than prevent it (Koven, 2004: 92) and could easily be manipulated by wily paupers with a knowledge of 'the system'. The COS instead saw its task as being 'to exclude as many people as possible from all forms of costly outdoor relief, which included cash, goods, and services' (Koven, 2004: 98). This was to be achieved through an increased focus on case records of clients and the central co-ordination of poor relief. This then, was perhaps the earliest example of a 'new', more efficient approach that could 'grip' both troublemaking families *and* local services, being touted as the answer to an overly generous system of poor relief. Family Action, the voluntary organisation that developed out of the COS, is supportive of and involved with the delivery of the Troubled Families Programme (see Holmes, 2015).

Concerns about a 'residuum' were also raised by the ill health of many recruits for the Boer War between 1899 and 1903 who came from poor, large families (see, for example, Morris, 1994: 25). No legislation or reforms were enacted specifically to counter the alleged threat of the residuum, and the popularity of the concept largely subsided following the gentlemanly behaviour of dock strikers in 1889 and the advent of the First World War, which led to full employment in England. Such developments led Stedman Jones to conclude that the residuum 'had never existed, except as a phantom army called up by late Victorian and Edwardian social science to legitimise its practice' (in Welshman, 2013: 17).

The concept of a residuum, however, proved influential in the subsequent constructions of the 'unemployables' in the 1900s and the 'social problem group' in the 1920s. Welshman (2013: 35) notes the concept of 'unemployables' was often used interchangeably with residuum and was thus a 'Trojan Horse concept' that helped to keep the idea of the residuum alive, providing 'fertile soil for the concept of the social problem group in the 1920s'. The idea of a social problem group, enthusiastically supported by the Eugenics Education Society, gained ground during the economic depression and time of high unemployment of the 1920s. Macnicol (1987: 300) notes that the arrival of mass democracy in 1918, an increasing concern about 'mental defectives' (sic) and the rise of both the Labour Party and the medical, health and social work professions, also played a role in the development of the concept. A 'Mental Deficiency Committee' (also known as the Wood Committee) report of 1929 contained, 'a famous passage which was to be quoted frequently by future supporters of the underclass concept' (Macnicol 1987: 302). The passage related to a 'group of families' that:

> would include, as anyone who has extensive practical
> experience of social service would readily admit, a much
> larger proportion of insane persons, epileptics, paupers,

criminals (especially recidivists), unemployables, habitual slum dwellers, prostitutes, inebriates and other social inefficients than would a group of families not containing mental defectives. The overwhelming majority of the families thus collected will belong to that section of the community, which we propose to term the 'social problem' or 'subnormal' group. (quoted in Macnicol, 1987: 302)

Macnicol (1987) and Welshman (2013: 65–77) both highlight the lack of robust research produced by the Eugenics Society, who went in search of the social problem group following the Wood report. Their inability to provide any real evidence in support of the existence of the social problem group led them to 'fall back on the argument that, while the existence of the group was self-evident, more research was necessary' (Welshman, 2013: 76). This undoubtedly contributed to the gradual demise of the concept. Other factors that played a part included the National Socialists' interest in eugenics in Germany, the outbreak of the Second World War, and the publication of the Beveridge Report of 1942. The evacuations of slum children during the war, however, provided the impetus for the concept of 'problem families' to emerge.

The Women's Group on Public Welfare *Our Towns* report (1943) is credited with being the first place where the phrase 'problem families' was first consciously used (Philp and Timms, 1957: vii). The report was written following concerns among members of the Women's Group about the condition of slum children who were evacuated from urban to rural areas from 1939. The introduction argued that the state of children arriving from slum areas proved that the 'submerged tenth' 'discovered' by General William Booth in the 19th century still existed in parts of England. This 'finding' led to discussion about, and criticism of, the effectiveness of state provision – mainly health and welfare services – for members of 'problem families'. This debate, in turn, led to the proposal of a new form of 'casework' with families, which paved the way for new forms of social work to develop. This style of casework, delivered by voluntary organisations such as the Family Service Units and Family Welfare Units, came to be known as 'friendship with a purpose' (Starkey 2000: 539) and Welshman (2013: 88) has noted how workers in Liverpool, for example, 'rejected a more professional approach, arguing that they were successful only in a "warm sympathetic relationship of friendship and involvement"'. It has also been observed that 'problem families' in reality meant 'problem' or 'feckless' mothers (Starkey, 2000) and the practical hands-on help offered by practitioners managed to locate the source of the family's

27

'problems' firmly within the domestic sphere that was, and still is, very much associated with 'mother's work'. Macnicol (2017) and Welshman (2017) have also highlighted similarities between the 'problem families' of the post-war era and the 'troubled families' of today.

The publication of *The Problem with the Problem Family* (Philp and Timms, 1957), written by two social workers, crystallised a number of the profession's concerns and Richard Titmuss, writing in the foreword to the book, gave a damning indictment of the 'evidence' supporting the concept:

> ... the debate about the 'problem family' has been conducted in a singularly uncritical manner. Precision has been lacking in the use of words and in the observation of phenomena has been generally lacking; heterogeneity has been mistaken for homogeneity; biological theories have obscured the study of psychological and sociological factors; the classification and counting of 'abnormals' has proceeded regardless of the need to set them in the context of contemporary social norms; in short, what knowledge has been gained from all these inquiries has not accumulated on any theoretical foundations.

While academics and members of the developing social work profession became increasingly sceptical and critical of the idea of 'problem families', the concept was more warmly received by health practitioners and policy makers, including Medical Officers of Health (Welshman, 2013: 92). In contrast to social workers, local and central government health professionals started using the term 'problem families' in the early 1950s and continued to do so until the 1960s and, in one area at least, the 1970s (Welshman, 2013: 91–2). By this time, the culture of poverty theory (Harrington, 1962; Lewis, 1959, 1965) was gaining traction in the USA and it would not be long before Sir Keith Joseph, the then Secretary of State for Health and Social Services in the UK, advanced his theory of 'transmitted deprivation'.

During a speech in 1972, Sir Keith Joseph asked why, despite years of full employment and long periods of economic stability since the Second World War, 'deprivation and problems of maladjustment so conspicuously persist' (in Welshman, 2012a: 1). Joseph believed that there was a phenomenon he referred to as a 'cycle of deprivation', whereby a small number of parents 'transmitted' their behaviours and lifestyle – and by extension their deprivation – onto their children, who then grew up to be the 'deprived' of the following generation.

Joseph argued that the process by which this transmission – or cycle – occurred, required further investigation and he established a Working Party that led to a large-scale research programme, delivered by the Department of Health and Social Security and the Social Science Research Council.

The research programme came to span eight years and produced a number of publications examining different aspects of deprivation. One of the first publications to arise from the programme was *Cycles of Disadvantage*, a review of existing literature (Rutter and Madge, 1976). The first sentence from the authors states 'The term "deprivation" must be one of the most overworked words in the English language' and they go on to note that

> The literature is full of countless articles and books on the nature, causes and consequences of deprivation and the research reports are outnumbered only by the emotional and polemical monologues and interchanges on a variety of theoretical, practical and political aspects of the topic. Much of the controversy is a consequence of the very diffuseness of the concept which is used by different writers (usually with force and conviction) to cover quite different issues and problems.

Highlighting previous work by one of the authors that proposed the term '"deprivation" had served its purpose and should now be abandoned', they argue, on the second page, that '[o]ur review of the writings on the topic of deprivation has strongly reinforced that view' (Rutter and Madge, 1976: 2). Resistance to the concept of 'transmitted deprivation' continued throughout the research programme and many of the individual projects and the related publications either avoided the concept altogether or were dismissive of it. One writer (Berthoud, 1983: 151) noted, at the end of the programme, that the 'hypothesis [of 'transmitted deprivation'] itself was a sort of burp from a debate about poverty and pathology that had been rumbling on for decades, if not centuries', but was equally critical of the research programme generally, in that it failed to keep the issue of 'deprivation' centre stage, and of the final report more specifically. The final report itself stated that 'All the evidence suggests that cultural values are not important for the development and transmission of deprivation' but did suggest that deprivation sometimes 'seems to lead to particular behaviours which may affect the chances of second generation members' (Brown and Madge, 1982: 226).

While Joseph's idea of a cycle of deprivation was subject to critical examination by academics, another theory of poverty was being advanced. Poor economic performance during the 1970s and a number of high-profile newspaper articles on 'scroungers' from 1976 onwards (Golding and Middleton, 1982) led many politicians and media commentators to conclude that an expansive welfare state led to a 'dependency culture' among recipients. Following a Conservative election victory in 1979 and influenced by a desire to cut state spending and assert the primacy of the market, the government 'nourished and sustained the idea of a dependency culture' and, given the 'social, economic and political context [it] ... was an idea whose time had come' (Taylor-Gooby and Dean, 1992: 25). McGlone (1990: 160) argued that the 'Thatcher government lacked any clear and well formulated policies for reforming the social security system', but was ideologically driven and 'committed to cutting public expenditure as part of its monetarist economic strategy'. Researchers examining the dependency culture found no evidence of separate cultures or values among people in receipt of state support and argued that 'any social security policy based on the notion of "dependency culture" is likely to be counterproductive' and that 'the notion obscures rather than assists our understanding of dependency' (Taylor-Gooby and Dean, 1992: 122–3).

At the same time that UK politicians and national media were discussing how to get to grips with the dependency culture, their counterparts in the USA were discussing welfare dependency and the associated concept of an 'underclass'. While the term 'underclass' was first used in this context by Ken Auletta (1981), a writer for the *New Yorker*, and the term was used by many scholars in different ways and for different purposes, it became most closely associated with Charles Murray, an 'unemployed political scientist of mediocre repute' (Wacquant, 2009b: 12), associated with the right-wing thinktank the Manhattan Foundation. Murray's book *Losing Ground* (1984) argued that generous welfare systems had created an underclass (although he rarely uses this term in this book) who simply responded to the 'new rules' of the game: 'We tried to remove the barriers to escape from poverty, and inadvertently built a trap' (Murray, 1984: 9). Just as scholars took issue with the idea of 'dependency culture' in the UK, a number of researchers who investigated evidence of an 'underclass', in Murray's terms, found little evidence to support his thesis (see Sherraden, 1984; Katz, 1989; Gans, 1995). This did not, however, prevent the Institute for Economic Affairs and *The Sunday Times* inviting Murray to the UK in 1989 to discuss the issue of an 'emerging British underclass'

(Murray, 1990). Murray announced himself as 'a visitor from a plague area come to see whether the disease is spreading', writing (1990: 42):

> With all the reservations that a stranger must feel in passing judgement on an unfamiliar country, I will jump directly to the conclusion: Britain does have an underclass, still largely out of sight and still smaller than the one in the United States. But it is growing rapidly. Within the next decade, it will probably become as large (proportionately) as the United States' underclass. It could easily become larger.

Murray's intervention, aided by the support of a national newspaper, prompted a strong and sustained response from British academics (see, for example, Dean, 1991; Bagguley and Mann, 1992; Robinson and Gregson, 1992; Mann, 1994; Mann and Roseneil, 1994; Macnicol, 1999). A second contribution from Murray in 1994, *Underclass: The Crisis Deepens*, focused on more recent changes that he perceived 'in the English family' (Murray, 1994: 102). Murray's consideration of these changes led him to the conclusion that '[a] top to bottom overhaul of the benefit system is necessary', which must start with the question 'What is it worth to restore the two-parent family as the norm throughout British society?' (Murray, 1994: 103).

The Crisis Deepens also provoked responses from British academics. It was highlighted by Kirk Mann (1994: 79–80) that 'the features of the underclass vary enormously':

> For some observers the underclass is young, homeless or rootless. Others see an underclass which is black, Hispanic or Celtic but usually welfare dependant. Illegitimate births, crime, low labour force participation, child abuse, drug dependency, women who are sole parents, alcohol abuse, physical or mental disability, begging or promiscuity are cited by some as the key features ... They are politically dangerous and threatening but simultaneously irrelevant or marginal. They are nimble enough to burgle any home and can run off after a 'bag snatching', but the disabled are also members of the underclass. Their morality is likely to infect the rest of society but they are isolated from society. The underclass have developed their own street language and culture but this differs between countries. In short the disparate observers who claim to be able to witness

an underclass are incapable of agreeing on what it is they have witnessed.

Elsewhere, Bagguley and Mann (1992: 122) queried the evidence base surrounding the underclass thesis and argued that the concept led to 'poor social science'. In 1996, Murray's two essays along with commentaries from academics were reprinted as *Charles Murray and the Underclass: The Developing Debate* by the IEA (Lister, 1996). In the foreword to this publication, Ruth Lister provided a comprehensive summary of some of the main weaknesses of the 'underclass' thesis and warned that 'the use of stigmatising labels is likely to lead to stigmatising policies' (1996: 10). She concluded that

> It is partly because the notion of an 'underclass' now carries such strong connotations of blame that I do not believe that it offers the means of reconciling structure and agency in helping us to understand poverty and thereby do something about it. (Lister, 1996: 12)

The debate summarised above appeared to have little direct or immediate influence or bearing on government policy in the UK, which was still occupied with tackling the broader idea of a dependency culture. The term, however, entered mainstream usage and became contemporary shorthand for the historical feckless and undeserving poor.

When New Labour entered office in 1997, they came armed with the new language of social exclusion (Fairclough, 2000), although links with the idea of an underclass remained. In Tony Blair's first speech as prime minister, he argued that there was a need to tackle 'what we all know exists – an underclass of people cut off from society's mainstream, without any sense of shared purpose' (in Welshman, 2012a: 234). While Blair continued to use the term 'underclass' relatively frequently, certainly in his early days of office (Levitas, 1998: 155–6), it was the concept of social exclusion that was formalised via the creation of the Social Exclusion Unit (SEU) in Whitehall. Levitas (1998) argued that, within the social exclusion agenda, there were competing, often contradictory discourses at work. She argued that a Redistributive Discourse quickly gave way to both a Social Integrationist Discourse, which valorised paid work as the solution to social exclusion, and to a Moral Underclass Discourse, which was:

> a gendered discourse with many forerunners, whose demons are criminally inclined, unemployable young men

and sexually and socially irresponsible single mothers, for whom paid work is necessary as a means of social discipline, but whose (self) exclusion, and thus potential inclusion, is moral and cultural (Levitas, 1998: 7–8).

Veit-Wilson highlighted similar inconsistencies and argued that within wider social exclusion discourses there were strong versions that emphasised structural issues and the role of society in doing the excluding, and weak versions that focused primarily on the behaviours of the excluded themselves as the cause for their exclusion (in Byrne, 1999: 4–5). Nonetheless, in keeping with their desire to see 'evidence-based policy' and implement 'what works', the Labour government established strong relationships with the London School of Economics and Political Science which saw the establishment of a Centre for Analysis of Social Exclusion (CASE). The SEU, with its 18 Policy Action Teams, was also prolific in producing research and policy reports across a number of different policy areas such as 'young runaways', 'neighbourhood renewal', 'teenage pregnancy', 'truancy and school exclusion' and 'anti-social behaviour'. In 2002, a separate Anti-Social Behaviour Unit (ASBU) was established in the Home Office to address increasing popular and political concern about an alleged minority of troublesome young people and families. Louise Casey, the government's 'Homelessness Czar' (Burney, 2009: 31) was appointed to lead the ASBU.

Responses to the ASB agenda from academics were swift and largely negative (Millie et al, 2005; Squires and Stephen, 2005; Hughes, 2007; Squires, 2008). Burney called it an 'elastic concept' (2005: 7), describing ASB as the 'hydra-headed monster that represented a spectrum of bad behaviour, from serious to merely irritating' (2005: 16) while Ashworth (2004: 263) suggested it was 'a vague term with a broad definition, which in the last few years has become a rallying call for some onerous and intrusive measures against individuals'. Burney (2005: 17) also highlighted that 'concerns about crime became focused on the fear and disruption attributed to a small number of families and individuals in hard-to-manage neighbourhoods of social housing'. Squires (2008) argued that the ASB agenda simply amounted to the 'criminalisation of nuisance', primarily among young people.

In his third term of office as prime minister, Tony Blair stated that he wanted to create a society of 'respect' (Millie, 2009: 1). A new Respect Task Force (RTF) was established in 2006, replacing the ASBU, but still headed by Louise Casey. A Respect Action Plan (RTF, 2006a) accompanied the launch of the Task Force, Hazel Blears was appointed as the Minister for Respect, and 'Respect became a banner attached to anything related to the menu of policies passing through the hands of the Task Force' (Burney, 2009: 33). Burney argues that the discursive shift from 'anti-social behaviour' to 'Respect' helped to highlight the increasing political concern with parenting practices and, more specifically, parental responsibility for children's behaviour and attitudes. The environmental and neighbourhood-based enforcement tools remained, but they were now accompanied by funding for local youth provision and parenting classes and support, as well as an expansion of Family Intervention Projects (FIPs) for the 'most challenging families' (Burney, 2009: 34).

FIPs, which are discussed in more detail in Chapter Six, began life as a single 'Families Project' in Dundee, run by the children's charity NCH Action for Children Scotland (Dillane et al, 2001). Following a positive evaluation, five Intensive Family Support Projects (IFSPs), using a similar model, were established in England in 2004, as part of the work of the ASBU. In 2006, and following mildly promising evaluations of the initial six projects (Nixon et al, 2006), the establishment of a 'national network' of Intensive Family Support Schemes was announced in the Respect Action Plan (RTF, 2006a). The plan called for a 'new approach' in working with the 'small number of households [who] are often responsible for a high proportion of antisocial behaviour'. This approach, mirroring that of the COS over 100 years previously, was designed as a response not just to the family's problems but also to the perceived inability of local services to address their problems:

> What makes the projects distinctive and different is that a lead person 'grips' the household and the range of services and professionals that are involved. This provides co-ordination and consistency for the household and a consistent message on the consequences of disengagement. (RTF, 2006a: 21)

The family intervention approach is based on a single keyworker who can 'get to grips' with the whole family and look at the family, working with them persistently and assertively, as well as helping with practical tasks and domestic chores. An RTF document (2006b: 2) setting out what FIPs were claimed that evidence supported a view that 'this small number of families need an intensive, persistent and, if necessary, coercive approach'. A 'twin-track' approach was thus advocated, one that combined help and support for families with the threat of sanctions and 'supervision and enforcement tools to provide them with the incentives to change' (RTF, 2006b: 2). FIPs would, the government claimed, 'ensure that the destructive behaviour which is so often passed from generation to generation, blighting not only these families but entire communities, is effectively tackled for the first time' (RTF, 2006b: 2).

At the same time that the ASB agenda was focusing on a small minority of troublemaking families, the social exclusion agenda was also shifting its focus. A report published in 2007 (SETF, 2007a) identified 140,000 families in Britain that were deemed to be 'at risk'. This report, which examined families experiencing multiple disadvantages and used data from the 2004–05 Families and Children Survey, was later to become a key document in the identification of 120,000 'troubled families' in England in 2011. 'At risk' effectively meant families experiencing five out of seven disadvantages (SETF, 2007a: 4) and who were, therefore, perhaps the most disadvantaged families in the UK. The seven disadvantages were:

- no parent in the family is in work;
- family lives in poor quality or overcrowded housing;
- no parent has any qualifications;
- mother has mental health problems;
- at least one parent has a longstanding limiting illness, disability or infirmity;
- family has a low income (below 60% of the median); and
- family cannot afford a number of food and clothing items.

Shortly after becoming prime minister in 2007, Gordon Brown closed the RTF and Louise Casey moved to a new job in the Cabinet Office, looking at community policing, although many of the RTF policies, including FIPs, remained, with some simply moved over to a new Youth Task Force. Brown remained supportive of FIPs and promised to further extend them to 'the 50,000 most chaotic families' (Brown, 2009) if Labour won the 2010 general election. The Conservative opposition, aided by the Centre for Social Justice thinktank and the national tabloid newspaper *The Sun*, were, in 2007, simultaneously pressing ahead with their own 'Broken Britain' narrative.

Following his unsuccessful stint as party leader, the Conservative MP Iain Duncan Smith reinvented himself as a social justice champion and established an 'independent' thinktank – the Centre for Social Justice (CSJ) – to explore the root causes of 'social breakdown' in the UK. When David Cameron became leader of the Conservatives, he established a number of policy groups to look at specific areas, including social justice. The CSJ provided the secretariat for this group, which was headed by Duncan Smith. In 2006, the CSJ published *Breakdown Britain*, an 'interim report on the state of the nation' (CSJ, 2006) and, a year later, followed it up with *Breakthrough Britain* (CSJ, 2007), which contained policy recommendations to the Conservative Party. In the foreword to the *Breakthrough* report, Duncan Smith argues that 'social breakdown is the greatest challenge we face' (CSJ, 2007: 4) and highlights what he has learnt from 'visiting many of Britain's most difficult and fractured communities' over the past six years.

> I have seen levels of social breakdown which have appalled and angered me. In the fourth largest economy in the world, too many people live in dysfunctional homes, trapped on benefits. Too many children leave school with no qualifications or skills to enable them to work and prosper. Too many communities are blighted by alcohol and drug addiction, debt and criminality and have low levels of life expectancy.

Cameron used the 'broken society' theme frequently in speeches and interviews (see Watt and Wintour, 2008), and referred to a by-election in Glasgow East as 'the broken society by-election' (Hencke et al, 2008). *The Sun* newspaper ran a Broken Britain campaign in 2008 and, in an interview with the newspaper, Cameron said 'I applaud *The Sun's* Broken Britain campaign. You are absolutely on to the right thing' (in Pascoe-Watson, 2008). The 'Broken Britain' narrative, focused on behavioural 'pathways to poverty', the putative negative 'effects' of living in social housing or 'welfare ghettos', and eliding 'family breakdown' with 'social breakdown' (see Pickles, 2010, for an example) has been subjected to extensive critique (Mooney, 2009; Lister and Bennett, 2010; Hancock and Mooney, 2012; Slater, 2014). Although Cameron used his last Conservative party conference speech before the 2010 general election to argue that our society was 'broken' because 'government got too big' (Cameron, 2009), Hancock and Mooney (2012: 59) argue, in contrast, that the broken society narrative legitimates increasing state intervention in the lives of poor people.

> Far from withdrawing from intervention in working class lives, the state, in the guise of welfare 'reform' to combat the broken society, is involved in earlier and deeper penetration of those lives and in particular in the lives of the most disadvantaged sections of society.

By the time that the Conservatives arrived in government, as lead partners in a coalition government in May 2010, the political focus was on responding to the economic crisis and implementing a series of austerity measures. The Coalition Agreement stated that the government would 'investigate a new approach to helping families with multiple problems' (HM Government, 2010: 19). While Cameron remained committed to promoting the importance of family in society (Cameron, 2010), it was not until riots erupted across England in the summer of 2011 that he promised that 'the broken society is back at the top of my agenda' (Cameron, 2011b). The next chapter highlights the way in which the concept of 'troubled families' emerged during the early days of the coalition and how it has developed, following the riots and the establishment of the TFP.

The more it changes ...

Poverty and, perhaps more specifically, poor people themselves have been a concern of government for at least 650 years. In tracing the backstory to 'troubled families' we can see many continuities between different concepts of the underclass and/or the undeserving poor, but also many differences and changes. While the rhetoric has often been about the alleviation of poverty and the improvements of living conditions, there has also often been a concomitant focus on the containment of certain sections of marginalised and impoverished groups, a situation that Wacquant (2009a: 295) has characterised as social policies often being as much about relief *from* the poor as it has been about relief *to* the poor. Politicians, government officials, researchers, charitable organisations and social reformers have often attempted to make a distinction between the various categories of the deserving and undeserving poor. The history of poor relief has thus been riven with tensions about how best to care for members of the 'deserving poor' – the 'hard-working families' or 'ordinary working families' (DfE, 2017) of today, and how best to control their wayward cousins, the 'undeserving poor', the 'underclass' or the 'most troubled families'.

Narratives about how expansive state provision and a generous welfare system can create a 'dependency culture', while simultaneously not addressing the needs of the 'underclass' have proven to be recurring themes. Such concerns first surfaced in Victorian times with the advent of the COS, and their argument that better co-ordinated service provision was required. Sir Keith Joseph wondered how, with rising living standards and relative prosperity, some families remained immune to this 'progress', while the Thatcher government embraced and 'nourished' the concept of 'welfare dependency' in order to reduce support for disadvantaged groups. Part of the issue with 'troubled families' has, according to the government, been the 'moral hazard in our welfare system – people thinking they can be as irresponsible as they like because the state will always bail them out' (Cameron, 2011a). Similarly, despite a radical restructuring of the welfare system undertaken by the coalition government, a specific programme for 'troubled families' was required, the government argued, because 'when it comes to these [troubled] families, these reforms are not enough' (Cameron, 2011b).

The simplistic umbrella labels given to the 'underclass' during various iterations of the concept have often masked competing and contradictory discourses, and provided shelter for concerns about a wide variety of social issues. Descriptions of the residuum and the social problem group often included long lists of tenuously linked groups and the particular problems that they faced and researchers highlighted how the concept of 'deprivation' was used to cover 'quite different issues and problems' (Rutter and Madge, 1976: 1). Kirk Mann (1994: 80) highlighted how the 'disparate observers who claim to be able to witness an underclass are incapable of agreeing on what it is they have witnessed' and Ruth Levitas noted at least three competing discourses within New Labour's focus on socially excluded groups, which initially included 18 different Policy Action Teams. 'Troubled families', as we have seen, have officially morphed from the criminal, anti-social and 'workless' families, to those who also experience health issues or have disabled members, have 'children in need', or experience domestic violence. Unofficially, 'troubled families' have also been linked with issues such as Islamic extremism, gang membership and organised crime. Local authorities, as we will see in Chapter Four, often used numerous different issues to identify the 'troubled families' in their area.

The role of the state in sponsoring or sustaining different constructions of the 'underclass' has been increasing in recent years. In earlier constructions, the idea of an 'underclass' was often advanced by those outside of government, such as researchers, social reformers and campaigning groups or voluntary organisations. More recently, however, the establishment of a research programme focusing on 'transmitted deprivation' by a Secretary of State, and an explicit policy focus in the 2000s on 'social exclusion' have seen this situation change. It was New Labour that helped to draw attention to the 'problem' of Anti-Social Behaviour and, subsequently, the 'problem families' that were supposedly responsible for a substantial proportion of it. The idea of 'troubled families' represents the culmination of this process, whereby the 'underclass' have become an officially recognised and identifiable group.

There has also, in recent years, been a (re)intensifying of the gaze on the 'family' in underclass discussions (Gillies, 2014). This gaze then leads to a focus on parenting and child rearing practices, which, in turn, leads to policies scrutinising the capabilities of working class women. It should be noted here that efforts to make working class women 'more respectable' have their own long history, going back over 200 years (Skeggs, 1997: 41–55). More recently, Sir Keith Joseph was concerned about deprivation that was 'transmitted' through the generations and Charles Murray's second intervention in the UK in 1994 focused on changes to the British family. The Labour governments of 1997–2010 shifted an initial broad policy brief around social exclusion and ASB to a more focused gaze on the 'most challenging families' (RTF, 2006a) and 120,000 families 'at risk' (SETF, 2007a) in their later years in office. Cameron's strong belief in the importance of family (see, for example, Cameron, 2010, 2011a, 2011b and 2014a) fits with traditional Conservative interests, which manifest themselves in the contemporary fixation with 'hard-working families', and a parallel concern about, the social consequences of 'family breakdown' and 'troubled families'. Gillies (2011) has highlighted how families are often viewed by contemporary politicians in terms of their *practices* such as child rearing, education and, especially in the case of 'problem families' under New Labour and the 'troubled families' of today, the all-round domestic competence of the household.

The tensions, contradictions and shifts in emphasis that have occurred over a prolonged period of time highlight that the concept of 'troubled families' did not materialised fully-formed and without contention. Instead, a number of fragments of previous ideas have come together, contributing to the creation of an official classification of 'troubled families'. Themes from longstanding concerns about an alleged 'underclass', expressed in different ways at different historical periods, have merged with contemporary political concerns and popular opinions. In recent years, then, traditional Conservative interests in the role of the family coalesced with an electorally successful 'broken society' narrative to produce a powerful discourse about the importance of 'the family' in addressing disadvantage. The largely accepted need for austerity has led to popular and uncritical support for policies that claim to save 'the taxpayer' money and that can reduce the size of government. The next chapter highlights how these circumstances, coupled with the riots of 2011, opened a 'policy window' for the creation of and sharp focus on a small group of 'troubled families' who were 'the source of a large proportion of the problems in society' (Cameron, 2011b), and the development of a wide-ranging interventionist and 'more efficient' policy programme from the state.

THREE

The opening of a policy window

As I see it, people who are trying to advocate change are like surfers waiting for the big wave. You get out there, you have to be ready to go, you have to be ready to paddle. If you're not ready to paddle when the big wave comes along, you're not going to ride it in. (Policy analyst in Kingdon, 1995: 165)

Introduction

This chapter traces the emergence of the concept of 'troubled families', from a single mention in a speech by David Cameron during the early days of the coalition government (Cameron, 2010), through to the establishment of a high profile central government policy with specific criteria for what constitutes a 'troubled family' and with 120,000 such 'troubled families' identified in local authorities across England. The chapter draws on work by the American political scientist John W. Kingdon (1995) who argued that certain issues moved up the policy agenda as a result of three different process streams – problem recognition; formation and refining of policy proposals; and politics – coming together or 'coupling' at key moments.

Kingdon noted that a variety of *problems* captured the attention of governments and the individuals working within them, representing the first process stream. Often, these problems would come to the attention of policy makers and politicians via focusing events – crises or disasters that 'reinforce some pre-existing perception of a problem ... that was already "in the back of people's minds"' (Kingdon, 1995: 98). There was also, Kingdon argued, a second stream – a 'community of specialists – bureaucrats, people in the planning and evaluation and in the budget offices ... academics, interest groups, researchers – which concentrates on generating *proposals*' (1995: 87, emphasis added), each with 'their pet ideas or axes to grind'. The third *political* stream, according to Kingdon, consisted of 'things like swings in national mood, vagaries of public opinion, election results, changes of administration, shifts in partisan or ideological distributions ... and interest group pressure campaigns'. Each of these streams operated largely, but not entirely, independently and came together only infrequently. Kingdon argued that it was the coupling of these streams at such moments or 'critical times' that were the key to understanding policy change and agenda setting – 'A problem is recognized, a solution is available, the political climate makes the time right for change, and the constraints do not prohibit action' (1995: 88).

Kingdon identified that these moments, these 'critical times', opened 'policy windows' whereby 'policy entrepreneurs' could push their favoured solutions and attempt to 'attach' them to the particular policy problem faced. Policy entrepreneurs, who can occupy a variety of positions or roles, are 'advocates who are willing to invest their resources – time, energy, reputation, money, – to promote a position in return for anticipated future gain in the form of material, purposive or solidary benefits' (1995: 179). Policy windows, Kingdon (1995: 88) argued, presented 'an opportunity for pushing one's proposals … open for a short time, when the conditions to push a given subject higher on the policy agenda are right'.

Kingdon's work offers a valuable framework in attempting to understand the shift from a government concerned with developing a light-touch Big Society approach to 'families that have never worked' to one that, via the 2011 riots in England, implemented and led a national programme to 'turn around' the lives of the 'most troubled families' in England. The chapter begins by examining the early coalition attempts to work with 'disadvantaged and dysfunctional families' against a backdrop of austerity and welfare reform, via locally-led 'Community Budget' pilots and the volunteer-led Working Families Everywhere project. The government response to the 2011 riots, and its focus on parenting failures, and the 'underclass consensus' (Tyler, 2013: 2) that emerged during the riots is then considered. In the months following the riots, the expansive Troubled Families Programme (TFP) was established and launched, and 'troubled families' became an official government title for families displaying or causing certain 'problems'. The roles of key individuals, such as Emma Harrison, David Cameron, Louise Casey and Eric Pickles, during these 'critical times' are also discussed before the chapter concludes with a summary of the emergence of the TFP and the strength of the official discourse surrounding 'troubled families'.

The emergence of 'troubled families'

The 2010 Conservative Party manifesto set out the ambition to 'make Britain the most family-friendly country in Europe' (Conservative Party, 2010: viii) and promised that a Conservative government would 'give targeted help to disadvantaged and dysfunctional families' (2010: 41). A chapter articulating how a Conservative government would make Britain more 'family-friendly' stated:

> We will help families with all the pressures they face: the lack of time, money worries, the impact of work, concerns about schools and crime, preventing unhealthy influences, poor housing. We will not be neutral on this. Britain's families will get our full backing across all our policies. (Conservative Party, 2010: 41)

The manifesto also set out how 'disadvantaged and dysfunctional families' might be supported, stating that a Conservative government would take Sure Start 'back to its original purpose of early intervention, increase its focus on the neediest families, and better involve organisations with a track record in supporting families' (Conservative Party, 2010: 43). There was also a pledge to 'set out a new approach to help families with multiple problems' (2010: 43).

The Conservative Party did not win the 2010 general election, but did form a coalition government with the Liberal Democrats. The coalition's 'programme for government' (HM Government, 2010) argued that this situation, where both parties were apparently willing to put aside differences in order to govern 'in the national interest', offered the best of both worlds, with family policy being used as an example of this pragmatic approach:

> We have found that a combination of our parties' best ideas and attitudes has produced a programme for government that is more radical and comprehensive than our individual manifestos. For example, when you take Conservative plans to strengthen families and encourage social responsibility, and add to them the Liberal Democrat passion for protecting our civil liberties and stopping the relentless incursion of the state into the lives of individuals, you create a Big Society matched by big citizens. This offers the potential to completely recast the relationship between people and the state: citizens empowered; individual opportunity

extended; communities coming together to make lives better. We believe that the combination of our ideas will help us to create a much stronger society: one where those who can, do; and those who cannot, we always help (HM Government, 2010: 8).

This document also stated that the coalition would 'investigate a new approach to helping families with multiple problems' (HM Government, 2010: 19). In October 2010, signs of this 'new approach' began to appear. The Department for Communities and Local Government (DCLG) announced that 16 local authority areas would be given control over local spending in their area 'free from centrally imposed conditions' (DCLG, 2010):

From April next year this first phase of 16 areas covering 28 councils and their partners will be put in charge of 'Community Budgets' that pool various strands of Whitehall funding into a single 'local bank account' for tackling social problems around families with complex needs.

The press release accompanying the announcement (DCLG, 2010) stated that around £8 billion was spent each year on around 120,000 families that have 'multiple problems', with this funding being distributed through different programmes and agencies. Eric Pickles, the Secretary of State for Communities and Local Government, argued that Community Budgets would tear down 'artificial barriers' and 'help better protect frontline services and help the most vulnerable' (DCLG, 2010). This approach was in keeping with wider rhetoric about localism and decentralisation, 'doing more with less', and the need to curb public spending to improve the government's finances.

In December 2010, just over six months after becoming prime minister, David Cameron spoke at an event organised by Relate, a relationship advice charity. In his speech, Cameron (2010) set out his government's 'family-friendly reform agenda', which would be about 'thoughtful, sensible, practical and modern support to help families with the issues they face'. Cameron stated that he was 'as aware as anyone about the limits of what government can do in this area' and was not going to introduce 'some bureaucratic system telling parents what to do', but nor was he advocating 'leaving families to get on with it in a hostile world'. Making it clear that he 'loathe[d] nanny-statism' and that he was 'not proposing heavy-handed state intervention', Cameron instead set out why he believed government, and policy makers, should be cognisant of the importance of 'family':

> The seeds of so many social problems – as well as success stories – are sown in the early years. Family is where people learn to be good citizens, to take responsibility, to live in harmony with others. Families are the building blocks of a strong, cohesive society. This isn't a hunch. A whole body of evidence backs it up. When parents have bad relationships, their child is more likely to live in poverty, fail at school, end up in prison, be unemployed later in life. It would be wrong for public policy to ignore all this. No one who wants to tackle some of our deepest social problems – and the massive economic costs they bring – has a hope unless they understand the importance of family.

It was in this speech that Cameron first publicly used the phrase 'troubled families', and he spoke at length about the problems they faced and how the coalition government would work with these families:

> For years we've known that a relatively small number of troubled families are responsible for a large proportion of the problems in our society. Maybe the parents have an addiction or have never worked in their life. Maybe there's domestic violence. Often the children are completely out of control.
>
> If we are honest, people's first instinct with these troubled families is to turn their backs on them. But that is self-defeating. The problems get worse. The misery increases – for them, their neighbours and society as a whole. Let's not forget that children are being brought up in these homes – children who through no fault of their own have inherited a life of despair. And let's not forget these families cost us a fortune – in benefits, social workers, police time and places in young offenders' institutes and prisons. Indeed, some estimates suggest that just 46,000 families cost the taxpayer over £4 billion a year – that is nearly £100,000 each.

Cameron went on to set the ambition that by the end of the parliament, he wanted to 'try and turn around every troubled family in the country'. This ambition was to be realised through a Big Society venture, relying on private and voluntary sector input and based on volunteers supporting 'troubled families'. Emma Harrison, the Chief Executive of the welfare-to-work company Action 4 Employment (A4E), was announced as the person who would lead the work to 'turn around' the lives of 'troubled families', with Cameron arguing that '[h]er approach is the complete opposite of the impersonal, one-size-fits-all approach that has failed so many families'.

Cameron promised to help Harrison 'pioneer a new way of doing things' that would be 'less bureaucratic, less impersonal, more human, more effective'. This would include working with the family as a whole and not just as individuals, although given the similarity of the approach to that adopted with 'problem families' in the 1940s, Garrett's (2007) critique of the 'pioneering' claims attached to Family Intervention Projects (FIPs), and the 'think family' approach of the previous government, it is unclear in what respects this approach would qualify as 'pioneering'. The approach would be piloted with 500 'troubled families' in different local authorities. Cameron further marginalised the role of government in this endeavour by stating

> Our side of the bargain of this: we will strip away the bureaucracy and give her, and the many others who we hope will follow her lead, the freedom she needs to make a difference. Her side of the bargain: to get these families back into work and on their feet.

Although 'troubled families' were never clearly defined by Cameron at this stage, Harrison's work, which came to be known as Working Families Everywhere (WFE), was focused on 100,000 families that had 'never worked'. The scheme would see a number of volunteer 'family champions' supporting families with multiple disadvantages into work, with Harrison (2010) saying that 'every family will have their own "Emma", able to use every existing resource to help them get going, face up to and sort out their problems, whether they be parenting challenges, poor health, debt, addiction, dependency or lack of motivation'. Following some initial media interest, the scheme, located within the Department for Education, operated outside of the media glare for much of its early stages.

At this stage of the coalition government's period in office, the main policy focus was on wider reforms to the public sector and the welfare state. Austerity had, in the words of Clarke and Newman (2012: 300) been 'ideologically reworked', from being an economic response required by the financial crisis of 2007–08, to a political response that 'focused on the unwieldy and expensive welfare state and public sector ... as the root cause of the crisis'. Political consensus prior to the 2010 general election about the need to cut public expenditure had, following the election, morphed into an assault on the welfare state with one commentator noting that the unprecedented attack, with harsh cuts being accompanied by a simultaneous wide-ranging restructuring programme, coupled with increasing demands on services, amounted to a 'double crisis' (Taylor-Gooby, 2013). The re-working of austerity and the attack on the welfare state was accompanied by a return of 'scroungerphobia' (Deacon, 1976; Shildrick and Macdonald, 2013) and the resurrection of the overly-generous state leading to 'welfare dependency' trope, with numerous politicians discussing families where two or three generations had 'never worked' (see Shildrick et al, 2012 for a comprehensive rebuttal of such vacuous claims). Stigmatising poverty porn television programmes (Jensen, 2013, 2014), such as *We All Pay your Benefits*, *On Benefits and Proud*, and *Benefits Street*, offering 'hardworking families' the opportunity to gawk at the lives of those who relied on social security payments for their income, helped to secure support for stringent cuts in support to those on out of work benefits. The WFE scheme and the Community Budgets pilot both fitted the narrative of needing to do more with less and presenting poor people themselves as the problem to be solved.

On 28 July 2011, the Permanent Secretary at the DCLG, Sir Bob Kerslake, wrote to local authority chief executives to inform them of 'a number of exciting opportunities to get involved' (DCLG, 2011a) with Community Budgets, and of the government's desire to expand the approach to new local authority areas and to help tackle different issues. Kerslake stated that Community Budgets were 'developing into a powerful tool to drive change' and that there was 'a belief in the concept'. The challenge now, he said, was 'to develop and apply it together and demonstrate its power through real change and improvement in service delivery, outcomes and efficiency'. The letter, which used the terms 'problem families' and 'families with multiple problems' interchangeably, spoke of a 'radical future' for Community Budgets and set out government plans both to expand the number of Community Budgets to 50 areas by April 2012 and to examine the potential for the approach to address other policy issues such as long-term care and environmental management. A little over a week after Kerslake's letter was sent, riots took place across England in August 2011. The problem of 'troubled families' was once again back in the media spotlight.

The 2011 riots

On 4 August 2011, Mark Duggan was shot dead by police in Tottenham. Peaceful demonstrations involving members of Duggan's family and his friends took place two days later outside Tottenham police station, following a lack of direct communication from the police and incidences of misinformation regarding the shooting being reported in the media. When senior police officers refused to meet with or speak to protesters, the situation escalated with police officers coming under attack from bottles and fireworks. The BBC reported that 'unconfirmed reports say the incident was sparked by a confrontation between a teenage protester and a police officer' (BBC News, 2011) although alternative explanations have been given (see, for example, Cadwalladr, 2016).

The rioting spread to other parts of London in the following days, as well as other cities and towns across England, including Manchester, Liverpool, Bristol, Luton and Nottingham. MPs were recalled from their summer holidays as a result of the unrest and, on 11 August 2015, the prime minister delivered a statement to parliament (Cameron, 2011c). Dealing initially and primarily with the incidents that led to the riots, the police response to it and the damage caused by those involved in the riots, Cameron eventually turned to what he called 'the deeper problem'.

> I have said before that there is a major problem in our society with children growing up not knowing the difference between right and wrong. This is not about poverty; it is about culture—a culture that glorifies violence, shows disrespect to authority and says everything about rights but nothing about responsibilities.
>
> In too many cases, the parents of these children—if they are still around—do not care where their children are or who they are with, let alone what they are doing. The potential consequences of neglect and immorality on this scale have been clear for too long, without enough action being taken. As I said yesterday, there is no one step that can be taken, but we need a benefit system that rewards work and is on the side of families. We need more discipline in our schools; we need action to deal with the most disruptive families; and we need a criminal justice system that scores a clear, heavy line between right and wrong – in short, all the action that is necessary to help mend our broken society.

Cameron's focus on the 'cultural' causes of the riots, a culture that glorified violence, one where lone parent families and lack of parental care are inextricably linked, formed part of what Tyler (2013: 2) called the 'underclass consensus' that surrounded the riots and their causes. She notes that this emerged in and from the responses of politicians and journalists, even while the riots were ongoing. In a similar vein, De Benedictis (2012) traced the 'feral parents' narrative that played out in some sections of the media, echoing Cameron's concerns about absent parents and disruptive families. Allen and Taylor (2012: 5) argued that popular debates surrounding the riots 'were suffused with a long-standing narrative of troubled mothers which refuelled debates around welfare dependency and the (un)deserving poor in an age of austerity' while Edwards et al (2012: 432) noted the 'orgy of family blaming' that followed the riots. Alternative explanations about contributory factors that might, for example, have highlighted the history of black men dying at the hands of police in Tottenham, or the potentially damaging effects of wide-ranging government cuts and increases in youth unemployment, were effectively crowded out.

Four days after his address to parliament, Cameron (2011a) gave a 'fightback' speech in his Oxfordshire constituency of Witney. He again eschewed structural or political issues as catalysts for the riots, stating that they were not about poverty, race or government cuts. Instead they were, in Cameron's eyes, about behaviour: 'people showing indifference to right and wrong, people with a twisted moral code, people with a complete absence of self-restraint'. Stating that the broken society was 'back at the top' of his agenda, Cameron promised that 'today and over the next few weeks, I and ministers from across the coalition government will review every aspect of our work to mend our broken society'. The speech contained numerous proposals across disparate policy areas, including: a promise to reform the police service and education provision; an echoing of New Labour language in calling for 'respect for community'; arguing for a welfare system that promotes responsibility; namechecking a National Citizen service for young people – a 'non-military programme ... that captures the spirit of national service'; and even promising a 'no holds barred' approach to 'the human rights and health and safety culture'. The riots, and the media and public response to them, thus acted as a 'focusing event' for the government, providing them with a 'policy window' for a more expansive, interventionist form of government to tackle the pre-existing problem of 'troubled families'.

Cameron once again focused on the issue of families and parenting and argued that it was only necessary to 'join the dots' to get a 'clear idea' of why so many young people were involved in the rioting:

> I don't doubt that many of the rioters out last week have no father at home. Perhaps they come from one of the neighbourhoods where it's standard for children to have a mum and not a dad, where it's normal for young men to grow up without a male role model, looking to the streets for their father figures, filled up with rage and anger. So if we want to have any hope of mending our broken society, family and parenting is where we've got to start. (Cameron, 2011a)

He stated that a 'family test' would be applied to all domestic policy and mentioned speeding up work to improve parenting, but he also paid particular attention to 'troubled families':

> And we need more urgent action, too, on the families that some people call 'problem', others call 'troubled'. The ones that everyone in their neighbourhood knows and often avoids. Last December I asked Emma Harrison to develop a plan to help get these families on track. It became clear to me earlier this year that – as can so often happen – those plans were being held back by bureaucracy. So even before the riots happened, I asked for an explanation. Now that the riots have happened I will make sure that we clear away the red tape and the bureaucratic wrangling, and put rocket boosters under this programme, with a clear ambition that within the lifetime of this Parliament we will turn around the lives of the 120,000 most troubled families in the country. (Cameron, 2011a)

The mention of Harrison's work prompted a renewal of media interest in the WFE scheme. *The Times* reported that the scheme would work to 'uncover a background of welfare dependency' (Sherman et al, 2011). In an interview with *The Sunday Times* (Driscoll, 2011), Harrison also claimed credit for the term 'troubled families':

> In the beginning he [Cameron] used the term 'problem families' – in that they're a problem to society – now he says 'troubled families'. Do you notice that? That's my word.

> These are not bad people, they are families who haven't got a clue.

Although she claimed that '[p]art of her deal with Cameron was that this vilification should stop', she still managed to pathologise and infantilise the families she was working with, giving one example of the 'transformative' power of her approach:

> I sat with them for two hours. There were cigarette ends and dirt everywhere, mattresses on the floor ... We had a real good chat. I said to them, "There's a chap who runs a charity shop in your local precinct, and he's asked if you'll come and help out tomorrow." They said, "Us? But people think we're scum."
>
> This family lived on crisps, chips – and cigarettes – but at the end of the day the manager told them they'd done a good job, and they had that good feeling you get from a job well done, and the mother went into a shop and bought some fresh food and cooked a meal. Her daughter nearly fell over. Now I might never get Mum back to work, but she can help her children, she can support the working family.

Other commentators were less effusive about the approach with one calling the scheme a 'small state fantasy' and a 'new government initiative dedicated to summoning paradise out of chaos' that 'conjures the image of workshy beasts lying in piles of Pringles and crack, waiting to be shouted at by Hyacinth Bucket, on top of the rest of their woes' (Gold, 2011). Cameron's 'rocket boosters' quickly fizzled out however, the 'small state fantasy' never materialised and, instead, the policy window provided by the riots saw a new policy for dealing with 'troubled families' emerge.

Although the launch of the TFP occurred in December 2011, plans for the programme had been put in place in the months leading up to the announcement. While giving evidence to the Public Accounts Committee (PAC) inquiry into 'troubled families' in 2016, Louise Casey told of how she had been asked to carry out a small review to understand whether the government could meet the prime minister's ambition, made in the speech to Relate in December 2010, to 'turn around' the lives of the 120,000 'troubled families'. In a good example of a 'policy entrepreneur' 'softening up the system' (Kingdon, 1995: 181) she stated that she reached the conclusion that they probably were not going to meet that commitment if they carried on as they were, and instead offered an alternative course of action:

> In fairness, I had said to them in the summer during which the riots happened – at a very low level; I was not doing a major review – "There are different ways you could look at this. You could do it writ large. In other words, do you actually want to really transform the lives, spend money and have a massive Government programme? Or you could do a classic line to take, which is that there are lots of ways Government is helping all these families, such as through early help." I said, "You've got two options here. Whitehall might try to get you to do the middle one. That will be a mistake." It was left there. The riots happened, and then I think they decided around September … (Public Accounts Committee, 2016a: 14)

The decision in 'around September' led to the announcement in October 2011 of Casey heading up a new Troubled Families Team in DCLG. In the week following the announcement on Casey's appointment, Pickles (2011), echoing the prime minister's robust rhetoric in the days following the riots, set the tone – and the pace – for the TFP during a speech to council leaders:

> Last week the Prime Minister announced a Troubled Families Unit in my Department led by Louise Casey. She will be working on an action plan for what needs to be done nationally and locally to deliver this ambition. That will include cutting the bureaucracy that gets in your way. And she'll be supporting and talking to you. To ensure that all across the country, councils and their partners are prioritising the activities and interventions which work. If you're wondering is this a threat to your independence – the answer is yes, it is a threat. It is a threat if you don't get on with things. Think of this as a race to deliver by 2015. If you motor along then we'll play catch up. But if we get there first – you'll find yourselves behind the agenda. And I'm sorry about people who tell me they've already got a programme that deals with this. Well, if it was all dealt with we wouldn't be here. One or two projects along the right lines isn't nearly enough to solve this problem. So be in no doubt – we are in a hurry, we mean to deliver. You

don't need to talk about it or show empathy. I want you to get on with it. And I know local government can get results. But understand – this isn't either or. We are going to deliver on this. So get moving.

Casey already had a reputation as someone who got things done, able to talk in blunt terms and cut through Whitehall red tape. Controversy has also followed her relatively closely. In 1999, while she was the head of the government's Rough Sleepers Unit, she told the *Observer* that homeless charities were 'servicing' and 'perpetuating' homelessness (Bright, 1999). Two years later, while still in the same role, she faced accusations that her unit had 'fiddled the figures' in order to meet a pledge to reduce the number of people sleeping rough by two-thirds between 1998 and January 2002 (BBC, 2001). It was reported that 'people were put in hostels or threatened with arrest overnight while counts were done' in order to keep the homeless figures artificially low (BBC, 2001). At the time, the *Independent* reported that:

> The claims stem from a meeting of 35 outreach workers who complained to their union, the TGWU, that they had been forced to help fix the count on 20 November. One hostel, Kingsgate House in central London, held a party that night, and allegedly encouraged residents to invite friends, many of them rough sleepers. A second London shelter, Bondway, is said to have converted its dining room into a temporary dormitory (Morrison and Symenliyska, 2001).

Casey denied the reports, stating that she had 'nothing to hide or be ashamed of' (BBC, 2001) and that 'we wouldn't get caught up in things like that to distort the figures' (Morrison and Symenliyska, 2001). In January 2003, 'Whitehall's least conventional civil servant' took over as head of the newly formed Anti-Social Behaviour Unit (ASBU), with her promotion being seen as 'a sign of Whitehall's new-found enthusiasm for civil servants who make things happen' (Walker, 2003). In 2005, Casey once again made the headlines for an expletive-laden after-dinner speech to senior police officers. She was quoted as extolling the virtues of working while drunk, threatening to 'deck' any civil servant who 'says bloody "evidence-based policy" to me once more' and made light of her language while acting in an official capacity:

> Excuse my language. I get lots of complaints about it. But you can't complain. It is an after-dinner speech. So you can

> write to Hazel Blears as much as you like. I'll just say 'after-dinner speech' and I wasn't even pissed ... (*Guardian*, 2005).

The furore surrounding the speech did not prevent Casey from being named as the head of the new Respect Task Force when it was launched a few months later. Although Gordon Brown moved her on from the RTF in 2009 when he was prime minister, she did not have to wait too long before being invited back into the heart of government, initially leading a review into 'the hotchpotch of schemes the government had set up on problem families' (Ramesh, 2012a) and then in heading up the unit that she herself had proposed to co-ordinate and streamline this activity.

Kingdon (1995: 180–1) suggested that policy entrepreneurs possessed qualities that fell into three broad categories. First, entrepreneurs had some kind of claim to a hearing – they were seen as experts, or possessing certain experience or knowledge that others might not necessarily have. Second, they were known for being politically savvy or for their negotiating skill that enabled them to exert greater influence than may otherwise have been the case. Third, and perhaps most pertinently in this example, Kingdon argued that policy entrepreneurs were persistent, with 'sheer tenacity' often paying off for successful entrepreneurs. Casey, as we have seen, possesses each of the qualities associated with successful policy entrepreneurship, and there is little doubt that she played a major role in advancing or 'pushing' the politics and processes behind the TFP.

The Troubled Families Programme

'Troubled families' became an official social problem on 15 December 2011, when David Cameron launched the Troubled Families Programme with a speech at Sandwell Christian Centre in Oldbury in the West Midlands (Cameron, 2011b). In contrast to his previous commitment (Cameron 2010) to 'strip away the bureaucracy' to help Emma Harrison develop her volunteer-led approach to supporting 'troubled families', Cameron, sensing the 'policy window' for a large government programme was now open, claimed that 'only government has the power ... to sort them out' and arguing that it would 'take a concerted effort from all corners of Government' (Cameron, 2011b).

The social turbulence caused by the riots and the government's need to be seen to be doing something required a stronger and more robust response than the 'Hyacinth Bucket' image of the WFE programme. Throughout the early stages of the construction of the concept of 'troubled families', the discourse surrounding and permeating it was reminiscent of Wacquant's argument that neoliberalism involved a *remasculinisation* of the state. It also lent credence to Featherstone et al's (2014a: 2) claim that there exists an approach of 'muscular authoritarianism towards multiply deprived families'. Cameron wanted to 'sort out' these families, Pickles was 'threatening' local authority leaders and Casey was well-known for blunt talking and 'getting things done'. This approach extended to the promotion of the intensive 'family intervention' model that would 'grip' not just families, but also the allegedly un-coordinated mass of services that was failing to turn them around.

'Troubled families' were not just brought into existence and given an official identity by the government, they were also 'quantified and coded by the state' (Bourdieu, 2014: 10). There were, according to the government, 117,015 'troubled families' (rounded up to 120,000), and each local authority was provided with an indicative number of 'troubled families' in its area. This estimate was arrived at using data from the Families and Children Survey in 2005, and population estimates and indices of deprivation and child wellbeing (DCLG, 2011b). Levitas (2012) highlighted that the FACS data, which led to the SETF (2007a) publication on 'families at risk', revolved around disadvantages such as material deprivation, low income, maternal mental health, and poor quality or over-crowded housing. She went on to argue that the figure of 120,000 'troubled families', characterised by crime, anti-social behaviour, educational truancy and worklessness in England, on closer inspection 'turns out to be a factoid – something that takes the form of a fact, but is not' (Levitas, 2012: 4). The misrepresentation of the research base was brushed aside by the government, with Casey suggesting that 'a lot is made of this, in retrospect, which needn't be' (in Gentleman, 2013) and that the most important thing was that she was 'getting on with the job', working with local authorities – giving them the criteria for 'troubled families' and working to help them populate their local database 'with real names, real addresses, real people'.

'Troubled families' were, at this stage, those who met three of the four following criteria:

- Are involved in youth crime or anti-social behaviour
- Have children who are regularly truanting or not in school
- Have an adult on out of work benefits
- Cause high costs to the taxpayer. (DCLG, 2012a: 9)

Despite the official number of 'troubled families' in England originating from data which included disadvantages such as poverty, poor housing, low skills and maternal mental health, none of these issues were explicitly reflected in the criteria used by the government to identify 'troubled families'. Poor families who might have been experiencing some of these issues but who did not, for whatever reason, meet three of the four criteria, would not be eligible for the TFP. Thus, entrance to the TFP was reserved for the 'troublemaking' or 'undeserving' poor, reinforcing the rhetoric that this was a programme targeting a small hard-core of 'neighbours from hell' cut adrift from mainstream society.

As well as the official criteria for being a 'troubled family', speeches by Casey and Pickles and DCLG publications offered an insight into the 'types' of families that would qualify as 'troubled' and what their shortcomings were. These were families that could not keep their houses clean, that could not properly care for their young children and/or could not control their teenage children:

> The help provided is often very practical and involves workers and families 'rolling up their sleeves' and 'donning the marigolds' – working alongside families, showing them how to clear up and make their homes fit to live in. (DCLG, 2012a: 21)

> Work with individual family members and group work with the family as a whole often looked at family relationships and communication as well as supporting parents with parenting positively, setting boundaries and routines and learning how to praise and motivate their children. (DCLG, 2012a: 12)

> This is all about making sure the mum is in control of her household and even with a 14- or 15-year-old teenager, quite often when they're looking at, you know, being sent down, right, who do they call for? Their mum. (Casey, 2013a)

The focus on improving parenting practices and providing domestic support is suffused with gendered assumptions about the (in)competence of mothers within 'troubled families' and, in some cases, the links have been made more explicit, as can be seen in the final quote above. Casey has also suggested that mothers in 'troubled families' have too many children (Winnett and Kirkup, 2012) and should be given contraception advice by family intervention workers (Swinford, 2013).

An accompanying rhetorical preoccupation with domestic violence almost slips into mother-blaming in Casey's suggestion that 'while those [women] who suffered domestic violence did not *actively* choose violent partners, they may be used to, vulnerable to, or not surprised by violence in partners' (Casey, 2012a: 50, emphasis added). The implicit and sometime explicit focus on maternal (in)competence and (lack of) control in 'troubled families' is entirely consistent with Starkey's observation, noted in the previous chapter, about the 'problem families' discourse in the 1950s:

> In spite of the use of the term 'problem family', what was really meant was 'problem mother'. The description which appeared to embrace all members of the family was used to mask a profoundly critical attitude towards poor, working class women. (Starkey, 2000: 544)

The political construction of 'troubled families' and the putative source(s) of their problems has implications for the type of work that is required to 'turn them around' and also for the workers tasked with carrying out that work. Family workers are expected to be able to 'roll up their sleeves' and 'don the marigolds'. They are also expected to be willing to get down on their knees and scrub floors and cook pizza, if necessary (Bennett, 2012), and demonstrate how to get children ready for school and 'out the door' (Casey, 2013a). As well as this maternal, 'caring' side to family workers, they are also required to demonstrate a 'tougher' side as well. They have to be prepared to be 'persistent, assertive and challenging', able to 'tell it like it is' to the families they are working with and threaten them with sanctions where non-compliance might be an issue. They have, in Casey's words, 'been around the block themselves, they won't take no for an answer' and often 'don't look and feel like officials' (in Hellen, 2014).

Just as the TFP has been positioned as policy response to past 'failures of the state' (see Crossley, 2016), the qualities of 'family workers' are juxtaposed against other street-level bureaucrats (Lipsky, 1980). The TFP, then, attempts to claim distinction for family workers, forging a new social identity for them that is contrasted against their supposedly lethargic, overly bureaucratic colleagues in the public sector. They represent the answer not just to 'troubled families', but also to a reputedly bloated, failing public sector that has been remiss in their dealings with 'troubled families'. Social workers, in particular, have been singled out for criticism. In Casey's eyes, social workers 'circle' families, armed with clipboards, 'assessing the hell out of them', 'writing reports about them' but never able to effect any lasting, sustainable change within the families (in Bennett, 2012). Social workers 'collude with [families] to find excuses for failure' (Casey, 2013a), and Casey has been clear that she is 'not running some cuddly social workers' programme to wrap everybody in cotton wool' (in Winnett and Kirkup, 2012). Casey has herself highlighted the difference between family workers and their colleagues when she gave evidence to a select committee and told them:

> we have staff and workers *who are extraordinary*. They walk into these families' lives; *they do not invite them to an office for an appointment with a letter.* They walk through the front door and into the front room past two extraordinarily difficult and dangerous-looking dogs that they hope are locked in the kitchen. They have to sit on a settee, often in a pretty rough environment with some very aggressive people, and, with kids not in school and people all over the criminal justice system and so on, they have to get them from there to there. I think that is extraordinary. (Communities and Local Government Committee, 2013: 5, emphasis added)

The ability to 'get stuck in' and get things done while being 'persistent, assertive and challenging' are all characteristics and dispositions that have been associated with Casey, who is known for having a 'tough streak' (Chambers, 2012) and for her 'plain speaking and habitual trashing of PC niceties' (Williams, 2012). Just as Emma Harrison suggested that each family would have its very own 'Emma' helping them in the WFE scheme, it appears that Casey believed that it was workers who shared her dispositions and attitude that were best placed to help 'troubled families' under the TFP.

Conclusion

The coalition government's desire to explore a 'new approach' to working with what they initially called 'disadvantaged and dysfunctional' families before turning to the phrase 'troubled families' progressed through a series of adjustments before it finally crystallised into the TFP. Prior to the riots in 2011, a number of small, largely un-coordinated and unconnected schemes had been in operation but the 'focusing events' of the riots presented a 'critical time' when strong government action was required, if not expected, by certain sections of the media and the wider populace. The riots presented an opportune moment when the *problem*, *policy*, and *political* process streams were all aligned for a proposed solution to 'troubled families'.

Such a 'solution' to the 'troubled families' problem was already available in Whitehall, owing to Casey's suggestion that 'a massive government programme' was the best way to meet the prime minister's commitment to 'turn around' the lives of the country's most 'troubled families', and the existence of the family intervention model. Casey, therefore, played a central role in the development of the TFP but the role of the riots should not be underestimated either. The TFP also carries the hallmarks of two other influential figures – Cameron and Pickles. Pickles' blunt talking and robust handling of local authorities reinforced Casey's rhetoric, while Cameron's traditional Conservative belief in the centrality of the family in social life also helped to shape the programme. Cameron himself is perhaps more closely associated with the TFP than he was with other social policies and programmes. It was Cameron who first spoke about 'troubled families', he announced the programme in December 2011 and, a few months later, he held an official launch at 10 Downing Street. A speech on families in August 2014 immediately preceded the publication of details of the expanded programme. Casey acknowledged that 'the fact that her appointment as head of the Troubled Families Unit was announced by David Cameron as "an important signal" and made a "big difference" to her authority to act' (Rutter and Harris, 2014: 8). It is instructive that none of these key individuals remain overtly involved in the second phase of the programme. Cameron has retired from politics altogether, Pickles is no longer a government minister and Casey went on to be involved in high profile, if similarly controversial, reviews on child sexual exploitation in Rotherham and community integration among migrant communities before announcing in April 2017 that she would be leaving government to 'take up new opportunities in the voluntary sector and academia' (DCLG, 2017b).

This chapter has highlighted how the concept of 'troubled families' has emerged as an official social problem, extending and strengthening the long history of the 'underclass' thesis discussed in Chapter Two. The influence of powerful individuals like Harrison, Cameron, Pickles, and Casey can be found in the emergence and development of discourses surrounding and permeating the concept of 'troubled families'. Casey, a senior civil servant who was trusted by both Cameron and Pickles, acted as the chief policy entrepreneur in ensuring that her 'pet proposal' (Kingdon, 1995: 165) was ready to go when the moment arrived. In Kingdon's classic book *Agendas, Alternatives, and Public Policies*, he quotes a policy analyst who uses a surfing analogy to argue that policy makers are waiting with their boards attempting to ride the big wave in.

While Casey rode the big wave of the TFP in, Harrison's WFE scheme and Community Budgets ebbed away. The WFE scheme was quietly closed with existing pilot areas blending their work into the new TFP when it was announced. Harrison stepped down from her role as Cameron's 'family champion' shortly after allegations of fraudulent practice at her A4E 'welfare-to-work' company. Community Budgets working with 'families with multiple problems' were effectively subsumed by the TFP, although new Community Budgets were developed that examined spending at a neighbourhood level and across a 'Whole Place' – a large number of multiple local authority areas. While these schemes kept the issue of 'problem' or 'troubled' families on the policy agenda, they existed largely out of the spotlight. The development of the TFP changed this dramatically.

The concept of 'troubled families' provides an example of the strength of official government discourse. 'Troubled families' have been given an official state identity. The government have identified how many 'troubled families' there are, and roughly where they can be found. There are numerous official government documents published on 'troubled families' including: the evidence base behind them; the 'problems' they both face and cause; the cost of them to 'the taxpayer'; and the best way of working with them. The former prime minister made a number of speeches about them and about how the programme that he launched was 'turning around' their lives. Family workers, largely employed by the state, were 'rolling their sleeves up', 'getting stuck in' and showing 'tough love' with these families, in their own homes, up and down the country every single day.

These actions have brought the concept of 'troubled families' to life in the eyes of the wider population. Feeding off a longstanding and populist belief in 'the underclass', and a contemporary preoccupation with poverty porn about 'scroungers' and 'benefit fraudsters', the government sought to link 'troubled families' with the causes of the 2011 riots and a wide range of other, often unconnected, social ills. Research highlighting the extent of multiple disadvantage was misrepresented to provide an evidence base for the existence of 120,000 troublesome, anti-social and 'workless' families. Bourdieu (1996: 24), in a rare foray into discussion of 'the family' specifically, argues that one:

> has to cease to regard the family as an immediate datum
> of social reality and see it rather as an instrument of
> construction of that reality; but one also has to ... ask who

constructed the instruments of construction that are thereby brought to light.

Bourdieu (1996: 25) argued that 'the family' was a 'well-founded illusion' and 'a fiction' because 'being produced and reproduced with the guarantee of the state, it receives from the state at every moment the means to exist and persist'. He noted that government officials, such as statisticians and social workers (as well, it should be said, as sociologists) helped to produce and reproduce this social reality by *acting on* this reality (Bourdieu, 1996: 25). Thus, every visit to a 'troubled families' house by a family worker, every PbR claim submitted for a 'turned around' family, every press release highlighting 'progress' in working with 'troubled families' helps to sustain and nourish the concept of 'troubled families', despite the shaky foundations on which the concept is built. The illusion of 'troubled families' that was initially produced by the state has, we see in the following chapters, been reproduced despite numerous criticisms and concerns. The next chapter explores the 'evolution' of the TFP into its second phase.

FOUR

The evolution of the Troubled Families Programme

When the general cueing effect produced by the sensitisation is combined with the type of free association in the 'It's Not Only This' theme, the result is that a number of other deviants are drawn into the same sensitising net. In the phase after the inventory, other targets became more visible and, hence, candidates for social control. These targets are not, of course, chosen randomly but from groups already structurally vulnerable to social control (Cohen, 2002: 64).

Introduction

The TFP was established specifically to 'turn around' the lives of the 120,000 troublesome and anti-social families that could be identified using the government's official criteria, with the government promoting the family intervention model as the best way of doing this. It was not long, however, before slippages from this original narrative began to emerge and it became clear during Phase 1 that many local authorities were struggling to find the requisite number of 'troubled families' in their area (Wiggins, 2012). Many were also choosing to work with families using existing universal services, and not necessarily rushing to adopt an intensive family intervention approach. It also was not long before it was announced that the programme would seek to work with an additional 400,000 families, once the original 120,000 had been dealt with. These families had been identified using new research and the 'massive expansion' (DCLG, 2013b) of the programme would also see new and expanded criteria introduced for the 400,000 extra families. A new approach to the PbR element of the programme was also announced for the second phase, one that required families to demonstrate 'significant and sustained progress' in order for local authorities to receive additional funding. Following intense criticism of the claims of success surrounding the TFP, the second phase of the programme operated out of the public limelight in its early stages before, in early 2017, it was announced that the programme was in line for a 'reboot' (Savage, 2017). In April 2017, the 'next phase' of the 'evolution' of TFP was announced, including a new focus on 'workless families' within the TFP and a further review of the PbR mechanism.

This chapter documents the evolution of the TFP from a high profile and relatively autonomous policy programme in its first phase, to one that currently occupies a much lower profile and that has been subsumed into a wider government initiative around workless families. The chapter progresses chronologically, with a discussion of the evolution of the programme within the first phase followed by an examination of new developments in the second and then the third phases. A discussion, focusing on continuities within the TFP and the programme's increasing emphasis on 'service transformation', concludes the chapter. The TFP, from 2015–20, was commonly referred to as the 'second phase' of the programme, but the announcements in April 2017 referred ambiguously to 'the next phase' of the programme. This is how these phases are referred to here.

Phase 1 (2011–May 2015)

The evolution of the programme began shortly after it was announced. Concerns raised by local authorities about the ability to identify the requisite number of families led DCLG to relax the criteria for what constituted a 'troubled family'. In August 2012, the *Local Government Chronicle* (LGC) reported that a number of authorities had queried the numbers of 'troubled families' allocated to them by DCLG (Wiggins, 2012), highlighting one authority where an initial data trawl had identified only around a third of the families they had been allocated by DCLG. The imposition of national criteria failed to take account of local demographics that affected the types of problems faced by many families. The LGC report quoted one officer as highlighting that their area had

> 'high levels of poverty ... a lot of families with working parents but on very low incomes, [but] relatively low levels of crime and anti-social behaviour, fairly good performance of children attending school and unemployment is not as high as some areas.'

Local authorities used a wide range of local criteria to help make up the local numbers they had been given and there was little oversight of what these criteria were. One authority initially used over 40 different local criteria to identify their 'troubled families' in the early stage of Phase 1. DCLG (2013a: 4–5) informed local authorities that they could use 'as many [local filter criteria] as you like' and that their 'only expectation is that these are high cost factors in your local area'. Many areas used loose criteria such as living in a disadvantaged neighbourhood, engagement with existing services, child protection issues or instances of domestic violence.

DCLG also relaxed the national criteria so that less 'troubled' families could be worked with under the programme. In guidance issued to local authorities in October 2013, it set out a number of ways in which local discretion could also be applied to the national criteria. By way of example, the guidance highlighted that although the national financial framework stated that families might be subject to an ASBO, an injunction or a housing-related ASB intervention in the last 12 months, families that had received a single letter about nuisance or ASB could also meet the national ASB criteria for entry to the programme (DCLG, 2013a: 1–2). The guidance also clarified that children who had 'been placed in specialist provision within a mainstream school for the purposes of improving behaviour' or who had 'a pattern of poor attendance that gives the Head Teacher an equivalent level of concern' (DCLG, 2013a: 3) could also meet the national education criteria of 'children not in school' (DCLG, 2012c: 3). School leavers could, according to the guidance, help local authorities to meet the criteria for success by making the educational element 'neutral' (DCLG, 2013a: 2). Thus, if any families were identified for the TFP through a combination of poor school attendance of one child, 'worklessness' and local filter criteria, they could be (and many were) deemed 'turned around' once that child left school, with no other change necessarily occurring within the household. In Derbyshire, for example, 108 families were claimed as 'turned around' simply because a child reached school leaving age; in Leicestershire the figure was 78; in Islington it was 84; in Suffolk it was 115; and in Middlesbrough it was 165.

Despite, or perhaps because of, these problems that local authorities encountered when attempting to find the initial 120,000 'troubled families', the families were also discursively linked to a wide variety of problems and problematic behaviours including: gang membership, dangerous dogs, runaway children, radical extremism and organised crime. In June 2013, when only around 1% of 'troubled families' had been 'turned around' by local authorities, the government quickly announced the 'massive expansion' of the TFP to include 400,000 more families in June 2013. When he announced the expansion, Eric Pickles claimed that the TFP was 'on track to turn around the lives of 120,000 families by 2015 and reduce the burden they put on the taxpayer' while Danny Alexander, the Chief Secretary to the

Treasury, stated that the programme was 'a radical example of how, by spending a bit more in certain areas, we can save much more in others' (DCLG, 2013b). The new phase was to begin in 2015 at the end of the original programme. The announcement was accompanied by two different press releases from the government on the same day, but little further detail was provided, save for information about an additional £200 million of funding that would help the 400,000 'high risk families to get to grips with their problems before they spiral out of control' (DCLG, 2013b). There were, at that time, no details on how the 'high risk' families had been identified, the extent of their problems or how they differed from existing 'troubled families'. A Freedom of Information request asking for details about the methodology used in identifying the extra families elicited the response that the number was 'an estimate based on information about a number of provisional criteria for identifying high risk families, and that these criteria may be subject to change following the conclusion of the policy formulation process' (Crossley, 2013a).

Just over a year after the initial announcement, further details on the 400,000 new families were published. They were no longer referred to as 'high risk' families and were instead now referred to as 'more' families to be worked with under the TFP. Families that could be included in the new expanded programme would have to meet two of the six following criteria:

- parents and children involved in crime or anti-social behaviour
- children who have not been attending school regularly
- children who need help
- adults out of work or at risk of financial exclusion and young people at risk of worklessness
- families affected by domestic violence and abuse
- parents and children with a range of health problems.

It was also announced that 51 'high-performing authorities', who had made the best progress in 'turning around' 'troubled families', would be 'early starters' in Phase 2, working with 40,000 families under the new programme a year earlier than planned (DCLG, 2014a). The details of the expansion were announced as the government published a report, *Understanding Troubled Families* (DCLG, 2014b), which drew on information gathered during the early stages of the first phase of the programme about the kinds of problems faced by 'troubled families'. In an interview with *The Sunday Times*, Casey stated that she had not expected the problems faced by 'troubled families' to be as extensive as they were and claimed that they were the 'worst families' and 'off the barometer in the number of problems they have' (Hellen, 2014).

At the same time that the high profile launch of the new phase of the programme was being announced, another development was taking place behind the scenes and out of the public eye. In a letter to local authority chief executives in August 2014, Casey highlighted that there were 'eligibility thresholds' for local authorities wishing to participate in the expanded second phase of the programme. Casey (2014a) informed chief executives that in order for local authorities to be 'eligible' for the second phase, DCLG would 'need sufficient assurance that areas are likely to hit their existing commitments to turn around all of their current allocation of troubled families by May 2015'. Local authority areas that were working with all of their 'troubled families' at the time of the penultimate PbR claims window for the first phase in January/February 2015, and who had turned around at least 75 per cent of them would be able to provide DCLG with the 'assurance' it required, and would therefore be eligible for participation in the expanded programme. Casey (2014a) went on to note that, where this performance threshold was not met, the local authority risked being prevented from participating in the second phase of the programme:

> If your area does not meet either of the above thresholds then we do hope that there will be an opportunity for you to join the expanded programme at a later point but, at this stage, I am unable to reassure you that this will be the case.

Three months later, in November 2014, Joe Tuke, the new Director of the Troubled Families Team at DCLG (following Casey's departure to lead an independent inspection into Rotherham Council), wrote again to some local authority chief executives stating that he remained 'worried that your council may not meet the levels of performance required in the current Troubled Families programme that will allow it to participate in the expanded Troubled Families programme' (Tuke, 2014).

Unsurprisingly, at the end of the first phase, all local authorities had met the eligibility thresholds and were able to participate in the second phase of the programme. Overall, according to the government, 99 per cent of 'troubled families had had their lives turned around by the end first phase of the TFP in April 2015' (DCLG, 2015a). Such success is unheard of across any social policy area, let alone one concerned with working with very disadvantaged and/or troublesome families, those who are often deemed 'hard to reach', at a time of cuts to local services and a range of welfare reforms that disproportionately affected some of the poorest families in the country. The official figures published by the government showed that the overwhelming majority of local authorities had worked with and turned around exactly the same number of 'troubled families' that they had been allocated by DCLG at the start of the programme in 2011. Not one 'troubled family' had slipped through the net or failed to respond to the approach of the TFP, in over 130 of the 152 local authority areas, according to the government figures. In the North East, for example, government figures stated that only three out of 7,285 'troubled families' across 12 local authority areas had failed to have their lives 'turned around' by the programme.

Not all of the 'troubled families' whose lives had apparently been turned around by the TFP had actually received any form of intervention under the programme, however. An investigation by the *Guardian* (Bawden, 2015) highlighted that less than 80,000 'troubled families' had received a 'family intervention' approach, with an identified keyworker involved with the family, and around 8,000 families in 40 local authorities had been 'turned around' without having any form of intervention whatsoever from a local authority. These families were 'turned around' through a process known on the TFP as 'data matching'. This involved local authorities trawling through data they held on families to find those that at some point were eligible for the programme but had managed to 'turn themselves around' without any support from the local authority through, for example, an adult moving into work or school attendance improving. Bawden also highlighted how local authorities had highlighted the importance of existing universal services, thus 'contradicting the government's portrayal of the TFP as the sole reason for families no longer being troubled'. Local authorities also disclosed that they had worked with far more families than the PbR figures suggested, but had not been required or expected to inform DCLG about this.

These findings highlight significant flaws with the claims made about 'troubled families' and the success of the TFP in 'turning them around'. The fact that families were able to 'turn around' their own lives highlights that they are not a homogeneous 'underclass' cut off from the rest of society requiring intensive state intervention. The data matching practice also raises the issue that some of those 'troubled families' that local authorities worked with, and received an 'attachment fee' for from DCLG, will not have been the same 'troubled families' whose lives had been 'turned around'. The continued use of existing, universal services to help 'turn around' families only undermines the government rhetoric about state failures of the past that had precipitated the creation of the TFP.

The putative success of the programme led to suggestions that the approach should be rolled out to other policy areas. The 2014 Budget namechecked the TFP in a section on the radical reform of public services and suggested that the government was looking 'to further reduce the waste and complexity of public services, whilst protecting outcomes for individuals', which could include services to 'better support the unemployed into work, vulnerable children and young people, people experiencing mental health problems' (HM Treasury, 2014: 25–6). The Institute for Public Policy Research (IPPR) published a report called *Breaking Boundaries* (McNeil and Hunter, 2015) calling for a 'Troubled Lives Programme' with a focus on working-aged individuals who experienced mental health, homelessness and addiction problems and Cameron suggested that the approach could be widened to child protection services (Cameron, 2015b). By the time that the second phase of the TFP officially started in May 2015, such proposals had not come to fruition.

Phase 2 (2015–20)

There were a number of changes that occurred during the shift from the first phase to the second phase of the programme but, in marked contrast to the first phase of the programme, the expanded second phase adopted a low profile from the outset. Progress on the first phase of the TFP was reported regularly following each PbR claims window, which occurred at three to four month intervals, with DCLG issuing press releases extolling the good work being carried out by local authorities. No updates were provided on the second phase of the programme, however, until an annual report was published in April 2017, nearly two full years after the second phase officially commenced and over three years after some families had begun being worked with by some of the 'early starter' areas.

Changes to the criteria for what constituted a 'troubled family' also led to changes to the financial framework associated with the programme, and how 'success' was measured. Under the new framework, families were required to make 'significant and sustained progress' against all of their presenting issues, or achieve a continuous employment outcome in order for a PbR claim to be triggered. Significant and sustained progress was to be measured against families' own Outcomes Plans, which were locally designed and differed from authority to authority, albeit with many similarities between them. DCLG guidance on such plans suggested that they would help to: set out the aims of working with the family or what was hoped would be achieved; determine whether or not significant and sustained progress against such aims had been met; and provide a framework whereby internal auditors could establish whether a proposed PbR claim was warranted (DCLG, 2015b: 25).

The success of the second phase of the TFP was to be considered more broadly, and in relation to three different issues. First, local authorities were required to support families to make significant and sustained progress or achieve continuous employment. Second, they were expected to capture a 'richer understanding of the families' (DCLG, 2015b: 10) through the National Impact Study and through Family Progress Data. Finally, they would be expected to be able to demonstrate the savings that accrued as a result of their work on the programme through the findings from an online troubled families Costs Savings Calculator.

The demand to 'capture a richer understanding' of the families involved prompted a number of local authorities to invest in new data management software packages. Data was required to help identify families using the wider entry criteria, to support and monitor the 'significant and sustained progress' that was required for PbR claims, and also to meet the needs of the National Impact Study. Private companies lined up to provide 'data solutions' and support for local authorities in identifying and 'tracking' their 'troubled families'. In one case, a local authority contracted with a US firm based in California best known for its work with the US military, the CIA and the National Security Agency to provide a data intelligence hub which would help with their local 'troubled families' work (Crossley, 2017a: 110–11). A new 'legal gateway' was established for the programme that allowed the Department for Work and Pensions to share data with local authorities, '*without the informed consent of those families*, for the purpose of identifying troubled families' (DCLG, 2015b: 43, emphasis added).

The amount of funding available for work with individual families was also reduced. In the first phase, local authorities were able to claim up to £4,000 for 'turned around' families, through a combination of attachment fee and PbR claim. In the second phase the total amount on offer to local authorities was only £1,800 in total – £1,000 attachment fee and a PbR component of £800. It was actually possible for 'troubled families' to have been worked with and 'turned around' under Phase 1 of the programme, *and still meet the criteria for a 'troubled family' under Phase 2*, but local authorities would not be able to claim funding for such families (DCLG, 2015b: 38–39). The payment to local authorities in Phase 1 that supported the costs of a Troubled Families Co-ordinator was doubled for most areas and re-badged as a Service Transformation Grant, which would help local authorities to roll-out the family intervention approach. This grant formed 'an essential part of the new programme's increased focus on driving public service transformation across all relevant local services' (DCLG, 2015b: 11). In order to ensure that local authorities were extending the family intervention approach and not relying on data matching or universal services to generate PbR claims, DCLG introduced the need for 'eligible families' to be 'receiving a whole family intervention' (DCLG, 2017a: 46). This meant that four criteria had to be met:

1. An assessment taking into account the needs of the whole family had taken place.
2. There was a whole family action plan in place.
3. There was a lead worker involved with and recognised by the family.
4. The objectives in the action plan were aligned to the local authority's Troubled Families Outcome Plan.

Local authorities were also supposed to prioritise those families that were 'most likely to benefit from an integrated whole family approach' and those 'families who are the highest cost to the public purse' (DCLG, 2015b: 9), meaning that local authorities could not actively choose to work with the 'easiest' or 'least troubled' families in order to generate PbR claims. The problem of 'creaming and parking' or 'picking off the lowest hanging fruit' has long been associated with PbR mechanisms and funding models that are 'outcomes based' (Lowe and Wilson, 2015), but the original PbR model for Phase 1 did nothing to address these issues.

Another obvious change was the type of families to be worked with. The first phase of the programme was characterised by a focus on families with members that allegedly caused problems to others, through disruptive and unruly children, criminality or adults being out of work. The second phase, with an increased focus on families that experienced health issues, or who had a child or children 'in need', who were experiencing financial exclusion, or where domestic violence was present, saw the focus shift onto families that were potentially experiencing problems themselves. Additional documents were published to support the greater involvement of health practitioners and health services in the expanded programme (DCLG, 2014c, 2014d, 2014e). The expansion in entry criteria for families was explained partly by many of the original 120,000 'troubled families' experiencing the additional problems, but also by the cost to 'the taxpayer' of families experiencing the additional problems. In an annex of the financial framework for the expanded programme, the financial case is made for three of the criteria for families entering the programme:

> The financial case for the prioritisation of employment outcomes for troubled families is compelling. Welfare benefits are the single greatest area of public expenditure on these families and the wider benefits of reducing welfare benefit dependency are felt across improvements in health, reductions in crime and local economic growth. (DCLG, 2015b: 18)

> Domestic violence and abuse has been a damaging and widespread problem for many of the families in the first programme. Its prioritisation in the expanded programme responds to clear and strong feedback from local areas and is reinforced by a compelling financial imperative; the consequences of domestic violence and abuse are felt across health, police, housing and Children's Services budgets. (DCLG, 2015b: 20)

> Health problems for troubled families are costly and pervasive. (DCLG, 2015b: 21)

Sitting behind the six headline criteria for families entering the TFP in the second phase were 29 different suggested indicators. Five of the six criteria included the potential for local professionals to 'nominate' families or family members for entry to the programme where there were, for example, 'problems of equivalent concern' to other indicators. This degree of discretion meant that a nomination or referral from a single professional meant that a potentially 'troubled family' met one of the criteria. Similarly, it was explicitly stated that where a single family member met two of the headline criteria, this was enough for the whole household to be categorised as a 'troubled family', as long as that individual concerned lived in the family home. A child with a disability or a Special Educational Need could potentially be referred by professionals across three different criteria relating to education, children in need and health problems. Almost any family with a family member with caring responsibilities for other family members could also easily meet the new expanded criteria. In effect, the new criteria meant that almost all families who came into contact with non-universal services, for whatever reason, could be made to 'fit' the 'troubled families' criteria, which was exactly what happened in local authorities (Crossley, 2017b).

Despite some of the significant changes to the programme listed above, many symbolically important elements of the programme remained. The new families, despite being identified using additional, and in some cases quite different, criteria, were still referred to as 'troubled families' and associated with all of the political baggage that accompanied that term. The expanded programme generated front page headlines on national newspapers such as 'Rise of new underclass costs £30bn' (Hellen, 2014) and 'Welfare Squads to Target Problem Families' (Little, 2014). Despite the wide range of new issues to be addressed under the expanded programme, there was no suggestion that the robust family intervention approach might not be the best way of attempting to address such issues. The SETF research into 'families at risk' that identified the original 120,000 families with multiple disadvantages highlighted that a 'whole family' approach might not be appropriate in instances that relate to the expanded programme:

> Some respondents to the review's call for evidence argue that a 'whole family' approach, especially when this may mean placing a family together 'in the same room to work out problems', may not be suitable in cases of domestic violence, child abuse or when a patient's right to confidentiality takes precedence. (SETF, 2007b: 29)

The expanded programme operated out of the limelight for its first two years. Much of the public attention on the TFP during this time remained focused on the claims of success and the controversy associated with the evaluation of the first phase. It was not until April 2017 that any progress on Phase 2 was reported nationally. An 'annual report' for the TFP – *Supporting Disadvantaged Families: Troubled Families Programme 2015–2020: progress so far* – was published, in keeping with new reporting obligations under the Welfare Reform and Work Act 2016. Alongside the report, five further documents were published: four of which provided information from the evaluation of the second phase, which was being carried out by Ipsos Mori (DCLG, 2017c, 2017d, 2017e, 2017f); and a fifth that acted as a toolkit to support 'service transformation' (DCLG, 2017g). The report and accompanying documents served two main purposes: first to provide an update on the first two years of the second phase of the TFP, including progress made in work with families; and second to highlight the 'evolution' of the programme into its 'next phase', which would see the focus of the programme shift once more.

There was no separate press release or spreadsheet setting out the progress made by local authorities during the second phase of the programme. Instead, this element of the report was relegated to the back of the *Supporting Troubled Families* document, after detail about the next phase of the programme and the characteristics of the families themselves (DCLG, 2017a: 49–56). In total, 185,420 of the 400,000 families had been worked with as at 28 March 2017. Of these, 43,813 had achieved 'significant and sustained progress' and 9,157 had achieved the continuous employment outcome. Local authorities were expected to prioritise those families that would be 'most likely to benefit' from a whole family approach and those that represented the highest cost to the 'public purse', and so the relatively slow progress made in 'turning around' troubled families, in terms of the programme timescales, could be explained by the complexity of the families involved. It should also be remembered, however, that the first phase of the TFP was supposed to have 'turned around' the 120,000 most complex and difficult families and the broad criteria for families under the second phase meant that many families with relatively minor problems could be classed as 'troubled families'. These headline figures, which received very little media or political attention at the time, mask a great degree of local variation which, once again, highlights inconsistencies between the national rhetoric surrounding the TFP and the reality revealed by scrutiny of the figures.

Local authorities had started on Phase 2 of the programme at three different times (September 2014, January 2015, and April 2015) depending on their progress under Phase 1, with the best performing authorities starting in September 2014. Dudley Council, for example, was one authority that started at the earliest date and had worked with 895 families in the two and a half years to 28 March 2017. Of these 895 families, Dudley claimed that only one of them had made significant and sustained progress, while 28 had achieved continuous employment. Essex County Council, who started on Phase 2 in January 2015 had worked with 3,740 families up to 28 March 2017, but *not one of them* had achieved continuous employment, while over 1,300 of them had made significant and sustained progress. Northampton Council, who started at the same time, worked with 1,941 families and claimed for two successes in achieving continuous employment, yet Enfield, who also started at the same time, claimed for 402 continuous employment outcomes out of 1,127 families worked with. Liverpool

City Council, one of the earliest starters had claimed for 138 families making significant and sustained progress by March 2017 out of 3,500 families worked with, while Leeds City Council, starting at the same time and working with 3,754 families, claimed for 1,350 families for the same outcome.

These local discrepancies and inconsistencies could be explained in a number of different ways, but there has not yet been systematic evaluation carried out regarding why some local areas performed well against one or the other outcome, while others were making relatively slow progress against either. In the absence of any definitive answers, the figures from the early stages of Phase 2 reinforce existing concerns about the claims made about, for example: the claims of uniform success across all local authorities in Phase 1; the rationale for the service transformation that has reputedly taken place under the programme; and the efficacy of the family intervention model for helping disadvantaged families with numerous different issues. These concerns did not, however, stop the government from pressing ahead with a slightly re-focused 'next phase' of the programme.

The 'next phase' (2017–20)

The foreword to the *Supporting Disadvantaged Families* report, written by the Secretary of State for Communities and Local Government, Sajid Javid, stated that the second phase of the programme was building on the strengths of the first but also highlighted a new direction of travel for the next phase of the programme (DCLG, 2017a: 4–5). A review of the PbR mechanism was announced that would shift the focus more towards helping families into work and the 'next phase' would also look to improve 'operational partnerships' between local 'troubled families' workers and colleagues in Jobcentre Plus. The closer linking of the TFP with 'worklessness' was also evident at a higher level, with the TFP apparently shifting from being a standalone, albeit cross-departmental, programme, to one that merely formed part of 'new plans to help workless families break the cycle of disadvantage' (DWP, 2017a: 49). The 'next phase' of the programme would see this element become a greater priority. This greater focus on 'worklessness' emerged despite the fact that a majority of families involved with the second phase of the programme were working families: only around 45% of 'troubled families' in Phase 2 were classed as 'workless'. While the entry criteria would remain the same, the prioritisation process would not, with the government 'encouraging local authorities to prioritise families experiencing worklessness, and two of the main disadvantages associated with worklessness: parental conflict (including domestic violence, which features in many cases of Children in Need), and serious personal debt' (DCLG, 2017a: 24).

On the same day that the annual report and associated documents were published by DCLG, the DWP published a report called *Improving Lives: Helping Workless Families* (DWP, 2017a). This document also set out how the 'next phase' of the TFP would align with broader government work to support families back into work, reduce parental conflict, reform elements of Jobcentre Plus and tackle dependency. The TFP would be re-focused so that it had 'an even greater emphasis on helping people back into work and tackling the disadvantages associated with worklessness' (DWP, 2017a: 4). Parental conflict, as well as becoming more of a priority in the TFP was to be addressed through 'the launch of an innovative new programme to support evidence-based interventions delivered by specialist organisations at a local level' (DWP, 2017a: 4). Jobcentre Plus would be expected to work more closely with local Troubled Families teams to better support people with complex needs, and dependency would be addressed through pilot approaches to support people dependent on drugs and alcohol back into employment.

There was, once again, a renewed emphasis within the TFP on service transformation with a self-assessment tool – the *Early Help Service Transformation Maturity Model* (DCLG, 2017g) – for local authorities published alongside the other 'troubled families' documents. In the foreword to the report, Joe Tuke highlighted the need for service reform using typically dystopian and deterministic examples:

> Providing effective support to a family early means that a family might see a GP, not turn up repeatedly in A&E; that parenting support is put in place before a child becomes at risk of being placed in local authority care; and that a mental health problem might be identified and treated before crisis point and before a parent feels they can no longer hold down their job, which in turn will have a major impact on the children. Transforming services means there should no longer be a host of unconnected services and professionals circling a family with their own assessments, thresholds, appointments and measures. (DCLG, 2017g: 2)

The Maturity Model included six different 'strands' of work: the family experience of transformed services; Leadership; Strategy; Culture; Workforce development; and Delivery structures and processes. The language in the document, in keeping with wider talk of 'transformation', was typically vague, if not entirely vacuous. Local authorities were encouraged to develop a 'shared vision', 'shared values', 'a shared culture', a 'shared commissioning framework', a 'shared focus on services' and 'shared or pooled budget arrangements'. The leadership strand highlighted the need for 'a common purpose across senior leaders to lead, design and deliver services that best meet local needs for families with complex problems' before going on to set out what 'leadership' in the context of local 'troubled families' work is:

> Leadership is about 'who' is leading transformation locally – a visible commitment to a shared cross-service vision to achieve sustainable outcomes for families, to transform services, to understand and manage future demand and meet the particular needs found in specific localities. (DCLG, 2017g: 17)

Local services were expected to be able to evidence their progression towards service transformation maturity and the word 'evidence' is itself used 116 times in the 38-page document. This emphasis on evidencing transformation to services stands in stark contrast to the lack of evidence relating to the efficacy or likely impact of the services themselves.

Although the focus on supporting 'workless' families back into work fits in with wider political and popular concerns about 'cultures of worklessness' and people enjoying the benefits lifestyle, there is little evidence about the extent of such problems. The trope of 'families that don't want to work' or where 'three generations have never worked' has long since been exposed as a politically expedient myth (Taylor-Gooby and Dean, 1992; Shildrick et al, 2012) that can engender public support for punitive welfare reforms. Similarly, the evidence base for a family intervention approach addressing the issue of unemployment or 'worklessness' is limited, to say the least. The final evaluation of the FIP projects established under new Labour highlight 'ambiguous findings' (Lloyd et al, 2011: 84) in relation to employment outcomes and, in total, only around 20 per cent of 'workless families' involved in that evaluation had successful outcomes in relation to finding work, the lowest rate of success across any of the issues FIPs attempted to address (Lloyd et al, 2011: 91).

Although both the *Improving Lives* and the *Supporting Disadvantaged Families* reports suggested that 18,000 families had seen adults move into work in the first phase of the TFP, the actual number at the end of Phase 1 was under 12,000, suggesting that less than 10 per cent adults in 'troubled families' in the first phase had moved off out of work benefits and managed to sustain continuous employment. The additional 6,000 families that the government was claiming credit for were those that had found work *after exiting the programme*. It is also worth remembering that many of these people will have found work themselves and will have only entered the TFP statistics as a result of the data-matching processes described earlier in the chapter. It should also be noted that different elements of the national evaluation of the first phase of the TFP found that the programme had no statistically significant impact on employment outcomes. The family survey found 'no statistically significant impact on adults being in work around nine months after the start of the programme' (Purdon and Bryson, 2016: 29) and a similar outcome in relation to families responses to questions about job seeking activity and expectations about finding paid work in the following year. The impact study (Bewley et al, 2016) provided an even more comprehensive summary of the impact of the programme on employment outcomes for participants:

> The clearest and most reliable estimates, bearing in mind the limitations of the data, were for impacts on benefit receipt and employment. Our analysis found no significant impact of participation in the Troubled Families programme on any of the key outcome variables. We found no significant impact on the proportion of adults claiming out-of-work benefits either 12 or 18 months after starting on the programme. This was also the case when focusing specifically on JSA [JobSeekers Allowance] or incapacity benefits. Participation in the programme also had no detectable impact on the number of weeks that adult family members spent on out-of-work benefits in the year following the date that they started on the programme. Nor did we find any impact on the likelihood that adults shifted from other out-of-work benefits to JSA. The analysis also suggested that participation in the Troubled Families programme had no impact on the likelihood that adults were employed 12 or 18 months after starting on the programme. The number of weeks spent in employment over each of these time periods seems to have been unaffected and we found no evidence that more intensive contact affected employment outcomes (Bewley et al, 2016: 20–21).

These findings, and the slow rates of families finding employment in the first two years of Phase 2 of the TFP, should not surprise us. The families who have been involved in FIPs and the TFP are often some of the most disadvantaged families in society. Many have low or no qualifications, and many have health issues or disabilities, both of which will make them less attractive to many employers. Many adults in 'troubled families' have caring responsibilities for other adults, for children with disabilities or health issues, or for pre-school children, which means that, in many cases, they are not expected to be looking for work. A minority of families will have such severe disadvantages or complex problems that work will not be an option for them until other aspects of their lives improve (see Shildrick et al, 2012: 45). The government did not publish the proportion of adults in 'troubled families' who were in receipt of Jobseeker's Allowance (JSA) in the TFPs first annual report. This figure could only be found in an accompanying report on 'local and national datasets' (DCLG, 2017c). This report highlights that only 18.7 per cent of adults in 'troubled families' on Phase 2 of the programme were claiming JSA – less than 1 in 5. In Phase 1 of the programme, data published by DWP revealed that JSA was the main benefit for just over a third of adults in 'troubled families', suggesting that employment may not have been an expectation or an option for up to around two-thirds of adults in these families (DWP, 2015: 6).

The presentation of these findings across different April 2017 documents is also problematic. Interesting, explanatory data, as highlighted above, is sometime not contained in main reports and is instead included in datasets that are less likely to be read. Even where statistics do feature, they are presented in a less than ideal way. A graph in the *Supporting Disadvantaged Families* report simply titled 'Steps taken towards getting a job' highlights that 62 per cent of respondents have not taken any steps towards finding employment in the previous 12 months (DCLG, 2017a: 31). The title of the graph makes no mention of the fact that this information applies only to the main carer in 'troubled families' households, many of whom will be living with adults in work, and many of whom will not have been expected or required to have 'taken any steps' towards securing employment. In another example, a section in a report on the family survey undertaken in the second phase of the programme states that there are a 'high proportion of workless households' in the TFP (DCLG, 2017d: 21). The section also states that this is a 'persistent' problem, with 'many' of the main carers having spent most of their time since leaving education out of paid work or never had a job. In fact, less than 3 in 10 main carers have spent most of their time out of work (29 per cent) and only 1 in 10 have never had a job. An alternative way of presenting the data would have been to highlight the persistently high number of adults in 'troubled families' in work and that, despite a number of societal, structural and familial challenges, 90 per cent of main carers in 'troubled families' had been in work at some point, and the overwhelming majority of them (over 70 per cent) had spent the majority of their time since leaving education in work. Such a portrayal, however, does not help to 'sustain and nourish' or reproduce wider discourses about 'troubled families', and disadvantaged and poor families in general. The TFP focus on 'workless families', which ignores the myriad reasons why adults in 'troubled families' are not currently in employment, can thus be viewed as part of a continued and expansive 'discursive strategy [that] is successful in feeding vindictive attitudes to the poor', as Levitas (2012a: 8) noted when discussing the original labelling of 'troubled families'.

Discussion

The Troubled Families Programme, originally tasked with 'turning around' the lives of 120,000 troubled families in a single term of parliament has evolved into a different type of programme since its inception, albeit one with many enduring features. The expanded criteria for the second phase of the TFP effectively operationalised and lent official credence to Mann's (1994: 80) argument, 20 years earlier, that members of 'the underclass' were 'nimble enough to burgle any home and can run off after a "bag snatching", but the disabled are also members'. The 'next phase' of the programme, announced in April 2017, sought to bring sharper focus to the work of the TFP by emphasising the need to support 'workless' families into employment. The criteria for identifying and prioritising families for the programme changed, the outcomes expected by the programme also shifted, but the name and the family intervention approach remained.

The continuing focus on 'families' – either 'troubled' or 'workless' – and on the family intervention approach deflects attention away from the quantity and quality of jobs on offer, and their suitability or otherwise for carers of young children and/or disabled or vulnerable adults. The potential consequences of poor, or insecure, or sporadic work on disadvantaged families' lives remained undiscussed. Poor quality, poorly paid, irregular work, often at unsociable hours in the early morning or late at night, accompanied by potential changes to benefits entitlements, does not always lead to less parental conflict or a greater, more sustainable income. The pejorative term 'workless' ignores the amount of domestic and caring work that takes place within 'troubled families', many of whom have young children and/or family members with health issues or disabilities. The continuing focus on the cost of 'troubled families' to 'the taxpayer' also neglects to acknowledge the value provided to the economy of the unpaid care taking place in 'troubled families'. The only kind of work that is valued is paid employment.

Although there is still a focus on families, there has also been a shift in the allegedly transformative aims of the TFP. As each phase of the programme has been announced, and as its profile and importance has dropped, there has been an increase in the extent to which the programme claims to be transforming and re-shaping local services. These announcements have, of course, been interspersed with or accompanied by research findings that highlight the lack of impact of the programme on numerous aspects of families' lives. Such findings have not yet suggested to the government that the family intervention approach might not be worth 'rolling out' and 'mainstreaming'. The transformation of local services that the government claims is taking place under the TFP suggests appears to be driven more by ideology than evidence.

The continuing marginalisation of issues of poverty, inequality and material deprivation in the 'troubled families' discourse helps to portray the issues faced by families as originating within the home, and also close off the opportunity to consider the influence of these structural factors on the lives of 'troubled families'. The government has successfully restricted the narrative to one that makes families responsible for their own circumstances and that prevents discussion of the government's own irresponsible behaviour towards disadvantaged families. It is to this issue that we now turn.

FIVE

The 'responsibility deficit'

> ... my mission in politics – the thing I am really passionate about – is fixing the responsibility deficit. That means building a stronger society, in which more people understand their obligations, and more take control over their own lives and actions. For a long time, I was criticised for talking about the broken society. But I believe that it's only by recognising the problem that we can fix what's gone wrong. And this summer we saw, beyond doubt, that something has gone profoundly wrong. The riots were a wake-up call – not a freak incident but a boiling over of problems that had been simmering for years. (Cameron, 2011b)

Introduction

When David Cameron (2011b) launched the TFP in December 2011, he remarked that the thing he was 'really passionate about' was 'fixing the responsibility deficit'. If we, as a country, were to address the 'broken society', Cameron believed that it was 'only by recognising the problem that we can fix what's gone wrong'. Cameron's focus was firmly on those families he labelled 'troubled' and the gaze of the TFP has remained firmly on those families and the activities of the workers tasked with 'turning them around'. Workers have been expected to 'look at the family from the inside out' (DCLG, 2012a: 4) in attempting to make 'troubled families' take responsibility for the circumstances in which they find themselves. The heart of the TFP remains on a supposedly strong relationship between different individuals and the 'service transformation' in local authorities that is being driven by the TFP. Such a perspective, Garrett (2013: 8) argues, 'under-theorises' the role of the state and, more specifically, central government, and means that the resolution of family troubles is 'entirely displaced onto micro-encounters' between workers and families. The 'private troubles' of hundreds of thousands of families are never viewed as the 'public issues' they undoubtedly are (Wright Mills, 1959).

Bourdieu's advice to be wary of 'pre-constructed' problems, and drawing on many other sociologists who advocated the need to 'study up' in different ways, encourages us to look away from the problems presented or created by the state. The focus in this chapter shifts from the emergence and evolution of the TFP to developments in other areas of social policy and welfare administration taking place at the same time. Drawing on work by Loïc Wacquant, the importance of the TFP in the crafting of a neoliberal state in the UK is discussed. Wacquant, writing primarily about the USA, argued neoliberalism was not just an economic doctrine, highlighting how traditional welfare functions and services were not just being rolled back under neoliberal policies, but were also being restructured and, in many cases, replaced by more interventionist schemes. The programme of austerity and the expansive raft of 'welfare reforms' pursued by the coalition government and then continued by the Conservative government following its election in 2015 are presented here, with particular detail paid to changes in eligibility for benefits and the increased conditionality attached to many of them. The centrality of 'the family' in the new developments is then discussed, with the government increasing its commitment to different forms of 'early intervention' in the lives of poor and marginalised families, with the rapidly expanding TFP at the vanguard of this development. Three important moments associated with the TFP are presented as exemplars of these neoliberal developments. The chapter concludes with a discussion of the real ambition of the TFP and a reflection on perhaps the most worrying 'responsibility deficit' in the UK today.

Beyond 'troubled families'

It is, or perhaps was, possible to view the TFP as an 'outlier' or an anomaly of a social policy, and not part of a wider programme of restructuring. The expansive and interventionist, centrally driven programme was launched at a time of supposed austerity when the 'big state' was decried and other forms of support from the state to disadvantaged groups were being scaled back. Localism and decentralisation were being promoted and the government was still attempting to get the idea of the *Big Society* off the ground. The programme was sold as being one that would transform the way the state engaged with 'troubled families', and was presented as being 'an opportunity to not repeat the failed attempts of the past', as Casey (2012a: 3) put it. It was time-limited and was initially relevant only to a relatively small number of families. At a time when welfare reforms and cuts to local government and voluntary sector organisations were making disadvantaged families' lives more difficult and precarious, the TFP, the public was told, was intent on intervening to turn their lives around, while simultaneously saving 'the taxpayer' vital funds.

This is certainly one perspective. If, however, we step back from the TFP and examine what has been happening in other social policy and welfare areas, a counter argument can be made. It is argued here that the TFP should not be viewed as a distinctive approach, or as a 'bespoke' policy programme, but instead as one that is entirely in keeping with wider developments in social policy and social work in the UK and other countries. Heeding Wacquant's call to think about neoliberalism *sociologically* rather than *economically* provides us with a framework through which to view developments across the bureaucratic field. Wacquant (2009a: 306) argues powerfully that:

> Whether singular or polymorphous, evolutionary or revolutionary, the prevalent conception of neoliberalism is essentially economic: it stresses an array of market-friendly policies such as labour deregulation, capital mobility, privatisation, a monetarist agenda of deflation and financial autonomy, trade liberalisation, interplace competition, and the reduction of taxation and public expenditures. But this conception is thin and incomplete, as well as too closely bound up with the sermonising discourse of the advocates of neoliberalism. We need to reach beyond this economic nucleus and elaborate a thicker notion that identifies the institutional machinery and symbolic frames through which neoliberal tenets are being actualised.

Such a standpoint, aligned with a historical perspective on the dual roles of the 'deserving and undeserving poor' enables us to examine the TFP and the UK government's programme of austerity and decentralisation through a different prism. Viewed in this way, the approach and development of the TFP comes to be seen as an integral part of recent efforts to recraft the state in the UK. Wacquant (2009a: 304–8) argued that, under neoliberalism, traditional welfare services and support from the state were being rolled back at precisely the same time that more interventionist strategies aimed at controlling disruptive or unruly elements were rolled out: 'the simultaneous retraction of its social bosom and expansion of its penal fist' (Wacquant, 2009a: 305).

He argued that while the 'remasculinised' neoliberal state 'embraces laissez faire' policies with economically powerful groups and individuals, the same approach was not employed in its relations with disadvantaged and economically deprived populations. Instead, Wacquant, argues, 'the soft touch of libertarian proclivities favouring the upper class gives way to the hard edge of authoritarian oversight, as it endeavours to direct, nay dictate, the behaviour of the lower class' (Wacquant, 2009a: 308). He goes on to highlight the policy language and political rhetoric that supports the expansion of neoliberal policies:

> The new priority given to duties over rights, sanction over support, the stern rhetoric of the 'obligations of citizenship', and the martial reaffirmation of the capacity of the state to lock the troublemaking poor (welfare recipients and criminals) in a subordinate relation of dependence and obedience toward state managers portrayed as virile protectors of the society against its wayward members: all these policy planks pronounce and promote the transition for the kindly 'nanny state' of the Fordist-Keynesian era to the strict 'daddy state' of neoliberalism. (Wacquant, 2009a: 290)

In his analysis, Wacquant highlights the 'shared historical origins of poor relief and penal confinement in the chaotic passage from feudalism to capitalism' (2009a: 291) and argues that the remaking of the state in the latter stages of the 20th century had seen two distinct spheres of the state – welfare and criminal justice – recoupled. Wacquant's focus was on the development of workfare programmes and the expansion of the prison population in the USA, although he also noted that there were other countries where similar developments could be found. The relevance to the TFP and wider developments in the UK and other countries should be apparent. Tyler (2013) has drawn on Wacquant's work in examining the 'underclass consensus' that emerged following the 2011 riots and Gillies (2016) has also drawn on his work to examine neoliberal developments in UK education. Hancock and Mooney (2012: 59) have previously argued that the rhetoric surrounding the 'broken society' did not allow for a withdrawal of the state, but instead 'encouraged earlier and deeper penetration … in the lives of the most disadvantaged sections of society'. Louise Casey (2016: 45), in an *example par excellence* of Wacquant's argument, has written that children's services, far from being a preventative service or a 'social bosom' in Wacquant's words, should act like 'a rapid and decisive SWAT team for when all else fails'. The next two sections sketch out some of the restructuring that has taken place in other bureaucratic fields in the UK and attempt to highlight the confluence between the aims of the TFP and those of other contemporary social policies. First, the attention turns to the withdrawal of the state from some its traditional welfare policy areas.

Rolling back support

Recent years have seen numerous attempts to subject the welfare state to 'radical reform'. Upon entry to office in 1997, Prime Minister Tony Blair reportedly asked Frank Field to 'think the unthinkable' about welfare reform and, in 2008, the Work and Pensions Secretary James Purnell faced severe criticism for increasing conditionality within the welfare system, being accused of introducing 'workfare' (Kirkup, 2008; Sparrow, 2008). In 2010, the coalition government published a White Paper, *Universal Credit: Welfare that works* (DWP, 2010), that, in the words of Iain Duncan Smith, marked 'the beginning of a new contract between people who have and people who have not' (DWP, 2010: 1). While this document focused on Universal Credit, introduced in an attempt to make the benefits system more straightforward and transparent, the coalition also introduced other significant changes to existing benefits, the conditions attached to them and how they were paid. A number of benefits, such as Child Benefit and some elements of tax credits, were frozen for three years while others were limited to increases of just 1 per cent for certain periods of time (see De Agostini et al, 2014: 10–13 or Beatty and Fothergill, 2016: 6–8 for lists of the main benefit and tax changes since 2010). The rate at which benefits were uprated was changed from the Retail Prices Index to the Consumer Prices Index, which one commentator noted was a move that would make 'the system significantly less generous to all claimants' (Hirsch, 2010: 6) and appeared to be a choice made 'principally to limit the cost of benefits to the exchequer' (Hirsch, 2010: 9).

A 'benefit cap' was introduced in 2013, and then reduced in 2016, limiting the total amount of benefits that any single household could claim. A spare room subsidy, popularly known as the 'bedroom tax' was also introduced for social housing tenants who were deemed to be 'under-occupying' their property. Some benefits, such as the Employment Maintenance Allowance and the Health in Pregnancy Grant, were cut completely. The campaigning charity Child Poverty Action Group estimated that a baby born in April 2011 would have been around £1500 worse off than one born in April 2010 as a result of the early coalition government welfare reforms (CPAG, 2011). The eligibility criteria for disability and incapacity benefits have been made more restrictive and some elements made time-limited and means tested (De Agostini et al, 2014: 11). In October 2016, an inquiry conducted by the United Nations Committee on the Rights of Persons with Disabilities (UNCRPD) into the impact of welfare reforms on disabled people concluded that there was reliable evidence that 'the threshold of grave or systematic violations of the rights of persons with disabilities' had been met (UNCRPD, 2016: 20).

As has been discussed, many 'troubled families' are in receipt of benefits where they are not expected to be looking for work. Where adults in 'troubled families' are looking for work, many of them have health issues and/or disabilities that will make it harder for them to find work in many cases. The lack of recognition of these extra challenges is in keeping with wider welfare reforms that took place in April 2017, at the same time that the TFP was repositioned to focus on 'workless families':

> From April, anyone newly classed by the Department for Work and Pensions as 'WRAG', or Work-Related Activity Group – people judged as so ill they can only take steps to prepare for future work rather than actually apply for jobs – will see their benefit shrink by £30 a week. That translates as a cut of nearly 30% (down to £73 a week) to a disability benefit already so meagre it's leaving a third of recipients struggling to afford food. (Ryan, 2017)

These changes to benefits, which also ignore the additional challenges faced by disabled people, were 'ending the distinction between healthy jobseekers and disabled people who – based on the government's own assessment – aren't "fit for work"' (Ryan, 2017). The *Guardian* columnist Frances Ryan, a vocal critic of the reforms, penned a passage relating to the change in benefits entitlement that could easily have been written about the 'next phase' of the TFP, arguing that 'the Conservatives are sending the message that having a debilitating disability doesn't mean a person needs specialist support or extra money, but simply a bit of motivation'.

The change to Employment Support Allowance (ESA) payments, which saw the withdrawal of £30 per week in the belief that it acted as a 'disincentive' to disabled people looking for work, was introduced despite some evidence, collected by disability and mental health charities and crossbench peers (Low et al, 2015), that suggested the cuts would have almost precisely the opposite effect that the government intended:

The overwhelming response from organisations and individuals who answered this question was *fundamental disagreement* that reducing the ESA WRAG payment would incentivise sick and disabled people to move closer to work. In fact respondents argued that *the reduction would hinder*, not help them take steps toward work. Many described the anxiety and stress that would entail from being pushed further into debt and poverty. Being consumed by these concerns would compound health (often mental health) conditions, meaning they would be *less able to take part in work related activity or look for work*. (Low et al, 2015: 8, emphasis added)

Rolling out interventions

In addition to these 'reforms', which have seen some benefits withdrawn entirely, the levels of others reduced, and new assessment procedures and changes to eligibility criteria, there has been a significant increase in the numbers of people penalised and sanctioned for not meeting certain conditions attached to unemployment and 'job-seeking' related benefits. Potential sanctions have traditionally played a limited role in the administration of social security benefits but, in the past 25 years, the rate and severity of sanctions has increased substantially. Dr David Webster, an honorary research fellow at Glasgow University has, in a series of publications and briefings drawing on historical documents and DWP statistics, highlighted these changes. In August 2014, Webster highlighted that around 7 per cent of people receiving Jobseeker's Allowance (JSA) had been sanctioned each month during the previous year. Figures for people claiming ESA were proportionately much lower but were increasing. Combined, Webster (2015: 1): argued, in the year leading up to March 2014:

an estimated total of 1,104,000 JSA and ESA sanctions were imposed, of which an estimated 149,000 were overturned on reconsideration/appeal, with claimants nevertheless having had payment stopped for weeks or months. The annual number of JSA/ESA sanctions has almost doubled under the coalition, while the annual number of cases of people losing benefits only to have them reinstated has quadrupled.

Webster (2015), in a comparison of which Wacquant would approve, has referred to the sanctions as 'an amateurish, secret penal system which is more severe than the mainstream judicial system, but lacks its safeguards'. He documented that, in 2013, more people were sanctioned through the benefits system than received fines through the criminal justice and court system. He also highlights that 'sanctioned benefit claimants are treated much worse than those fined in the courts' (Webster, 2015) and points out that sanctions are generally applied to poor people and they tend to result in almost total loss of benefit income for a period of at least two weeks, despite a system of 'hardship payments'. Webster suggests that sanctions push people off benefits, but not necessarily into employment of any kind, least of all good quality, and secure work. He goes on to expound some of the other consequences of sanctions:

> Sanctions undermine physical and mental health, cause hardship for family and friends, damage relationships, create homelessness and drive people to Food Banks and payday lenders, and to crime. They also often make it harder to look for work. Taking these negatives into account, they cannot be justified.

At the same time that sanctions have been preventing people from claiming the benefits they are legitimately entitled to, the increasing stigmatisation surrounding benefits claimants and the continuing complexity of the system means that many people do not claim the benefits that they are entitled to receive. The 'ideological re-working' of austerity (Clarke and Newman, 2012: 300), from an economic response to a financial crisis to a political response to a bloated and over-generous welfare state, has seen intense public scrutiny fall upon people claiming out-of-work benefits. 'Scroungerphobia' has returned and people living in poverty themselves often 'morally condemn "the poor"' (Shildrick and Macdonald, 2013: 285). Research around the increased stigmatisation associated with claiming benefits reported that 'quantitative and qualitative evidence suggests that stigma is playing a role in explaining non-take-up of benefits and tax credits' with around 25 per cent of respondents to a survey highlighting stigma as a reason for delaying or not claiming benefits (Baumberg et al, 2012: 3). Official government statistics (which the 'troubled families' turned around figures are not) suggest that around 40 per cent of people entitled to JSA do not claim the benefit (DWP, 2017b: 1). In total, the government estimated that over £12 billion of benefits remained unclaimed in 2015/16.

Funding to, and support for, other elements of the welfare state have also seen fundamental changes and restructuring. Numerous structural changes have taken place, for example, in both the health and education fields, with more private sector providers involved in the delivery of public services in these areas (see Bochel and Powell, 2016). The role of the state in the education system is being scaled back, with the expansion of the academies system and the introduction of 'free schools' removing schools from local authority oversight and central government requirements and regulations. These shifts highlight how the public policy fields of many of the traditional functions of the state – welfare support, health, social care, education and housing – are experiencing significant reform, with new conditions attached to the receipt of support. This restructuring does not, however, feature in the 'troubled families' story. None of these changes are highlighted, or reflected upon in TFP documents. The state is stepping back from certain functions, but it is simultaneously 'stepping up' in other areas, most specifically in its numerous 'early interventions' in family life.

The state has a longstanding interest in family life (Thane, 2010) and, as we have seen, this has increased in recent years. New Labour's initial policy focus on tackling child poverty and implementing large scale programmes gradually came to focus on efforts to 'responsibilise' small groups of 'problem' or 'at risk' families. When Cameron was prime minister he made several speeches about the importance of families, claiming that they are 'the building blocks of a strong, cohesive society' (Cameron, 2010) and that 'whatever the social issue we want to grasp – the answer should always begin with family' (Cameron, 2014). In a speech on improving children's life chances in 2016, Cameron (2016) claimed that 'Families are the best anti-poverty measure ever invented … [t]hey are a welfare, education and counselling system all wrapped up into one'. The proposal to withdraw Housing Benefit entitlement from some 18–21 year olds from April 2017 (see Wilson, 2015) and the suggestion by a government minister, when answering questions about a crisis in social care provision, that people have as much of a responsibility to look after their parents as they do their children (Asthana, 2017), highlights the potential centrality of 'the family' in future housing and social care policy fields as well.

Cameron's speech on life chances included numerous mentions of the importance of getting things right in 'the early years'. This policy focus on the 'early years', and its derivatives such as 'the foundation years', legitimises state 'early intervention' in the lives of disadvantaged families with small children (see, for example, Allen and Smith, 2008; Field, 2010; Allen, 2011a and 2011b). The focus, grounded in questionable neuroscience 'evidence' (Wastell and White, 2012; Gillies et al, 2017) has been critiqued as being 'a future oriented project building on elements of social investment and moral underclass discourses' (Featherstone et al, 2014b: 1739).

In the coalition government's first child poverty strategy (HM Government, 2011), Sure Start centres were repositioned as being services that 'targeted' the 'most disadvantaged families'. The same document linked the recruitment of an extra 4,200 health visitors to other work focusing on the 'most disadvantaged families', or those with 'multiple problems' (HM Government, 2011: 4). It has also been argued that as well as being 'mother's friend', health visitors are also now expected to be involved in 'identification, surveillance and early intervention of a wider set of vulnerabilities facing children and young people that expand the scope of their gaze beyond more traditional health and developmental concerns' (Peckover, 2013: 120). The introduction of the Family Nurse Partnership (FNP) in 2007, designed to support young mothers and pregnant women in their parenting through a programme of intensive home visits, 'a psycho-educational approach and a focus on positive behaviour change' (FNP, no date), provides another example of the state's increased reach into family life. The FNP website alludes to the 'moral underclass discourse' basis that Featherstone et al (2014b) highlighted, stating that it is a 'preventive programme [that] has the potential to transform the life chances of the most disadvantaged children and families in our society, helping to improve social mobility and break the *cycle of intergenerational disadvantage*' (FNP, no date, emphasis added).

In an intriguing parallel with the TFP, the official evaluation of the FNP found that the programme was 'no more effective than routinely available healthcare' in improving any of the primary outcomes of the programme, which included reducing smoking in pregnancy, increasing birth weight and reducing rates of emergency attendance or hospital admission for any reason (Building Blocks Study Team, 2015: 10). The researchers concluded quite starkly that there was 'little advantage' to be gained from adding the FNP to existing service provision for young mothers. The evaluation reports from the early stages of the second phase of the TFP note that the TFP and the FNP are the 'only two family programmes with major funding from central government' (DCLG, 2017c: 1). This leaves the government in the unenviable position of having independent evaluation teams struggling to find any impact whatsoever from its only two major family programmes.

This intense gaze on, and increased state intervention in, the 'most disadvantaged' families can also be found in other policy fields. The government has attempted to speed up and increase adoptions for children who are taken in to care and, when he was prime minister, Cameron (2014) stated that he was 'determined to do everything we can to unleash this adoption revolution in our country'. Academics have pointed out that although non-consensual adoption practices can be found in other countries, 'no other EU state exercises this power to the extent that England does' (Gupta et al, 2015). Researchers examining the link between deprivation and child welfare interventions have noted 'substantial inequalities in rates of state intervention in family life between areas and population groups linked to relative deprivation' and that 'gross inequalities in children's life chances are being acted out through child welfare services' (Bywaters et al, 2014: 9–10). There is, they argue a 'systematic link between levels of deprivation and a family's chances of being the object of powerful state interventions' (Bywaters et al, 2014: 10), while others have noted that poverty is 'the elephant in the room' in discussions and practice around child neglect (Gupta, 2017). Put simply, children living in neighbourhoods identified as 'deprived' in the UK have a far greater chance of being the subject of a Child Protection Plan or being looked after in out-of-home public care than children in more affluent neighbourhoods (Bywaters et al, 2014, 2015).

At a fringe event at the Conservative party conference in October 2015, the Health Secretary Jeremy Hunt, suggested that a 'draconian' approach was required to tackle childhood obesity. He reportedly told the audience that the 'huge success' of the TFP meant that government had a 'direct line to 300,000 of the most under-privileged families in the country', and that there would be a higher proportion of obese children in those families (in Demianyk, 2015). This 'draconian' approach to tackling children's health issues demonstrates why children's rights groups and charities in the UK are concerned about a 'serious erosion' of children's rights at the current time (Owen, 2013).

In addition to these developments, there have been proposals to expand the reach of the 'troubled families' approach, highlighting efforts to integrate principles in one social policy into other areas as part of the 'transformation' of local services. The expansion of the TFP into its second phase brought an extra 400,000 families into the programme and it also sanctioned the inclusion of families who were not 'troublesome' to others. The new criteria mean that families with disabled or sick children, or those facing financial hardship can easily be officially labelled as 'troubled families', in the process becoming recipients of 'the most intensive form of state intervention there is' (Cameron, 2016). There have also, as noted in the previous chapter, been suggestions that the approach should be extended to working-age individuals without children, with the think-tank IPPR advocating a 'troubled lives' programme in a document appropriately called *Breaking Boundaries* (McNeil and Hunter, 2015). The report proposes a new programme 'targeted at approximately a quarter of a million individuals who experience two or more of the following problems: homelessness, substance misuse and reoffending' (McNeil and Hunter, 2015: 3). The expansion of the 'troubled families' or 'family intervention' approach into other policy fields has not happened in any high-profile way at the time of writing, although there is evidence that local authorities are using some of the principles involved in 're-designing' of their services due to financial pressures (White and Day, 2016). The 2017 annual report of the TFP also announced that the next phase of the TFP would see continued 'alignment of the programme with Children's Social Care reform' (DCLG, 2017a: 23). It should, however, also be noted that recent publications exploring options and opportunities for the future of children's services by the Association of Directors of Children's Services and the Department for Education mention the TFP only in passing, or not at all (see, for example, DfE, 2016; Selwyn, 2016).

These wide-ranging reforms and restructuring efforts help to demonstrate the shifting shape and focus of the state in the UK. It is three symbolically potent moments, however, that can perhaps provide the best evidence to support Wacquant's theory of the remasculinisation of the state and the simultaneous rolling back of Keynesian welfare policies and structures and rolling out of more punitive, targeted interventions.

In June 2013, barely a year after the TFP had begun in earnest, the 'massive expansion' of the programme was announced, as discussed in Chapter Four. The announcement also included news of extra funding of £200 million for the first year of the second phase of the programme, which would run in 2015/16. The announcement was made as part of a Spending Review which saw local government lose £2.1 billion worth of funding from central government over the same period (HM Treasury, 2013: 10; Butler, 2013) and a further £350 million reduction in welfare spending, on top of over £21 billion already announced by the government since 2010 (HM Treasury, 2013: 7–8). In a near perfect illustration of Wacquant's (2009a: 304) argument that the 'rolling back' and 'rolling out' of the state occurs simultaneously, the UK government announced that it was expanding what was ostensibly a fiercely interventionist programme in the same document that it announced a significant loss of funding for local services and reduced welfare payments to disadvantaged groups.

In March 2016, the Welfare Reform and Work Act 2016 saw substantial elements of the Child Poverty Act 2010 repealed, including the commitment to eradicate child poverty by 2020 and the requirement to report child poverty statistics to Parliament on an annual basis. The Child Poverty Act was even retrospectively renamed as the Life Chances Act. In place of the requirement to report child poverty figures, new reporting obligations were introduced, including: reporting requirements on 'workless households' and educational attainment of children at Key Stage 4; and an obligation to report on progress made by 'troubled families' that have been 'supported' by local authorities. Once again, at precisely the same time and in the same document that commitment to material support for impoverished families was symbolically withdrawn, the commitment to a more expansive, behaviourist and punitive approach to disadvantaged families was advanced and enshrined in legislation.

Finally, in April 2017, when the 'next phase' of the TFP was announced, it came as part of a wider government agenda on 'helping workless households' (DWP, 2017a). While the TFP was being refocused, new claimants of ESA were losing £30 per week as part of 'welfare reforms' that aimed to remove 'disincentives' to disabled people who the government deemed had the potential to (re)enter work. Important financial support from the state, which recognised the extra costs that disabled people often incur, was recast as just another example of a bloated welfare system that inhibited entrepreneurialism and prevented people from 'fulfilling their potential'.

Conclusion: 'Learning to be poor'

Cameron's statement that the thing he was 'really passionate about' was 'fixing the responsibility deficit' thus needs to be examined in the wider context of recent state activity. The coalition government undertook a programme of neoliberal statecraft in the UK, across different bureaucratic fields, with the TFP located as a central part of that project. Wacquant (2009a: 304) has argued that this state crafting includes 'the punitive containment of urban marginality through the simultaneous rolling back of the social safety net and the rolling out of the police-and-prison dragnet and their knitting together into a carceral-assistantial lattice'. In the UK, welfare reforms, curbs on public spending and cuts in support to disadvantaged and vulnerable groups have been implemented hand-in-hand with more interventionist policies, usually aimed at disadvantaged populations, such as the TFP. These 'early intervention' approaches form:

> part of a modernising new managerialist approach to governance in which social values and moral issues are reduced to technical rationality, cut adrift from political debate involving interests and power, while social justice, material conditions and social inequalities are obscured from view. (Edwards et al, 2016: 1–2)

Sanctions and conditionality in the welfare system have increased dramatically in a worrying meeting of 'welfare' and 'justice' policies, no doubt aimed at 'responsibilising' marginalised groups. Poor families with children have been subjected to numerous forms of powerful state interventions that have attempted to change the way they behave without taking the resources they possess, or the effects of structural inequalities, into account. History repeats itself. People living in poverty have been castigated for not behaving more like the middle classes. The strength and resilience of many working class families, and especially women and mothers, has been misrecognised as a failure to live up to middle class standards and priorities, with interventions designed to help them become more 'respectable' and 'deserving' of state support. The list of unsuccessful state attempts to improve the lives of marginalised groups by attempting to change their behaviour now includes the TFP.

The 'responsibility deficit' that should be most troubling to us, as a society, can be found not among the dominated and disadvantaged groups engaged in the TFP, but in those occupying positions of power within our society. If we believe that failings and problematic cultures can be handed down from generation to generation, then perhaps it is the intergenerational 'intellectual poverty' (Cohen, 2002: 172) of our society, and specifically its politicians, that should most trouble us (Paul Gilroy also spoke of a 'poverty of the imagination' following the political response to the 2011 riots). Politicians have consistently abdicated responsibility for the effects of their limited thinking and unambitious policies on the lives of people who do not have enough resources to enable them to always cope with everything that society expects of, and indeed throws at, them.

It is not, as Cohen (2002: 172) noted in *Folk Devils and Moral Panics*, that there is 'nothing there' when someone or some group is labelled as troublesome. There are, at the current time, many families facing many problems, with many of them predicted to be made worse by government policies and reforms. But the government explanation and reaction to the problems faced and, in some cases, caused by marginalised families is fundamentally inappropriate, misplaced and inadequate. Troublesome or 'deviant' behaviours cannot be addressed in a social vacuum, with a mean-spirited, behaviourist 'family intervention' approach as the only recourse. Changes to the material circumstances of families and to the structural inequality that pervades our society, are necessary. In discussing the concept of the 'culture of poverty' that emerged in the USA in the late 1960s and early 1970s, William Ryan wrote about the impact of the concept on policy responses to poverty. His words still have relevance for 'troubled families' discussions today:

> If poverty is to be understood more clearly in terms of the 'way of life' of the poor, in terms of a 'lower class culture', as a product of a deviant value system, then money is clearly not the answer. We can stop right now worrying about ways of redistributing resources more equitably, and begin focusing our concern where it belongs – on the poor themselves. We can start trying to figure out how to change that troublesome culture of theirs, how to apply some tautening astringent to their flabby consciences, how to deal with their poor manners and make them more socially acceptable. (Ryan, 1971: 118)

If previous iterations of 'the underclass' were often parts of attempts to 'constrain the redistributive potential of state welfare' (Macnicol, 1987: 316), the official label of 'troubled families' can perhaps best be understood as part of an attempt to craft a new, neoliberal state. It is in this context that the TFP has emerged, 'pioneering' a new set of relations between the state and some of its most vulnerable citizens. It should be viewed as an integral part of an irresponsible programme of neoliberal statecraft across numerous policy fields that has seen different marginalised groups – such as disabled people, lone mothers, and unemployed individuals – targeted by a raft of welfare reforms that have served to stigmatise poor and vulnerable communities and vitiated their material circumstances. It acts, along with the other high-profile reforms or policies mentioned, as 'fleet vehicles for broadcasting the newfound resolve of state elites to tackle offensive conditions and assuage popular resentment toward derelict or deviant categories' (Wacquant, 2009a: 312). The real ambition of the government, far from being to 'turn around' the lives of the most 'troubled families', amounts to little more than encouraging them to learn to be poor (Ryan, 1971: 112–35), and to be well-behaved, quiet and inexpensive while doing so. The family intervention model is the perfect vehicle with which to achieve this aim.

SIX

'This thing called family intervention ...'

What we know works is this thing called family intervention and what it does is basically get into the actual family, in their front room and if actually the kids aren't in school it gets in there and says to the parents I'm gonna show you and explain to you exactly how to get your kids up and out every single day and then I'm gonna make you do it. And if you don't do it, there are gonna be consequences. (Casey, 2013a)

Introduction

A constant feature of the Troubled Families Programme, throughout its various phases and its 'evolution', has been the promotion of the family intervention model as the best way of working with 'troubled families'. This model has remained central to the TFP even when the entry criteria for 'troubled families' has changed and the outcomes expected of the programme have been tweaked. This chapter explicates the history of the family intervention model, initially by going beyond the reputed origins of the approach in Dundee. International and historical approaches that share significant features with the family intervention model are examined before the origins and development of the 'Dundee model' are considered in detail. The chapter follows the development of the family intervention approach as it was piloted in six projects across England in the early 2000s and subsequently rolled out as a 'national network' of Family Intervention Projects (FIPs) in 2006. The continued development of the approach under the TFP is then examined, with a focus on some unacknowledged changes from the Dundee model, as well as some troubling continuities. A discussion drawing attention to the neglect of structural issues in family intervention work concludes the chapter. The chapter also highlights how the approach, developed ostensibly to work with a very small number of troublesome families at risk of eviction, has, in practice, worked with a wide range of families, with issues such as poverty, disability and vulnerability often being far more prevalent than deviancy and delinquency. Some differences between policy rhetoric and professional practice are also highlighted in this chapter, but this issue is discussed in the following chapter in more detail.

The historical and International context

The family intervention approach has been presented as a radical departure from previous attempts to work with 'troubled families'. The original FIPs were described as pioneering projects (Nixon et al, 2006), and Louise Casey (2012a: 3) declared that the TFP presented an opportunity to develop a new way of working that would not repeat, or add to, past failings. And yet, just as there is a long and undistinguished history of ideas about an 'underclass' in our society, there is also a long and undistinguished history of attempts by the state to intervene in their lives in an effort to 'correct' their behaviour. Such attempts can be found not just in the UK, but across different countries and, indeed, different continents.

Chapter Two highlighted how, in the late 1800s, the COS believed that a more co-ordinated and efficient approach to support for paupers was required to ensure that wily applicants did not play the myriad services and organisations off against each other. Koven (2004: 59), highlighting early examples of 'entry criteria' for programmes and a desire to see 'multi-agency working', notes how, in 1866, an 'influential Anglican clergyman John Llewelyn Davies':

> called for the creation of a system of district visitors [who] would carefully investigate and determine the worthiness of each applicant and ensure that charities worked in concert with one another.

There are also particularly strong similarities between the family intervention approach and the 'friendship with a purpose' (Starkey, 2000: 539) approach that was adopted with families in the 1940s and 1950s. Welshman (2013: 86) notes that the developing interest in 'casework' with families advocated by the Pacifist Service Units in the early 1940s 'relied on the personal relationship between workers and clients, but which nonetheless stressed the value of practical help of a physical nature'. In highlighting the gendered focus on mothers in the 'problem family' narrative, Starkey (2000: 549–50) expounds the practical help and 'intensive family casework' offered by Family Service Unit workers:

The form of intervention they developed became known as intensive family casework and emphasised the importance of building close links with the family, in nearly all cases with the mother, and establishing a pattern of close supervision – so close that some were visited two or three times a day or even more. Treatment was directed towards remedying faults thought to be characteristic of the failing mother and emphasised the successful performance of such tasks as getting the children out of bed in time to go to school and taking them there; washing and ironing; regular fine-combing, and if necessary deinfestation, of children's hair; cleaning and cooking; putting the children to bed at a reasonable and regular time. The task of a good mother was not just to organise her own life, but to establish regular habits in her children.

Social historians have also noted the establishment of residential units to help re-train wayward families, such as the Brentwood Centre for Mothers and Children, near Stockport, which only closed in 1970 (Welshman, 2013: 203; Lambert, 2017). Residential projects formed an important part of the early FIP projects, and there are also strong similarities with projects developed in other countries. In setting out the history of a century of supervision of families in the Netherlands, van Wel highlights a number of different residential projects that sought to re-educate families before returning them to the wider community. For example, in the 1920s, 'inadmissible families' who 'neglected their living surroundings, had rent arrears, and/or were associated with disturbances' could be sent to a 'living school' which 'consisted of new brick houses and a club centre with a reading room, public baths, and a laundry' and where 'a female housing inspector supervised the residents' (van Wel, 1992: 149). In the 1940s 'socially ill families' were sometimes sent to '"family residences", which were artificial, isolated camps in the countryside' (van Wel, 1992: 152). These camps were used to re-house anti-social families evacuated from urban areas that had been damaged by bombing during the Second World War. Van Wel (1992: 151–2) notes:

In this coincidental way, the central government became involved in the care of antisocial families. The camps were seen as the perfect context for curing socially diseased families. Assistance measures were planned to bolster a wide range of living skills, such as housekeeping, sewing, management of food, hygiene, infant care, child-rearing and cultural practices.

More worryingly, there are strong similarities between the residential units advocated in the early stages of the family intervention model and the ways in which 'asocial families' were dealt with in 1930s Germany. In an examination of Hashude, an 'asocial colony' in Bremen, Lisa Pine (1995: 185) sets out how advocates of such colonies believed that "'asocial families" could be socially engineered, through the imposition of strict control and surveillance, into "valuable" members of the "national community"'. Work was undertaken with 'the entire family' and part of the rationale for such work was to 'reduce public expenditure' on 'asocial families' (Pine, 1995: 186). Pine noted that Hashude, which was on a far larger scale than the residential units proposed by the early FIPs, 'was the most significant experiment in the area of housing "asocials"', representing a 'last chance' for the most troublesome families to be 'reintegrated' into their community. Families generally stayed there for a year and, if they could demonstrate improvement, they were 'released into "normal" society' (Pine, 1995: 186).

More recently, a number of different models of family support or family intervention or 'whole family working' have been developed across different countries. A Brighter Futures model developed in New South Wales, Australia, in 2005 revolved around 'a case manager who, working collaboratively with families, assessed family needs, designed family support plans and brokered and organised services, childcare and sustained home visiting' (Churchill and Fawcett, 2016: 310). Other contemporary examples of similar ways of working with disadvantaged families can be found in France (Martin, 2015; Join-Lambert, 2016), and the Netherlands (Knijn and Hopman, 2015).

From Dundee to Westminster

There is no acknowledgement of these domestic or international forerunners within rhetoric surrounding the TFP and it has been pointed out that Louise Casey, despite being a History graduate, does not have a particularly strong grasp of the history of state intervention in family life (Welshman, 2012b). Instead, the government traces the origins of the family intervention approach back to a single voluntary sector project in Scotland that officially began in November 1996 (Dillane et al, 2001: 11).

The Dundee Families Project (DFP) was established following a successful attempt to intensively support a single family that was at risk of eviction and homelessness. The official evaluation of the project (Dillane et al, 2001) noted that, in the mid-1990s, Dundee had around 23,000 council houses. The authors state that 'like any significant public sector landlord, Dundee has problems with the behaviour of some of its tenants' (Dillane et al, 2001: 8), which suggests that people that live in privately rented or privately owned accommodation do not cause problems for their landlords or neighbours. In order to give 'some idea of the scale of the problem', the report notes that around 800 complaints about neighbour nuisance were received by Dundee City Council (DCC) in 1996/97. This equates to around 3.5 complaints per 100 properties. In the same year, the council 'took the *first step* in legal action (service of a notice seeking possession) in around 150 cases' (Dillane et al, 2001: 8, emphasis added). The authors note that 'This rate of around 20 per cent is fairly typical for a city authority' (Dillane et al, 2001: 8). A rate of '20 per cent' sounds quite high, and suggests that the 'problem' of anti-social behaviour or 'neighbour nuisance' is quite high. An alternative reading of the 150 figure is that just over half of one per cent of DCCs tenants received a relatively minor form of a temporary legal notice being served on them. In 1993, a total of 20 families, less than one tenth of one per cent, were evicted by DCC for anti-social behaviour. A subsequent drop in evictions was put down to 'enthusiasm' for legal action declining:

> Interviewees said part of the reason for this fall in evictions was that the legal process was slow and the outcome uncertain, because the Sheriff had to be convinced that the action was reasonable. In the meantime, the families were still living in council housing and often continued to cause havoc and misery to their neighbours. Sometimes neighbours were afraid to act as witnesses due to fears of reprisals. In a number of cases, no legal action was taken and the problems continued. (Dillane et al, 2001: 8)

There was also general agreement that eviction was not always the most helpful course of action for the families involved. The council often had a duty to re-house such families elsewhere, or the families ended up in private rented or temporary accommodation, or staying with friends or family, which, in many cases, would not have helped to improve their situation. Tensions, resource constraints and competing priorities between different local services meant that families often did not receive the support they needed or faced decisions that made their circumstances more difficult. There was recognition among local services that existing arrangements and working practices were not satisfactory and an alternative way of working with such families was sought.

According to the evaluation, one family with a 'history of severe anti-social behaviour' proved to be the catalyst for a different approach. The family was evicted in 1992, and after they were declared intentionally homeless by the DCC Homelessness Team, social workers intervened on the family's behalf. Housing staff were reluctant to re-house the family and so a 'compromise' was struck, with the following story (Dillane et al, 2001: 10–11) being told by a housing officer involved:

> 'The proposal was put that Social Work should take on a house and manage this house and put in the support and, after a period of time, if things went well, Housing would consider housing this family on a permanent basis. Now at that point the Social Work refused to take on the house saying that they were not landlords and it is not their responsibility ... So it got kicked about for a bit longer and then another compromise was reached in that we would invite a third party to take on tenancy of the house. Barnardos agreed to take on the property ... Various supports were put in from Barnardos and from Social Work and some of the housing issues were addressed in terms of the anti-social behaviour ... plus debt issues with the Housing Department. After something like about 6 months there had been a remarkable change in this family and everything was going well. The kids were at school and things were progressing and she had made payments towards the debt and it was then agreed ... to re-house the family. ... So the long and the short of it was that this was seen to work.'

It was decided that this model was worth exploring further, and could work with more families. Local services were supportive because 'the situation was not unusual' (Dillane et al, 2001: 11). Barnardos decided against remaining involved with the project, for unspecified reasons, and NCH Action for Children Scotland replaced them as a partner organisation. Funding was sought from the Scottish Office for Urban Programme in 1993, the project was established in 1995, and it officially opened in November 1996.

The aims of the project shifted from an early focus on those families that had already been evicted to one that provided a more preventative approach to working with a wider group of families that were deemed to be nuisance or anti-social. NCH also wanted to increase the numbers of staff and the rates of pay because, in the words of one interviewee 'we wanted to get a better quality of staff; we wanted to hire people who could actually make some difference to families' (Dillane et al, 2001: 16). The DFP, when it was launched, offered three different forms of service to families who had been evicted or were at risk of eviction:

- A core block, which provided accommodation for up to four families. This was the most intensive form of support – and surveillance – and was restricted to the most vulnerable or troublesome families that had been evicted from their homes.
- A small number of dispersed flats that provided 'step-down' accommodation for families to move into from the core block, or for families that had been evicted but did not require 24 hour support or surveillance.
- An outreach service for a larger number of families in their existing accommodation, where there was a risk of eviction by the City Council due to anti-social behaviour.

The staff involved with the DFP were clear about the approach that was required, according to the evaluation of the project:

> Staff saw key elements of the Project's approach to be the expectations for the family to accept responsibility for their behaviour and agree on the identified areas that need to be addressed. This was done by developing an honest and direct working relationship with each family member. The work of the agency was premised on a systematic, holistic assessment process and joint 'contracting' about what is to be done. (Dillane et al, 2001: 16–17)

Local and national media reporting of the project – using terms such as the 'sin-bin' and 'Colditz' to describe the residential core block – meant that residents living close to the DFP were concerned about the development of the project and what impact it might have on their local area, with an Action Group opposing the opening of the project. By the time the evaluation started in 1999, it was felt that the early negative perceptions of the project were beginning to be turned around, and most of the residents interviewed as part of the evaluation were ambiguous about the location of the project. Media reporting also changed and the Labour Government's Social Exclusion Unit report on anti-social behaviour (SEU, 2000: 84) stated that the project was 'unique in terms of housing and social work practice and has worked successfully with 70 families'. The Chartered Institute of Housing also conferred a 'Good Practice' award on the DFP (Dillane et al, 2001: 14).

The families worked with were usually poor, with only two parents in paid employment from 34 family cases assessed for an interim report. Around two thirds of the families were headed by a lone parent and around half of the families had records of drug and/or alcohol misuse (Dillane et al, 2001: 41). Anti-social behaviour was listed as at least a partial factor in the referral of around two thirds of these cases, but this covered diverse issues such as stealing, verbal abuse, neglect of property, neighbour disputes and violence. In two cases, families were reported to be the victims of intimidation by others (Dillane et al, 2001: 40). Health problems within families were not generally recorded by the DFP and there is no mention of the word 'health' in the chapter on families worked with by the project, which includes reasons for referral and characteristics of the families. During interviews with 20 families involved with the DFP, however, the evaluation team established that eight of them had health issues of varying severity (Dillane et al, 2001: 57). Seventy per cent of the young people interviewed by the researchers stated that they had been bullied at school (Dillane et al, 2001: 58).

Bearing in mind the DFP has been highlighted as the model for a national network of FIPs in England and the family intervention approach recommended for the TFP, one would expect to see very promising and robust findings from the research. This is not the case. The team of evaluators noted that of 56 closed cases of families that had worked with the DFP, 59 per cent had resulted in 'successful' closures, 18 per cent in 'unsuccessful' closures, and 23 per cent in changed circumstances that prevented either a 'successful' or 'unsuccessful' outcome (Dillane et al, 2001: 43). Furthermore, there was a marked difference between the success rates of the different elements of the project: the core block and dispersed tenancies strands were each successful with around 82 per cent of cases, while the outreach service was only successful in around 56 per cent of the families it worked with (Dillane et al, 2001: 43). Put another way, nearly half of the families worked with from a preventative 'early intervention' perspective, before eviction, did not achieve a successful outcome following their involvement with the DFP, according to the official evaluation of the project. This is despite a key criterion for entry into the programme being a desire to change. An assessment process was seen as being a 'cornerstone' of the project and 'maximum participation by the family was seen as an essential element' of the process (Dillane et al, 2001: 29). Therefore, families that did not want to engage with the project were viewed as being potentially problematic or were resistant to the approach in some way, and were excluded from the project. (See Gregg, 2010, for a fuller discussion of the findings from the Dillane et al report.)

In 2003, six 'pioneering local authorities' (Nixon et al, 2006: 9) in England established anti-social behaviour Intensive Family Support Projects (IFSPs). Five of these projects (Blackburn with Darwen, Bolton, Manchester, Oldham and Salford) were developed in the North West in partnership with NCH (now Action for Children) and one was set up by Sheffield City Council. Although the specific approaches of the projects differed, depending on local contexts, they were all explicitly based on the DFP (Nixon et al, 2006: 9) and the new IFSPs delivered broadly the same range of dispersed and outreach services provided by the DFP, although only three provided a core residential block for families. Casey highlighted her role in this development at an appearance before the Public Accounts Committee (2014: 35), stating 'I was working under a previous administration when we set up family intervention projects and brought them down from Dundee into England'.

A two-year long evaluation of the IFSPs, collecting data in 2003/04 and 2004/05, reported that although some of the families were involved in criminal behaviour, the majority of the cases concerned low-level but persistent nuisance behaviours (Nixon et al, 2006: 9). The authors of the report state that the 'cumulative impact of such behaviour on neighbours should not, however, be underestimated' and go on to note the action taken prior to referral to the projects. In 2004/05, around 39 per cent of families worked with had received either a verbal or written warning and around 33 per cent had been issued with a Notice of Seeking Possession (NOSP) in relation to their anti-social behaviour, at the point of referral. In 2003/04, only 17 per cent of families had been served with a NOSP at the point of referral. Only 8 per cent of families entering IFSPs in 2004/05 were the subject of eviction proceedings. Family members with Anti-Social Behaviour Orders (ASBOs) were found in around one sixth of households in both periods.

It is worth putting these figures into context. This was at the height of Labour's high-profile efforts to tackle anti-social behaviour and in the years immediately following the establishment of the ASBU. The fact that 67 per cent of families referred to the projects had not received anything more than a verbal or written warning about their behaviour should surprise us. Around 28 per cent of families referred to these 'pioneering' intensive anti-social behaviour (ASB) projects had not even received a verbal warning about their behaviour (Nixon et al, 2006: 70). Ninety-two per cent of families worked with by the IFSPs were not at risk of eviction when they were referred. Six out of ten families (60 per cent) were reported by project staff and/or referral agencies to be 'victims' of ASB (Nixon et al, 2006: 11).

The evaluation also reported a wide range of health needs and vulnerability in the families worked with, with around 80 per cent of adults experiencing poor mental or physical health and/or substance misuse (Nixon et al, 2006: 11). Depression affected nearly 60 per cent of adults. Around 30 per cent of children in families had learning difficulties and nearly 20 per cent of them experienced mental health issues or depression (Nixon et al, 2006: 56). Children in the families were described as 'amongst the most disadvantaged in the country' (Nixon et al, 2006: 11). In 47 per cent of cases domestic violence was reported as an issue, either historically or ongoing. In five out of the six projects, the clear majority of families were headed by 'single lone female parents'. In Sheffield, 89 per cent of families were headed by single females. In discussing the impact of the projects, the authors of the evaluation wrote:

> Given the levels of need associated with families referred to the projects, it might be anticipated that project interventions would only be partially successful. This was not the case. Indeed, the study findings relating to outcomes at the point at which families left the service indicate that, for the vast majority of families, the projects had helped them achieve *remarkable changes* (Nixon et al, 2006: 14, emphasis added).

In the *Executive Summary* of the evaluation report, readers are told that 'findings in the report are based on an analysis of statistical data collected from project case files in relation to 256 families, consisting of 370 adults and 743 children' (Nixon et al, 2006: 10). Four pages later, the evaluation reports that in over 85 per cent of families, ASB had 'ceased or had reduced to a level where the tenancy was no longer deemed to be at risk at the point where the family exited the project' (Nixon et al, 2006: 14). This sounds impressive, but it neglects to include the fact, mentioned earlier, that only 8 per cent of families were at risk of eviction upon entry to the programme.

The evidence of the impact of the interventions, however, was drawn from just 54 closed case files. This information is not presented in the

Executive Summary of the document; instead, it is first mentioned on page 117 of the report (Nixon et al, 2006: 117). Of these 54 cases, project workers assessed how families had not 'fully engaged' with the projects (Nixon et al, 2006: 118) with: 48 per cent being 'fully engaged'; 28 per cent 'partially engaged'; 17 per cent disengaged; and 7 per cent becoming ineligible for support. The figure of 85 per cent reduction in families' ASB comes from the 41 families in the 54 case files that were deemed to have 'fully' or 'partially' engaged with the projects. Including the 14 families that did not engage or whose circumstances changed in this analysis would change the reduction figure from 85 to around 64 per cent. Focusing on positive findings from families engaged in the programme and marginalising the (non) impact of the interventions on families that did not engage as much is a highly misleading way of reporting the 'impact of the interventions'. It should also be noted that the six families (15 per cent) who fully or partially engaged in the programme but did not achieve a reduction in ASB actually saw an increase in instances of ASB and 'for five of these families the risk of homelessness remained very high' (2006: 119). This information was tucked away on page 119 of the report.

A further evaluation report on the original six 'pioneer projects' examined the longer-term outcomes of families involved with the projects (Nixon et al, 2008). This report focused on the outcomes for 28 families that had worked with IFSPs. Of the 28 families included, 21 were interviewed and data was accessed on seven others via interviews with agencies such as housing providers (Nixon et al, 2008: 14). Six of the families were described as having exited the IFSPs 'recently' and it was acknowledged that this made it 'harder to establish the longer-term impact of the IFSP interventions' (Nixon et al, 2008: 14). The evaluation suggested that 12 of the 28 families had seen 'resoundingly successful outcomes' while six achieved 'more mixed outcomes' (Nixon et al, 2008: 108). For those families for whom 'success' was only partial, it was noted that 'there was evidence of a continuing lack of social inclusion and on-going unmet support needs resulting in negative impacts on their quality of life and well-being' (Nixon et al, 2008: 38). For eight families, involvement in the IFSPs had made no difference, with their lives still 'dominated by complaints about anti-social behaviour, homelessness or risk of eviction, and family breakdown' (Nixon et al, 2008: 108). For these families, problems were often associated with the behaviour of one person in the family and, according to the authors, 'the behaviour of the children appeared to be symptomatic of structural disadvantage, combined with long-standing cognitive and psychological problems, which had not been addressed by welfare and educational agencies at an earlier stage' (Nixon et al, 2008: 44). Families reported that they had been the victims of crime and ASB and were living in fear since exiting the projects. Once again, these statistics suggest that the families involved in the projects were not a hardcore of troublemakers or 'neighbours from hell', a point that the authors themselves made when they highlighted that:

> Contrary to popular belief, the evidence suggests that rather than constituting a distinct minority distinguishable from the 'law abiding majority' families tended to conform to the norms and values of the communities in which they lived. (Nixon et al, 2008: 63)

The report concluded that there were 'beneficial outcomes associated with IFSP interventions' but that there were also 'limitations of this approach' (Nixon et al, 2008: 110). They also stated that it was 'too early to make claims with any certainty about the longer-term sustainability of the changes that IFSPs had helped engender' but, by this time, the projects had already been rolled out under the Respect Action Plan in 2006.

The 'sexed-up' (Gregg, 2010: 11) success of the IFSPs provided the impetus for the launch of a 'national network' of 53 FIPs under the Respect Action Plan, published by the Respect Task Force (RTF, 2006a). Even the number of FIPs 'launched' was exaggerated as White et al (2008: 3) noted that only 34 of the 53 FIPs were 'set up from scratch' or underwent 'radical transformation', while the remaining 19 had existed prior to 2006. In a section on 'Impact' in an accompanying document on FIPs (RTF, 2006b), the 85 per cent reduction in ASB reported by Nixon et al (2006: 14) was reproduced, along with similarly impressive figures around reduced threat of possession action and improvements in school attendance. Disregarding the evidence that families involved in the IFSPs did not constitute a 'distinct minority', and were often vulnerable themselves, the Action Plan referred to families as 'problem families' and stated quite unequivocally that:

> Problem families can disrupt the quality of life of whole communities and make the lives of residents around them miserable. It is in the interest of all of us to ensure that the small minority of families who are responsible for a high proportion of problems, radically change their behaviour. (RTF, 2006a: 21)

Although the Action Plan referred to Intensive Family Support Projects, when the 'roll-out' occurred, the projects had undergone a name-change and they became known as FIPs. Key features of the approach including 'gripping the problem', 'gripping the family' and 'gripping all the other agencies' (RTF, 2006b). Accompanying Home Office webpages augmented the shift from a discourse that prioritised support and highlighted vulnerability to one that was far more punitive and assertive in its approach. Louise Casey was quoted on one government webpage titled 'Innovative new help to tackle "neighbours from hell"' as saying that 'problem families' 'cause untold misery to those who have to live alongside them and destroy entire neighbourhoods with their frightening and disruptive behaviour' (Home Office, 2007). She also stated that the FIPs would 'grip families' and were 'proven to turn families around'.

More evaluations were commissioned, again many of them showing some signs of success with families who both met the referral criteria and engaged with the work. But again, these successes were qualified. An evaluation of the design, set-up and early outcomes from the FIPs noted that 'a substantial proportion of families (35 per cent) were still engaged in ASB when they completed the intervention' (White et al, 2008: 6) and high levels of health problems remained (2008: 4). A Monitoring and Evaluation report highlighted that 15 per cent of families offered an intervention had failed to engage at some stage of the project (NatCen, 2010: 5). While positive outcomes associated with ASB and security of tenancy were achieved for around 60–70 per cent of families, issues such as mental health, drug or substance misuse, and concerns about child protection were less positive, with a minority of families experiencing these issues seeing any improvement (NatCen, 2010: 6). There was a one percentage point drop (from 76 per cent to 75) in 'workless households' and a two percentage point reduction (from 43 per cent to 41) in the proportion of adults who were unemployed. These less positive outcomes highlight that there are challenging structural issues that intensive 'gripping' of families is unlikely to address.

At this time, FIPs and the intensive approach they allegedly brought with them were in the ascendancy, despite Gordon Brown's decision to close the RTF when he became prime minister in 2009. Headline figures from evaluation reports were promising, with caveats and limitations of the research approaches remaining largely undiscussed. The types of problems that could be addressed by intensive approaches began to be broadened out. An evaluation of 'intensive family interventions (formerly known as Family Intervention Projects or

FIPs)' (Dixon et al, 2010: 5) noted that the aim of such interventions was to 'work with the most challenging families and tackle issues such as ASB, youth crime, inter-generational disadvantage and worklessness in families' and to 'turn around these families'. The widened remit of FIPs was reflected in the development and establishment of different types of intensive interventions that focused not on ASB but on child poverty and youth crime in 2009. Dixon et al (2010: 11) noted the reach of these services across the country and also stated that two more types of intervention had been launched in 2010:

> As of March 2010 there were 68 ASB family interventions, 32 Child Poverty family interventions and 150 Youth Crime family interventions across England ... In June 2010, two new types of family interventions – one part-funded through Housing Challenge and the other focusing on women offenders – were established.

As discussed in Chapter Three, the coalition government committed to investigating a new approach to working with families with multiple problems. While this involved support and challenge from volunteers under the Working Families Everywhere (WFE) programme, the riots saw Cameron's government return to the same old 'pioneering' approach that New Labour had 'discovered' in Dundee.

Family Intervention in the Troubled Families Programme

In Cameron's launch speech on 15 December 2011, he lamented the fact that, in traditional services 'no-one sees the whole family; no-one grips the whole problem' and spoke glowingly about the work of a FIP in Smethwick, that he had visited that morning. He highlighted the story of a single family to demonstrate what the FIP approach could deliver:

> In Smethwick ... you can see just what persistent and intensive work can achieve. The Family Intervention Project worked with one family whose criminality and anti-social behaviour had spiralled out of control. Police visits to their home were happening almost every day – to follow up on reports of anti-social behaviour, to arrest one of the children or to check up that curfews were working. The story of the misery that one family can caused one small area is all too familiar. The breakthrough came when

the mother admitted to the housing officer that she was struggling to cope at home. The Family Intervention Project gave the family a key worker, who over the next 9 months helped the family transform its behaviour. The change is lasting too – there are now no calls to the police, the teenage children are engaging with school, the younger children are more settled. (Cameron, 2011b)

Alongside the 'gripping' of families and services, families were once again referred to as 'neighbours from hell' and Cameron promised to 'turn troubled families around'. Cameron, sounding like he had just read Labour's Respect Action Plan, spoke of how 'a relatively small number of families are the source of a large proportion of the problems in society'. The TFP was positioned, just as FIPs had been, as a response to the failing of traditional services to help or 'sort out' families experiencing multiple problems. A single worker would see 'the family as a whole and get a plan of action together, agreed with the family'. A further evaluation of outcomes from FIPs that Cameron referred to in his speech, and published by the Department for Education on the day of the launch, 'identified eight core features of the FIP model that were viewed as critical to its success' (Lloyd et al, 2011: 12):

- recruitment and retention of high quality staff;
- small caseloads;
- having a dedicated key worker who works intensively with each family;
- a 'whole family' approach;
- staying involved with a family for as long as necessary;
- having the scope to use resources creatively;
- using sanctions alongside support for families;
- effective multi-agency relationships.

While the rhetoric was familiar, a number of differences between the model of family intervention introduced under the TFP and previous iterations could also be found. The PbR mechanism, which rewarded local authorities for families achieving certain behaviour changes, was new. There were 'entry criteria' which, at first glance, were far clearer and more formal than the local referral and decision-making processes that operated within FIPs. The scale of the programme was vastly increased as well. The intention was to work with 120,000 troubled families, which equated to around 13 times the 8,841 families worked with by FIPs between February 2007 and March 2011 (Lloyd et al, 2011: 1). In contrast to the small local projects, often delivered by voluntary sector organisations, the TFP was a national policy programme, designed and monitored by central government, and delivered largely by local authorities across England. These inconsistencies relating to the family intervention approach under the TFP continued.

Casey responded to a short but critical examination of the establishment of the TFP in the *British Medical Journal* by stating that the government was 'not prescribing Family Intervention Projects or any other model' (Casey, 2012b). However, later that year, a report produced by DCLG examining 'the evidence and good practice' around work with 'troubled families' identified the family intervention model as being central to the TFP. The report, *Working with Troubled Families* (DCLG, 2012a), was accompanied by an online announcement that stated 'Louise Casey calls for family intervention approach', and highlighted her 'endorsement' of the approach (DCLG, 2012c). The report mentioned no other approaches or models of working with families.

The report identified 'five family intervention factors' – the 'key features of effective family intervention practice stand out from both the evidence and from discussions with practitioners' (DCLG, 2012a: 14) – but made no mention of the 'eight core features' identified in the final research report on FIPs (Lloyd et al, 2011). The five factors were:

- a dedicated worker, dedicated to a family;
- practical 'hands-on' support;
- a persistent, assertive and challenging approach;
- considering the family as a whole – gathering the intelligence;
- a common purpose and agreed action.

While some of original 'core features' were echoed in the newly identified 'factors' (such as a whole family approach and a dedicated worker), there were some that were not well reflected in the five new factors. For example, core features identifying the importance of resources – recruitment and retention of high quality staff; small caseloads; and staying involved with the family for as long as necessary – were eschewed in favour of more pragmatic (and cheaper) dispositions such as 'practical "hands-on" support' and a 'common purpose and agreed action'. The belief in the value of well qualified staff stemmed from the original DFP, but here, in its latest iteration, the qualifications and/or experience of staff were marginalised in favour of a more muscular 'persistent, assertive and challenging approach'.

Another change that is reflected in the shift from the 'core features' to the 'five factors', but also elsewhere in the document, is the view that the family intervention model can be delivered in a less intensive way. The *Working with Troubled Families* publication set out the 'three basic models' that existing FIPs were using to deliver their services to families. These three models – family intervention, family intervention light, and family intervention super light – set out how family intervention, previously viewed as resource intensive work with small numbers of very challenging families, could be delivered to a much larger number of families, by workers with much higher caseloads. The family intervention light model suggested that it was possible to deliver 'an intensive intervention' to families by workers with caseloads of up to 15 families. No indicative caseloads are mentioned for the family intervention super light model, which sees workers remain in their existing services (despite the view that those services have been part of the problem of 'troubled families') but workers having more than 15 families to work with are unlikely to be able to work with them intensively, nor can they be helping all families get their children ready for school, for example.

This dilution of the intensive family intervention approach never made it into the wider public discourse surrounding the TFP. Instead, the focus remained on an approach that was characterised by, and whose success depended on, its intensity. For example, Cameron (2016), shortly before the end of the first phase of the programme, called the TFP 'perhaps the most intensive form of state intervention there is'. The evaluation of the implementation process for the first phase of the programme suggested a diversity of approaches from local authorities to delivering the TFP with one main challenge being that 'scaling-up family intervention was "diluting" practice' (White and Day, 2016: 5). Other divergences from the official rhetoric included workers: co-working some cases; working with families with low levels of need; working with large caseloads and mixed caseloads involving 'non-troubled families'; and providing support to families even after they were deemed to have been 'turned around' (see White and Day, 2016: 26). Many local authorities chose not to establish or expand a separate family intervention team and instead opted for 'hybrid', 'virtual' or 'embedded' models where cases were allocated to workers across a wide range of services, many of whom had existing relationship with families. In one local authority that had a dedicated family intervention team, workers located in 12 different services were involved in delivering the TFP (Crossley, 2016: 136).

Discussion

Advocates of the family intervention model have largely ignored the long history, across different countries, of the state attempting to intervene assertively in the lives of disadvantaged families and other marginalised groups. As we have seen in this and previous chapters, approaches that share many features of the family intervention model can be found across various different countries, often going back over 70 years. While this historical perspective highlights some enduring similarities, there are also some shifts and departures from previous models. Indeed, tracing the shorter history of the family intervention approach illustrates that the 'family intervention' that allegedly takes place within the TFP often bears little resemblance to the 'Dundee model' that it is explicitly based on. Elements of the rhetoric surrounding the approach have proven to be more enduring than the actual practice.

The approach was originally developed by a partnership between a Scottish local authority and a voluntary organisation, in response to concerns about existing service provision to a small number of families at risk of eviction. It now apparently underpins an England wide approach developed by a central government department in Westminster, which purports to have 'turned around' the lives of nearly 120,000 families already, and is aiming to do the same with 400,000 more by 2020. The rhetoric of 'intensive support' has gradually been replaced by 'intervention'. The model that was supposed to help tackle ASB has more recently been promoted as a model for working with violent extremists, domestic abusers, children who have run away from home, and vulnerable working age adults without children. It has been linked to policy agendas such as child poverty, relationship support, 'financial exclusion', childhood obesity, workless families and those who have 'a range of health problems'. Small projects, with local referral processes, have been replaced by a central government policy programme with official criteria for families that can be worked with and the outcomes that are required of them. Voluntary sector agencies, viewed as central to the original DFP and IFSPs, have increasingly been marginalised as the state has become more instrumental in delivering family intervention work.

The original three-level model, including core residential blocks for around 3–4 families, has been replaced with a new three-level model that advocates 'family intervention super light' and caseloads of upwards of 15 families per worker. A desire to employ high quality staff with small caseloads has fallen foul of an austerity-driven model that prefers instead to employ workers who are prepared to 'tell it like it is' and 'roll their sleeves' up, or that develops a 'virtual' team of workers based in a wide range of existing services. Once these shifts are understood, the term 'family intervention' risks being seen as an empty signifier – a 'model' that has no agreed, widely accepted meaning beyond some kind of more or less co-ordinated and supposedly 'efficient' work with severely disadvantaged families.

As well as the above shifts and discontinuities, there are some areas where elements of the family intervention model have remained more constant and enduring, some of which are returned to in later chapters. At the same time that politicians and policy makers have remained keen to dress family intervention up as a 'new' or 'pioneering' way of working, marking a radical departure from previous models, practitioners have, at various stages, remarked that this is not really the case (see, for example, Nixon et al, 2006: 85–6; Crossley, 2016: 135–6). The very small numbers of genuinely 'troublesome' or anti-social families has remained relatively stable, even when the family intervention approach has been scaled up to work with over half a million families. At the same time, the minority of putatively troublesome families are still more likely to face poverty and severe and complex health problems than to exhibit delinquent behaviours. According to the government's own evaluation, 'troubled families' were more likely to contain an adult with a mental health issue than they were to have had a police callout, or any other crime or ASB related issue, in the previous six months (Whitley, 2016: 17–18).

The focus on short-term outcomes has remained, along with celebrations of 'success' that are not always supported by research evidence or evaluation data, an issue which is discussed in more detail in the following chapters. The 'success' that has been achieved by the family intervention model, in its various iterations, has usually been defined by officials and policy makers. Enabling a family to sustain a tenancy, avoiding legal action, getting a child back into school, improving parenting skills, reducing often already low levels of ASB and nuisance and 'making progress to work' have all, at various times, been used as 'official' indicators of success, or of families whose lives have been 'turned around'. Not once, across any of the iterations of the family intervention approach, has a family moving out of poverty been used as an indicator of a successful intervention. The model attempts to change or improve almost everything except the material circumstances of families, the resources that they have access to, and possibly the one thing that could make a genuine difference to the quality of their lives: a good, secure income. It attempts to teach families how to be poor.

In 1959, in discussing the Younghusband Report into social work education, Barbara Wootton highlighted the importance of money in addressing the issues that social workers faced with their clients every day. She argued, in terms that are still relevant today, that:

> The problems associated with birth or death, with sickness or with the inability of people to get on with one another are not in themselves confined to any one social or economic class. But in nearly all these problems the economic element bulks large in that, with money, solutions can be found that are impossible without it. The social worker trudges up the steps of tenement dwellings but is seldom seen in the lifts of luxury flats, simply because the inhabitants of the latter do for themselves, or pay other people to do, the jobs that the social worker does for those less well endowed with the world's goods. (Wootton, 1959: 259–60)

Wootton was irritated by social workers attempts to 'glorify their profession' (1959: 258) and by the 'extreme silliness or the intolerable arrogance' that 'disfigured' much social work writing at that time that portrayed social workers as able to 'resolve the problems which have defeated the human race since the day of Adam and Eve' (Wootton, 1959: 253). These arguments ring true today, when we are told that 'persistent, assertive and challenging' family workers have allegedly 'turned around' nearly 120,000 of England's most 'troubled families', at a time when other issues affecting disadvantaged families, such as homelessness, child poverty, and the numbers of children being taken into care have been getting worse. Wootton's proposal to improve the lot of, or in today's parlance to help 'turn around', the families she was writing about was, and unfortunately remains, truly pioneering and innovative:

> Until we have abolished mental and physical illness, poverty and overcrowding, as well as such human frailties as jealousy and self-assertiveness, many of the problems presented are frankly insoluble. But they can often be alleviated, and most of them, it is worth noting, would be a lot more tolerable if those afflicted with them had a lot more money. (Wootton, 1959: 252)

SEVEN

Street-level perspectives

A street-level lens provides strategies for investigating questions of common interest ... Its central task is to expose the informal practices through which policies—and by extension social politics and social relations—are effectively negotiated, although rarely explicitly so. It seeks to make visible and understandable informal organizational practices that otherwise can escape analytic scrutiny and even recognition (Brodkin, 2011: i200)

Introduction

Government policy does not always get enacted without getting slightly muddied along the way, and political rhetoric does not always tally with the realities of practice. Practitioners do not always do exactly what is expected of them, and there is a long history of research that explores the complex world of policy implementation and 'street-level bureaucracy' (Lipsky, 1980). Previous chapters have focused on the role of a small number of powerful people, and the official documents they write or commission, and the speeches and interviews they have given that have 'set the scene' for the TFP, and provide the framework within which it must operate. It is these publications and proclamations that are reported in the media and read by members of the wider populace. The day-to-day life and operationalisation of the programme, however, involves hundreds, if not thousands of other, less powerful people working away from the public eye to help 'turn around' or improve the lives of 'troubled families'.

While local authorities and family workers have been spoken about in glowing terms by influential individuals such as Cameron, Casey and Javid, when the surface is scratched, workers do not always agree with all aspects of the policy they are asked to implement. Similarly, local authorities have often exercised the discretion afforded to them in their implementation of the TFP. This chapter examines the daily conduct of the TFP, drawing on a wide range of research that has been conducted with people involved in the delivery of the programme. The chapter begins with a discussion of 'street-level bureaucracy', a widely used concept that draws attention to the 'murky waters' of policy implementation, and its relevance to the TFP. Some recent research involving street-level bureaucrats in the UK is then sketched out, along with a slightly fuller discussion of research that examined local practices in the FIPs that preceded the TFP. The attention then turns to research that has been carried out with local practitioners involved with the TFP, including research undertaken in three different local authority areas that examined the daily life of the TFP and the relations between different agents involved in delivering the programme. These three authorities are anonymised here as Northton, Southborough and Westingham. The chapter concludes with a brief discussion of the ways in which local workers subvert and resist some of the rhetorical elements of the TFP, and the extent to which such resistance troubles the dominant policy narrative of the misbehaving 'troubled families' that require an intensive family intervention approach is also discussed.

Street-level bureaucracy

Michael Lipsky coined the phrase 'street-level bureaucracy' to highlight the central role of street-level practitioners, such as social workers, teachers, youth workers, housing officers, police officers, health workers, and so on, in implementing social and public policies. He argued that 'the actions of most public service workers actually constitute the services "delivered" by government' (Lipsky, 1980: 3) and that each encounter with street-level bureaucrats 'represents an instance of policy delivery'. Lipsky also highlighted the extent of discretion that frontline workers actually have, despite efforts to regulate their work more closely. He highlights that police officers 'cannot carry around instructions on how to intervene with citizens, particularly in potentially hostile encounters' (Lipsky, 1980: 15) and the same applies to a host of other roles. Teachers do not have a step-by-step guide on how to deal with each different situation that arises in the classroom, nor do social workers have a standard script that they must adhere to during home visits. Such discretion and autonomy is particularly important in the TFP, as workers are expected to know when to be 'persistent, assertive and challenging' and when to be more supportive of families, or when and how to work on their behalf in dealings with other agencies. The coalition government's wider focus on localism and decentralisation ensured that no statutory duties or new legislation were enacted in respect of the TFP in its first phase. While the government identifies what constitutes a 'troubled family', albeit with varying degrees of local discretion, and also what outcomes are required of the families, how local authorities work, and indeed what individual practitioners do, with 'troubled families' is largely up to them. The programme remains voluntary, with no official sanction for families that refuse to engage with it (despite rumours of plans to impose sanctions on families that did not engage with the programme – see Stratton, 2013), and workers thus often have to be persuasive and creative in how they 'sell' the programme to families they need to work with.

Lipsky is by no means the only person to identify the potential for policies to be delivered in ways that were not always consistent with their original aims. In a classic work called *Implementation: How Great Expectations in Washington Are Dashed in Oakland*, Pressman and Wildavsky (1984: xviii) suggest that problems in achieving policy goals are often 'of a prosaic and everyday character', noting that it should not be underestimated 'how difficult it can be to make the ordinary happen'. Drass and Spencer (1987: 278), in examining probation officers accounts of their exercise of discretion, proposed 'a theory of office ... a "working ideology" which consists of typologies of deviant actors and appropriate processing outcomes, as well as rules which link the two'. Researchers in the UK in recent times have also noted the potential for a 'governmentality gap' (McNeill et al, 2009: 419) in social work and 'counter agency' (Prior 2009) among frontline workers. Researchers have also highlighted tensions that occur in the space between the design of a policy and its delivery. Bourdieu suggested that the social and welfare functions of the state constituted its *left hand*, with the more technocratic, fiscally minded functions forming its *right hand*. He argued that social workers and other 'base line judges' were 'agents of the state ... shot through with the contradictions of the state' (Bourdieu et al, 1999: 184), but that these contradictions open up 'a margin of manoeuvre, initiative and freedom' (1999: 191).

Work by Pearson has noted the 'industrial deviance' performed by social workers in carrying out their jobs and achieving the desired ends. In *The Deviant Imagination* (1975), he explored the 'ambiguous politics of social work' and refers to social workers as 'social policemen', 'social tranquilisers' and 'professional Robin Hoods', who take part in 'moral hustling'. These 'ambiguous politics' include the dual (and sometimes competing) commitments to individual clients and to wider society, and negotiating the balance between care and control. The expansion and dispersal of discipline and a culture of control (Garland, 2001) means that social workers, often employed or funded by the state, are expected to carry out some controlling functions of the state. These functions sometimes conflict with the original aims and the wider ethics and values of social work, and has led to social workers being called 'reluctant policemen' (Burney, 2005: 115) and 'agents of social control, disguised stormtroopers of the state' (Cohen, 1985: 130).

The exercise of discretion among social workers, family workers and other street-level bureaucrats in the UK in recent times has been the subject of numerous research studies. For example, Del Roy Fletcher (2011), in work carried out in Jobcentre Plus offices highlighted the 'inconsistent and discriminatory' responses to Jobseeker Mandatory Activity pilots where local responses largely depended on the resources and time available to local staff. Sarah Alden (2015) interviewed workers in statutory homelessness services in 12 local authorities where an increase in service users occurred at the same time that resources were falling as a result of austerity measures and reforms. She 'found evidence of unlawful discretion', which she 'attributed to a complex mesh of individual, intersubjective, organisational and central-led factors.' Research examining the 'multi-agency' partnership approaches to tackling anti-social behaviour of the Labour governments in the 1990s and 2000s highlighted the difference that demography, geography, and history can play in localised approaches to ASB (Burney, 2005), while others have highlighted tensions between different partner organisations as a result of competing priorities and institutional attitudes (Matthews and Briggs, 2008; Edwards and Hughes, 2008).

A number of research articles have explored the work carried out by FIP workers and their efforts to 'modify the intended outcomes of national policy' (Parr and Nixon, 2009: 101). These authors go on to note that 'rich case study data serves to illustrate the ways in which local actors reinterpret formal policy agendas in order to create alternative discourses which both challenge and, in turn, influence national strategies' (Parr and Nixon, 2009: 102). In discussing FIPs as 'sites of subversion and resilience', Parr and Nixon highlight that local FIP workers 'drew attention to the underlying causes of disruptive and damaging behaviour' (Parr and Nixon, 2009: 108), and 'developed an alternative conceptualisation of "the problem" of ASB', seeking to locate the issue of ASB in wider discourses of social exclusion. Central government, on the other hand, took the symbolic step of establishing a distinct Anti-Social Behaviour Unit (ASBU) in 2002, promoting the issue of ASB from its previous home as a policy strand in the Social Exclusion Unit. Parr and Nixon also discuss the local characteristics – the project manager's professional background or local governance arrangements, for example – that influenced local practice and service delivery. In a reverse of the usual direction of subversion and negotiation, the authors note that, as the local projects, with ostensibly 'supportive' approaches, became seen as increasingly important in efforts to tackle ASB, 'a process of bargaining occurred' and they were re-positioned by central government as part of a 'tough approach' (Parr and Nixon, 2009: 114) to 'problem families'. This included the discursive shift from being *Intensive Support* projects to *Intervention* projects.

Elsewhere, the same authors have set out how local FIP workers saw themselves as 'plugging a gap' in local service provision rather than 'gripping' local agencies (Parr and Nixon, 2008: 170) and that there was a 'varied and contested way in which local stakeholders constructed the role of FIPs together with the anti-social subject'. They conclude that:

> Paying attention to the localised development and operation of policies facilitates a more nuanced understanding of the manifestation of the FIP policy and reinforces the view that to properly debate anti-social behaviour policy, we need to look at the practices of those who implement policy, not just the policy text itself. (Parr and Nixon, 2008: 174)

The differences between FIP practice in Scotland and England and the process of policy transfer has also been discussed by researchers. They noted that 'in English FIPs families were routinely threatened with sanctions to secure their initial cooperation', with these 'overtly disciplining practices stand[ing] in stark contrast to the professional ethos evidenced in the Scottish projects' (Nixon et al, 2010: 318–19). FIPs have also been described as 'sites of social work practice' where the design of a local FIP had provided staff 'with an opportunity to engage in the kind of creative practice that proceduralization, bureaucracy and managerialism have made impossible to achieve in mainstream social work arenas' (Parr, 2009: 1257). Just as FIPs provided fertile ground for exploring the street-level negotiation of dominant discourses surrounding 'problem families', the TFP itself has also offered researchers an opportunity to examine how local practitioners have responded to a high-profile, and controversial, policy aimed at similar families.

Street-level perspectives in the Troubled Families Programme

The alleged success of the TFP has been attributed to the enthusiastic embrace the programme has received from local authorities and their workers. In the early stages of the programme, Eric Pickles lauded the 'fast and unanimous level of take-up' from local authorities, which he claimed showed 'that the Government has got the confidence of local councils'. Louise Casey has regularly thanked workers and when the 99% success of Phase 1 was announced, she said that 'councils and key workers deserve enormous credit' (DCLG, 2015a). The various evaluation publications associated with the TFP have often promoted the 'service transformation' that is taking place under the programme. Some local authorities have reciprocated, and have themselves claimed to be carrying out tremendous work.

In the North East, the elected Mayor of North Tyneside stated that they were 'honoured' to have Louise Casey present to a conference they had arranged and also believed that the 'new way of working intensively with targeted families is already making a real difference' (North Tyneside Council, 2014). Newcastle City Council (2015: 3) appeared similarly enthused, with the Cabinet Member for Children and Young People highlighting the 'success' of the programme in the city:

> This is a tremendous example of council staff working with other agencies to make a real difference to the lives of thousands of parents and children who were facing many difficult challenges. By focussing our efforts on providing support targeted at their needs, we have helped them to turn their lives around ... The Newcastle Families Programme is real success story, showing how cooperation across different agencies can deliver better results, despite the cuts.

In the South East, local authority 'strategic leaders' published a document that espoused the 'vision, tenacity and dedication of staff working on the programme [which] has been second to none' (SESL, 2013: 2). The document – *Implementing the Troubled Families Programme in the South East of England* – promoting the work that was taking place in the South East claimed that the region was 'home to examples of national best practice' and that the purpose of the report was 'to showcase some of our transformational work and tell a few success stories' (SESL, 2013: 6). In London, a similar document produced by the capital's local authorities suggested that they 'have offered a successful demonstration of how agencies can work with those with complex and multiple issues' and had shown 'how freeing up local authorities from the central control can spark local initiative, local innovation and results' (London Councils, 2014: 4). Local authorities from across England submitted case studies of 'troubled families' they had 'turned around' to DCLG, which proudly displayed them on its website (DCLG, 2014f). Ten local authorities or associated bodies submitted evidence to the Public Account Committee inquiry into Troubled Families, many of them highlighting the positive work they had carried out.

There is also support from some local authorities and individuals for the more robust aspects of the family intervention approach advocated by central government. Louise Casey and David Cameron, supported by government publications, and intermediaries such as media organisations and voluntary sector agencies, have advanced the idea of a distinctive, more muscular, family work approach associated with the TFP. For example, Birmingham City Council bemoaned the lack of official sanctions involved with the TFP in its first phase and its Director of Children's Services, Peter Duxbury, was quoted as saying 'We'd like to be able to say you'd lose social housing entitlement or some of your benefits [if you refused], but it would need legal change' (in Wiggins, 2012). Similarly, Bristol City Council (2014), in an internal newsletter, promoted the approach of one key worker who explained how he managed to 'get through the front door' of a woman with mental health issues:

'When mum was finding it hard to manage her mental health I would often have to leave a whole morning or afternoon to visit as it has sometimes taken over an hour of banging on the door to get in to the house. Persistence has got me in the door even on bad days.'

However, the idea of a new breed of 'persistent, assertive and challenging' workers bursting free from previous bureaucratic straitjackets begins to look problematic when a 'street-level lens' (Brodkin, 2011: i200) is used to examine this idea. The pronouncements of successful and innovative work discussed above do not necessarily tell the whole story. As was demonstrated by research carried out in FIPs, local interpretations of policies around problematic and anti-social families often differ markedly from the national rhetoric. There is, then, no distinctive family intervention approach, and the practice on the ground often reflects the varied backgrounds of the workers who implement the TFP.

There is now a growing body of evidence surrounding the implementation of the TFP in different local authority areas. Researchers have highlighted the differences between 'government discourses' and 'keyworker discourses' (Bond-Taylor, 2015), especially in how families were worked with. Others have noted how a desire to avoid the term 'troubled' in their local work led to a minority of staff in two local authorities not knowing they were working on the TFP even though they were identified as keyworkers on the programme (Hayden and Jenkins, 2014: 642). A research study examining the perspectives of young people who had been involved with the TFP suggested that, even where families had been officially 'turned around', 'there were strong indications of "trouble ahead"' (Wenham, 2017: 150) for the young people involved due to the withdrawal of support from the local authority while a number of significant issues remained unresolved. Another study in a Northern city highlighted that there was 'no shared, city-wide understanding of keyworking' (Ball et al, 2016: 270) and that descriptions of what keyworking involved 'were rarely consistent'.

The intention is not to attempt to repeat or explicate this body of work here (see also, for example, Hayden and Jenkins, 2013; Bunting et al, 2015; Crossley, 2016; Wills et al, 2016; Bond-Taylor, 2017; Nunn and Tepe-Belfrage, 2017). Rather, the intention for the remainder of this chapter is to focus on elements of local 'troubled families' practice that have to date received slightly less attention, such as the bureaucratic demands that are placed on workers and the continuing importance of existing universal and specialist local services. This approach, which shifts the focus from street-level bureaucracy and the exercise of discretion in work with families to the constraints faced by workers and the strategies needed to overcome barriers, is hopefully in keeping with the wider focus of this book.

Many frontline participants in Northton, Westingham and Southborough had been employed in similar roles prior to becoming family workers or family intervention practitioners. Their backgrounds included play work, youth work (often with young people who had offended, or were at risk of offending), education welfare, teaching, social work, early years and family work, and many practitioners had experience across a number of these roles. This was also the case with their supervisors or managers, many of whom had extensive experience across a range of social welfare services including youth work, youth offending, social work and educational welfare. Some managers believed that their previous work had 'led' them to the 'troubled families' agenda or that their previous professional interests had coalesced in their new role.

This feeling was widespread, despite the different reasons for entry into the field from different participants. For example, some participants in Northton and Westingham were family workers as a result of redeployment processes within the local authorities and

Sam, a Children's Services Manager (CSM) in Westingham, noted that the programme had helped to sustain jobs for some employees whose services were affected by cuts and job losses. Employees who faced possible redundancy as a result of cuts to their services were thus able to secure, to a greater or lesser extent, employment within new 'troubled families' teams or positions. Many of these new positions were precarious, dependent as they were on continued government funding for the TFP. Some participants also saw family work as a stepping stone to other positions and careers, often social work.

The workers, however, did not make any special claims to distinction or superiority over any of their colleagues in different services or organisations. They did not suggest that their approach or their skills or backgrounds were somehow different to colleagues working in other fields or with similar families on more specific issues. One manager believed that the skill set of her (family intervention) team was no different to that of other children's and family teams within Westingham. Some of the workers who took on the role of 'lead' or 'keyworker' with 'troubled families' remained in their substantive posts and also worked with families or individuals who did not meet the 'troubled families' criteria, with their work effectively spanning more than one policy field. While some workers acknowledged that aspects of their work had changed, others stated that, despite the grand claims that the TFP represented a new approach, much remained the same. Many participants in Northton and Westingham highlighted that the exhortation to 'think family' (Cornford et al, 2013) and 'whole family' models pre-dated the TFP by a number of years. In Westingham, one manager spoke of feeling 'a bit like a fraud' when discussing the way that the government presented the TFP as something novel.

Workers and local authorities were, however, afforded some discretion around how to implement and operationalise the TFP locally, as long as they met the targets set by government: how the TFP was implemented locally was therefore of secondary importance to ensuring the aims of the programme were achieved. In keeping with Parr's (2009) findings about social workers employed in FIPs, workers talked about enjoying greater freedom or flexibility in how they worked with families than they might have enjoyed previously, or in other areas of work. In Westingham, workers from different service areas, such as Connexions, were nominated as the 'keyworker' when a family required a single-service intervention, which undermines the rhetoric of workers working holistically with all family members. In Northton, where a family intervention style team had been expanded using funding related to the TFP, lead workers were still spread across

12 different service areas. Youth Offending Team (YOT) workers involved with the programme in Northton suggested that they saw little difference to what they were doing with cases identified as 'troubled families', and those that weren't. For example, 'Team Around the Family' (TAF) meetings operated for both, and one worker stated that she tended not to make a distinction in how she worked between the two. Where differences between current and previous practice were expressed, these were often couched in terms of changes to bureaucratic or statutory constraints and expectations with a more focused approach required, albeit not one that was necessarily more muscular or authoritarian.

Largely ignoring Eric Pickles' exhortation to be 'a little less understanding' (in Chorley, 2012) with 'troubled families', workers articulated far more sympathetic views towards the families they worked with. They were keen to discuss a number of ways in which their approach differed from the dominant rhetoric of a muscular, assertive form of intervention that 'grips' families. Workers who were supposed to 'not take no for an answer' spoke of small numbers of families that refused to engage for a variety of reasons and where they could not 'get a foot in the door'. These families were often already involved with other agencies such as children's social care services, and their engagement with that service was not voluntary. It was widely accepted that very troublesome and/or criminal families were not being worked with under the TFP because it was viewed as inappropriate to do so. Sarah, in Westingham, said 'we identified that some of our families were actually too dangerous to work with' and Claire, a worker in Northton, spoke of these 'notorious families' being 'parked with the idea of going back to them and having another look'. While these families represented a small minority of the families that could potentially be worked with, these were also the families that most closely matched the dominant national stereotype of 'troubled families'.

A respectful approach towards families was thus found in workers' practices. Just as workers were prepared to accept 'no' for an answer from families, workers spoke of gentler ways of working, which highlighted a 'governmentality' gap between the muscular interventions craved by Cameron and Casey and the practices of some family workers. Workers also discussed how they would send out letters to families before attempting to make an appointment or before calling at the family home. Where contact with the family had not been made prior to an initial home visit, workers described tentative approaches which included checking that it was an appropriate time to call and, if not, offering alternative dates and times for return visits.

'Erm, and you can't, you know, you can't impose it on people. So all you can do is try and say, well there's other, what about, I could help you with work, have you got issues about housing, you know, and try to explore stuff. Better in person than over the phone, erm, and I'll always, even if they still say no, because it is voluntary and you're not about kind of trying to harass people, erm, I'll still always send them a letter saying, you know, thank you for talking to me, here's a little bit more about what we do.' (Jacqui, Youth Worker, Northton)

Workers or managers from all three locations often presented their approaches more akin to 'hand-holding' or 'walking with families', rather than 'gripping' them, suggesting a subversion of the 'muscular authoritarianism' (Featherstone et al, 2014a: 2) preferred by the government:

'But the difference we make is, we can come in and support them through it and show, teach them how to do it, show them how to do it. Hold their hand while they do it and then they learn how to do it and they reduce that, erm, anxiety and they gain in confidence to be able to do it.' (Jess, CSM, Southborough)

'Like yes, walk beside them. Yes, hold their hand but don't make them dependent.' (Emma, CSM, Westingham)

Despite the rhetorical emphasis at a national level on embodied hands-on domestic work undertaken by family workers, this did not appear to be central to the everyday practice of many workers and workers can only be in one place, and with one family, at any one time. They therefore cannot be helping more than one of the families they work with domestic chores or routines on any given morning or evening. Again, given the diversity of family 'problems' that are covered by the 'troubled families' umbrella, it should not be surprising that the simplistic narrative of workers who need do little more than 'roll up their sleeves' and 'model' good parenting to effect dramatic change does not fare well under empirical examination. While managers in Northton highlighted how they had needed to draw up new guidelines to assist workers who were willing to carry out small repairs and home improvements with the families they worked with, there were different approaches from workers within the authority to helping out with domestic work:

> 'Generally the ones that will go in and start cleaning the floors are the older members of the team, who are family support workers originally. I mean they're now family intervention workers but they've come from a family support background. So they're, they used to be based in children's centres and then they've moved into, they're the ones that you tend to find will go and clean the house. Whereas, obviously, I'm from a social work background, I'm not about creating a dependency. I'm about empowering people to change their own lives and improve things for themselves.' (Pam, FW, Northton)

Across the different locations, there was also a mixed reception to the issue of domestic work. The need to observe or help with breakfast or bedtime routines was not a priority issue for many of the families that workers were working with, although some did state that it was required in some of the families. Most workers believed that although the ability to work 'intensively' with families was an important aspect of their work, this did not necessarily translate into intrusive practices at intimate times in daily routines. Instead, workers focused more on the extensive and time-consuming support that families often needed when navigating other services and agencies who were involved in their family life in different ways.

In a majority of interviews, workers highlighted the advocacy work and negotiations they undertook on behalf of families, often with colleagues in their local authority or with housing providers, health professionals and/or private sector companies such as utility companies and debt agencies. Workers did not suggest they 'gripped' or attempted to 'grip' other services, but they did highlight the administrative and stereotypically bureaucratic nature of much of the work of frontline family workers. Cameron (2011a) in his speech at the launch of the TFP argued that 'troubled families are already pulled and prodded and poked a dozen times a week by government' and the TFP was needed to establish 'a single point of focus on the family: a single port of call and a single face to know.' In reality, families remained engaged with numerous other agencies and the family workers spent a large amount of time drawing on existing relationships and developing new networks, discussing disparate issues with other service providers. This inevitably meant that much of the focus of their work was less on 'the family' and more on 'services to families'. Family workers, in effect, became an asset to the families – possessing the requisite knowledge, resources and networks to engage with the state more effectively than families often could themselves.

The focus of such multi-agency working often remained on the quick resolution of individual or family issues rather than longer-term changes in the relations between families and different organisations. Correspondingly, all three local authorities provided small budgets for workers to draw on in their work with families. Some workers valued this facility and used it to purchase household equipment and goods such as beds, duvets and washing machines for families, while others rejected it as a form of 'cheating' or as an illegitimate shortcut to achieving family change. There was, in some cases, resentment that money was available to 'throw at families' simply because they met the 'troubled' criteria, while there were also suggestions that it merely presented another way for families to 'play the system'. As well as addressing some of the material deprivation found within families, workers also used the funding to improve access to some services, either through commissioning packages of support for family members or supporting them with travel costs to access existing services that were otherwise out of their reach. At times support and advocacy was also inflected with coercion and conditionality:

> 'it's not about having a magic wand and throwing money at people. But, erm, money does help and it helps if, you know, they're in dire financial need and can't put food on the table and, you know, don't have something to sit on, don't have a mattress. You know, to be able to go, do you know what, I can probably help you with that, erm, it's a good engagement tool, erm, bribe, if you want to.' (Susan, Youth Worker, Northton)

> 'So I saw the money as a bit of a barrier. Some agencies saw it as a bit of an open door for families. So they'd go in and they'd say, oh yes, we'll spend thousands on you. And I'd be like, no we're not because we've got to do this first. Sometimes it's a bit of a bargaining tool.' (Daisy, FW, Southborough)

In some cases, workers highlighted how other state agencies often increased the pressure on families while others also expressed frustration that they were able to advocate successfully with partner agencies when families' attempts to negotiate or discuss issues had been unsuccessful:

'So they'll do, you know, they'll, and I will fight their corner, particularly, you know, it is difficult for parents, with regards to, some head teachers are very challenging. Erm, some housing officers are really, their mind is already made up before they've even walked in that door, erm, you know. A lot, the, the families themselves have a lot of prejudice to overcome in some of the services. And sometimes just having me next to them, asking those questions that they were probably thinking about asking but wouldn't dare because the head teacher would shoot them down or, you know. I'll kind of be their voice in some ways.' (Claire, FW, Northton)

Workers were also keen to highlight that they attempted to work with families in an empowering way, encouraging family members to take small steps with initial support from the worker, in order that they would be able to make similar or greater steps on their own at a later date. At times, however, the version of empowerment that was practised by workers appeared to be perilously close to the 'responsiblisation' agenda that national government rhetoric advocates (see also Bond-Taylor, 2015). Empowering work often coalesced with suggestions on how family members could address or resolve their own problems and therefore reduce future demand on state services:

'And I think that if we continue to work the way that we are at the moment ... we will empower those families to make those changes, so that they don't keep coming back to us, which will then allow us to work with the new families.' (Sally, CSM, Southborough)

'But it's quite obvious in what, in the way we support families, that we're looking to empower and motivate and, erm, like I use a lot of motivational interviewing strengths based approaches.' (Pam, FW, Northton)

Some workers also highlighted how the initial assessment phases of the family's needs were empowering as they encouraged families to prioritise the issues that were important to them. Arguing against this thin conceptualisation of empowerment, Bond–Taylor (2015: 378) suggests that family workers should 'reflect upon the extent to which family participation in the process merely legitimates existing power relations under a veneer of empowerment discourses'. Attempts to reconcile these tensions led to a form of dissonance experienced by workers involved with the programme. An exemplar of this can be found in Vicky's articulation of how she develops plans with families she works with in Southborough, where inconsistencies and tensions can be found at almost every stage:

'What we try and do, hopefully, everybody, but what I try and do is empower people ... We discuss it and I use my, erm, techniques to really get them to see what the benefits are of change. And we're looking for what they feel is a problem, rather than what we feel is a problem. Every family is different and just because you think that should be done that way, it doesn't necessarily mean it's so. However, you know, child protection is always paramount, so we would always look at that.

'So it's about looking at needs, looking at healthy behaviours and attitudes. And also, what we're mainly looking at, we've got criteria, obviously, that we have to cover, which is, you're probably aware of it, the worklessness, mental health, erm, you know, domestic violence, those type of things we're looking at. Erm, attendance for children at school, which is a biggy. Erm, you know, so we bring all of that in. And what we would then do, once we've built the rapport, is we'd look to, erm, develop, erm, a plan of action. And that would be very much owned by the family. So, and we set it up together, we discuss it, we make sure it covers our remit, anything else that the family needs on there, we're quite versatile with that. Erm, and they would take ownership of the action plan but we would support them through that.

'Erm, yes and that's the main thing. So we'd be looking at when we can do it, how we can do it, that type of thing. With regards to the children, we would be setting up meetings, to make sure everybody's involved. So it would be pulling in all of the professionals that we feel could be a benefit to that family. And I do think that's one of our main roles. We're not an expert in everything, you know, but it's about sitting down with a family. They trust you, and then you say, OK, we're going to pull in these different professionals, from DWP, from, erm, debt charities, from housing, we pull them all in and we say, come on, we've got to look for a solution here. And that's what's really good about the job as well, that we are seen to do that role.'

Bond-Taylor's concept of a 'veneer of empowerment' is helpful in highlighting the absence of thicker, more critical constructions of empowerment in discussions with family workers. There was no mention of empowering families to challenge structural or systemic issues in the interviews with participants. The absence of 'the social' in the wider 'troubled families' rhetoric, and the primacy afforded to 'the family', is once again significant here. The 'troubled families' discourse encourages narrow procedures, focused on individual families, and workers' ability to smooth the passage to pre-determined short-term outcomes through 'established channels' of service delivery (London Edinburgh Weekend Return Group, 1980: 23–5). The gaze of the worker (and by extension the state), in terms of problems and solutions, remains firmly fixed on the family. Critical, reflexive practice is often all but impossible in such situations.

Many participants, while reluctant to explicitly blame families for their circumstances, did echo the 'inter-generational' rhetoric associated with 'troubled families' at a national level. Even when prompted during interviews for their views on what lay behind individual issues such as truanting, unemployment, substance misuse or mental health problems, parental or generational influence was almost always offered as an explanation, rather than any societal or structural factors:

> 'Well everything and anything. Non-school attendance, domestic violence, horrendous domestic violence, err, that's massive. Mental health, huge. Erm, unemployment, erm, housing issues, err, drug and alcohol. I mean drug and alcohol are in here, it's a huge, huge issue. Erm, social isolated, learning difficulties, learning disabilities, erm, bullying, absolutely everything. The whole thing's linked, the whole thing. The toxic triangle thing, you know, everything's linked, everything's, yes, generations.' (Becky, FW, Westingham)

> 'What I'm trying to say is, erm, there's a culture where some families, grandparents have never had employment.' (Lisa, FW, Westingham)

A small minority of workers did, however, break through the focus on families and acknowledge the *grande misère* (Bourdieu et al, 1999: 4) experienced by many 'troubled families' and sought to re-insert structural issues such as poverty, deprivation and poor quality housing into discussions about the troubles experienced or caused by families. At the same time, they recognised that the TFP left little room to discuss such issues (see also Hayden and Jenkins, 2014: 642; Crossley, 2016: 138–9):

> 'A lot of them are trapped in a cycle of poverty. And I know politically, we're not supposed to discuss things like that. But it's poverty underlying everything, it really is.' (Susan, Youth Worker, Northton)

> 'Housing, there isn't housing, Southborough is very, very poor, in terms of what there is available locally. There aren't council houses and the ones that there are have all been sold off. And flats and bedsits, they're horrendous, landlords are awful, rents are high.' (Maggie, FW, Southborough)

Workers also spoke of a far higher number of families where positive outcomes were not achieved despite their best efforts and where cases were closed for negative reasons. In some families, despite the involvement and support of a family worker, family life did not improve or the situation worsened, with referrals to child protection teams a common reason given for family workers stepping back from working with families:

> 'I would say, well speaking of my caseload, I would say probably a third end successfully, that's being optimistic ... because, erm, more often than not they step up or, erm, or they disengage or, you know, I've got a couple that I'm still working with that I started working with when, when I started the job, the one that I've been with for eighteen months, for example.' (Daisy, FW, Southborough)

> 'Well I've just finished working with a family who I've worked with for a year. And the mum has developed a dependency on myself as a support worker ... In this particular case, I think this mum will come round again to us, I do, erm. So, err, but she's with social care at the moment. I referred her to social care. I've always kept her

up to speed. She knows the reasons why she's there. She knows the level of support they're going to give her.' (Lisa, FW, Westingham)

The intense focus on 'the family' in the 'troubled families' rhetoric leaves little scope for discussion of the mundane, everyday bureaucratic negotiations that family workers are compelled to carry out in order to support the families they are working with. The TFP was supposed to be a programme that represented a slimmed-down altogether more efficient way of working with troublesome families. The family intervention approach has been portrayed as an antidote to modern social work practice which Casey has characterised as involving workers holding clipboards, 'circling families' and 'assessing the hell out of them'. The programme is apparently driving 'service transformation' in local government. And yet, in addition to the everyday discussions and work with colleagues in other departments and services, workers highlighted the amount of additional bureaucracy, record keeping and paperwork that was required for the TFP.

While the extent to which other services engaged with the local 'troubled families' work varied both within and between the different fieldwork sites, there was strong consistency in the amount of new, local multi-agency working arrangements and bureaucratic processes that had been established to support the implementation of the TFP. Northton established two new multi-agency groups to oversee its local work: a steering group that originally met fortnightly and then moved to monthly meetings oversaw the day-to-day work of the programme; and a business group, comprising of more senior individuals from the same agencies represented on the steering group, which took a more strategic, long-term view of the programme. Westingham and Southborough both developed neighbourhood or area-based models for their local 'troubled families' work, which again involved multi-agency meetings to discuss different aspects of the work.

In Westingham this involved a variety of different services agencies making referrals of families who potentially met 'troubled families' criteria to a central point, with this referral then being checked and passed to the relevant neighbourhood co-ordinator who disseminated the family details and referral notes to different services and organisations, who were tasked with collating any information they held on the family. Five different multi-agency neighbourhood forum meetings took place each week to discuss up to around 20 referrals in each area. One such meeting that I attended saw 13 attendees from different services and organisations discuss 18 different families, with the person chairing the meeting reading the notes on the referral form out to the meeting for every family being discussed. Other services then gave their views on what should happen, which agency should take the lead, and which intervention should be 'offered'. In one case, the forum simply referred a family back to the agency that had referred them. When discussing another family, a social worker asked 'Anyone got any ideas?' after relating her previous contacts with the family. The meeting lasted two and a half hours and did not feel entirely symbolic of a new, pared-back, almost perfect system for 'turning around' the lives of the most disadvantaged families in the country.

In many cases, family workers felt that the recording and monitoring requirements of the TFP often undermined their ability to work constructively with families. When asked about frustrations with their job, numerous workers highlighted paperwork and recording as the issues that stood out, with data collecting requirements increasing in the second phase of the programme. Workers spoke of keeping a 'chronology' of every contact with the family and every action carried out on their behalf or related to their case. Summaries of events at home visits and discussions during telephone calls with both family members and other services were recorded on computer databases so that the state's involvement with 'troubled families' could be tracked. As well as this local administrative burden, workers, managers and analysts also highlighted the amount of information they were required to extract from the family to meet the needs of the national programme. Family Monitoring Data, required for the national evaluation of the TFP, amounted to 55 different pieces of information (where applicable) on each family member and this information was typically recorded at three stages of work with a family: on entry to the TFP, when a PbR claim was made, and when the family case was closed by the local authority. In addition to this information (which was changed to Family Progress Data under the second phase of the TFP), local authorities also collected data for their own local evaluations and for other purposes. Northton, at the start of Phase 2 of the TFP, collected 95 different pieces of information on families, for six different monitoring or reporting purposes.

The issue of informed consent and the sharing of data concerned a number of workers and managers, and confutes the notion that a key factor in the TFP is the shared 'trust' that exists between families and workers. In the early stages of the programme data was 'trawled' or 'washed' to produce a list of allegedly 'troubled families' who were often then discussed at multi-agency meetings. Participants highlighted how this process often led to families with very minor or historical 'troubles' being discussed as possible 'beneficiaries' of the TFP without their knowledge, including one family in Westingham where a child had once stolen a chocolate bar. Similarly, under Phase 2 of the programme, participants expressed unease at the amount of data that was required by central government and family's knowledge of and consent to that data being sent:

> 'And I really struggled with that initially, the families that were being discussed at the meetings, were being discussed via a data trawl of the Government's criteria.' (Emma, CSM, Westingham)

> 'So I went back to legal and said that this question was on and we do not have explicit consent from these families, to share this information with National Troubled Families Team. What we do have is consent from the families to share information in relation to putting in place a package of support.' (Janet, CSM, Northton)

Conclusion

Interviews from a range of research studies with workers and managers in local authorities involved in the delivery of the TFP highlight 'the complexity of interactions concealed beneath the apparent monotony of bureaucratic routine' (Bourdieu, 2005: 140). While it would be unhelpful and similarly simplistic to talk of a divide between national policy rhetoric and local practice, there were substantial differences – a 'governmentality gap' (McNeill et al, 2009) – between the approach promoted by central government and that which was carried out by workers employed by local authorities and their partners.

Where government rhetoric has promoted the idea of an ahistorical, highly individualised family worker, workers involved in the programme in Northton, Westingham and Southborough highlighted long backgrounds in either similar work or in similar institutions and explained the extent to which they relied on colleagues in their teams and in other services to help them with their work. In place of the 'can do' attitude and 'hands-on' work carried out in family homes afforded primacy by the likes of Cameron and Casey, a more stereotypical bureaucratic approach was articulated by workers, which involved navigating rules and procedures and negotiating with fellow street-level bureaucrats. Where differences were articulated, they were framed in terms of greater freedom and flexibility offered by the programme, rather than any distinctive dispositions or capabilities possessed by family workers, or acquired by them upon entry to their role.

However, these subversions were all relatively minor alterations to policy that did little to trouble the national portrayal of the TFP (Crossley, 2016). They did not, as DuBois (2014: 39) has observed, 'contradict the rationales of official policy' and effectively ended up serving its goals. They were thus all examples of 'safe oppositions', occurring within the 'black box' of policy implementation, which enabled workers to exhibit autonomy and discretion within the boundaries allowed by the TFP. In Bourdieusian terms, these practices can be viewed as 'legitimated transgressions' (Bourdieu, 2005: 132) or:

> *partial revolutions* which constantly occur in fields [and] do not call into question the very foundations of the game, its fundamental axioms, the bedrock of ultimate beliefs on which the whole game is based. (Bourdieu, 1993: 74, original emphasis)

Family workers that participated in the research discussed above believed in the value of their work and have not doubted the idea that family work of some description was necessary for the families that they were working with. They attempted to play the 'troubled families' game in the best way they could, given the environment in which they were operating. They lived with the ambiguity of their work and often resisted the politically charged elements of the TFP, such as the idea that they were 'turning around' the lives of the families they worked with. What was at stake, for them, then, was not the idea of family intervention or family work with marginalised or 'troubled families' per se, but the form that that work took.

There is no room, however, for such nuance or complexity in the 'troubled families' story told by the government. As such, the daily work with families, in whatever form it takes, unfortunately only serves to strengthen the popular view that it is only by intensive and direct work with families that their lives can be 'turned around'. The daily routines of family workers and colleagues in other service areas thus help to produce and reproduce 'the reality' of 'troubled families'. They are, unfortunately, part of the work of the production and reproduction of 'troubled families' that the state is engaged with. Their resistance to elements of the programme and their rejection of some of the more stigmatising aspects of it have not 'troubled' the bigger picture surrounding the TFP. The more successful workers are in subverting or resisting problematic elements of the programme, the more the government is able to claim that its 'persistent, assertive and challenging' approach is working.

EIGHT

Research: 'help or hindrance'?

> The idea of a group of feckless, feral poor people whose pathological culture and/or genes transmitted their poverty to their children, can be traced from the Victorian 'residuum' through theories of pauperism, social problem groups and multiple problem families to the underclass arguments of today. ... The problem of poverty was blamed on 'bad' genes before the Second World War and on 'bad' culture after the discrediting of the eugenics movement by the end of the War. These ideas are unsupported by any substantial body of evidence. Despite almost 150 years of scientific investigation, often by extremely partisan investigators, not a single study has ever found any large group of people/ households with any behaviours that could be ascribed to a culture or genetics of poverty. This failure does not result from lack of research or lack of resources. (Gordon, 2011)

Introduction

Researchers have played a prominent part in the history of debates and discussions about a supposed 'underclass' and John Macnicol (1987: 316), a social policy academic who has done much to chart the history of the 'underclass' thesis, has noted that a 'recurring feature' of these debates is the need for more research to be carried out. It was Charles Booth, an early social researcher, who was one of the most influential individuals involved in the 'discovery' of the residuum' in Victorian times and it was US academics from different disciplinary backgrounds whose work was influential in propagating the concepts of a 'culture of poverty' and an 'underclass'. Keith Joseph, the Secretary of State for Social Services who advanced the idea of 'transmitted deprivation', argued that the phenomenon required further examination, and established a large research study spanning eight years.

This chapter examines some of this research involvement in previous iterations of the underclass before turning to the relationship between the concept of 'troubled families' and research. The misrepresentation of the research behind the original figure of 120,000 'troubled families' is explored in detail, before the attention turns to other uses and misuses of research in the 'troubled families' agenda. Louise Casey's engagement with research is highlighted, including her own writing for academic journals, her *Listening to Troubled Families* report and critiques of it, and the case of a survey that she used in conference speeches to make the case for 'radical reform' that turned out not to exist. The focus then turns to the government's use of case studies as 'evidence' of the need for, and success of, the TFP, and the way that data from the official evaluation has been interpreted and presented by the government. This discussion involves a detailed analysis of criticisms that were aimed at some of the researchers involved in the evaluation during the Public Accounts Committee inquiry into 'troubled families'. The chapter concludes with a discussion of how the government's approach can be linked to other developments in similar social policy fields, and how critical research about the TFP can provide alternative perspectives on it.

Researchers and the 'underclass'

The involvement of researchers and academics with ideas about an 'underclass' and concepts similar to 'troubled families', on both sides of the argument, can be traced back as far as the ideas themselves. Charles Booth, who is perhaps better known for his investigations into poverty in London in the late 1800s and the colour-coded maps that he produced than his interest in a 'social residuum', wrote about a class of 'so-called labourers, loafers, semi-criminals, a proportion of the street-sellers, street performers and others', including criminals who worked and homeless people (in Welshman, 2013: 27). Welshman argues that traces of an interest in the 'residuum' can be found throughout Booth's writings.

Another historian, Ross McKibbin, has argued that some of the earliest female social researchers in England were articulating a theory similar to the 'culture of poverty' argument made by Oscar Lewis, but predating his work by around half a century. He believes that 'give or take a tape recorder' (McKibbin, 2002: 190) the techniques that Lewis employed in talking to families in Mexico in the 1950s were almost identical to those used by Helen Bosanquet and Margaret Loane in the UK at the turn of the 20th century. McKibbin also discusses the work of a third woman, Lady Florence Bell, and states that, together, '[t]hey were all three probably the most accomplished Edwardian practitioners of a cultural sociology' (McKibbin, 2002: 167) who were particularly interested in issues of poverty and social class. Although their work in

England was overshadowed by the survey-based work of influential male investigators of the same period, and was not necessarily well-received, McKibbin claims that the culmination of their work came in Lewis' theory some 50 years later.

Seebohm Rowntree, who undertook similar investigations to Booth in York at the turn of the 20th century, has been credited with advancing structural explanations of poverty and disadvantage. Even when highlighting the number of people who experienced 'secondary poverty', by which he meant deprivation occurring because of a sufficient income being spent on other things, either usefully or wastefully, Rowntree (in Welshman, 2013: 46) identified structural factors that might cause poverty in these circumstances:

> Housed for the most part in sordid streets, frequently under overcrowded and unhealthy conditions, compelled very often to earn their bread by monotonous and laborious work, and unable, partly through limited education and partly through overtime and other causes of physical exhaustion, to enjoy intellectual recreation, what wonder that many of these people fall prey to the publican and the bookmaker?

Researchers involved with the Eugenics Society attempted to prove the existence of a social problem group in the 1930s, without success, and with criticisms aimed at a number of their investigations and the publications they generated. The quality of evidence supporting the debate about the 'problem families' of the 1940s and 1950s has also been critiqued with Richard Titmuss, as discussed in Chapter Two, arguing that whatever knowledge had been gained from numerous inquiries and investigations was 'not accumulated on any theoretical foundations'.

The idea of a 'culture of poverty' emerged out of social scientific writing on poor people at a time of widespread social changes in the USA during the post-war years. Focusing primarily on black communities and migrant groups, a number of scholars in the 1950s and 1960s advanced 'culture' as an important aspect of poverty and poor communities that required further investigation. In 1952, 'slum culture' was used to examine differences in educational attainment (Davis, 1952) and, a short while later, 'lower-class culture' was proposed as an explanation for 'gang delinquency' (Miller, 1958). Oscar Lewis, a social anthropologist, first advanced his idea of a 'culture of poverty' in 1959 following fieldwork in Mexico and developed this concept further in a number of different publications (Lewis, 1959, 1961, 1965). A number of strong critiques and counter-arguments were aimed at Lewis's theory (see, for example, Roach and Gursslin, 1967: Valentine, 1968; Gans, 1970; Leacock, 1971; Ryan, 1971) with many arguing that his research was weak and his theory deflected attention away from structural issues affecting poor communities and instead assisted a focus on alleged behavioural shortcomings and failings among the poor themselves. Lewis' biographer, Susan Rigdon, was particularly critical, arguing that:

> in reading Lewis on the culture of poverty, one sees not the results of a reasonably systematic analysis of his data but a mosaic of shards culled from the literature of anthropology, psychology, psychiatry, sociology and economic history, as well as from novels about the poor. (Rigdon, 1988: 171)

Sir Keith Joseph, in advancing his theory of a 'cycle of deprivation' called for more research to be carried out to understand the process by which deprivation was 'transmitted' between generations. While he acknowledged that his theory was not supported by robust empirical evidence, he also pointed towards several studies, of varying quality, that he argued supported his views (see Welshman, 2012a). The response from academics involved with the large scale Social Science Research Council (SSRC) that Joseph established was robust, with many of them producing research and reports that ultimately questioned the idea of a 'cycle of deprivation', and which instead highlighted the social structures and institutions that served to keep many families in the same conditions over prolonged periods of time.

There was a strong response to ideas about an 'underclass' and the way in which the term was used in the USA in the 1980s and 1990s (see, for example, Sherraden, 1984; Katz, 1989; Gans, 1995) and a similarly strong response awaited Charles Murray, a key proponent of the concept when he visited the UK, as discussed in Chapter Two. Although Tony Blair used the term 'underclass' in his years as prime minister, it was the concepts of social exclusion and anti-social behaviour that were conflated in the Labour government's latter focus on 'problem families' which led to the family intervention model being rolled out across England. As discussed in Chapter Six, the evidence supporting family intervention is not as compelling as has often been made out. The most robust interrogation of some of the early findings of the FIP evaluations was provided by David Gregg, who argued that they were a 'classic case of policy-based evidence' whereby research findings were (mis)represented to support particular policy agendas. He noted:

> the discontinuities between the headline government claims for FIP success, the strong caveats and reservations of the three FIP evaluation teams over a decade and the marked weaknesses in evaluation methodology and database quality. (Gregg, 2010: 15)

Gregg also highlighted that three different evaluation teams had called for better and longer methods of data collection in relation to the family intervention approach, but these were largely ignored by government. Instead, and as we see in the next section, the government argued that no more research was necessary when it came to solving the 'problem' of 'troubled families'.

'Joining the dots': research and 'troubled families'

In 2007, the Social Exclusion Task Force (SETF) published a report on *Families at Risk*, which drew on a range of data and evidence to highlight different disadvantages such as income inequality, poverty and health. The report argued that progress against poverty was such that 'the government is now in a position to focus its attention on the complex needs of a small minority of families who face multiple and entrenched problems' (SETF, 2007a: 4). Presenting new analysis of the Families and Children Survey (FACS) conducted in 2004 with around 7,000 families, the report suggested that there were approximately 140,000 families experiencing 'multiple disadvantages', or those that experienced any five or more out of seven disadvantages. As noted in Chapter Two, those seven disadvantages were:

- no parent in the family is in work;
- family lives in poor quality or overcrowded housing;
- no parent has any qualifications;
- mother has mental health problems;
- at least one parent has a long-standing limiting illness, disability or infirmity;
- family has low income (below 60% of the median);
- family cannot afford a number of food and clothing items.

This was the research presented by the government as evidence of 120,000 'troubled families' in England, linked to crime, anti-social behaviour, truancy and school exclusion, and an adult in the home being in receipt of out of work benefits. In his 'fightback speech' following the 2011 riots, David Cameron (2011a) reasserted his ambition to 'turn around the lives of the 120,000 most troubled families in the country'. Cameron argued that it was only necessary to 'join the dots' to realise that it was these families, and the lack of parenting authority within them, that had been a major factor in the riots. Four days later, Matt Barnes (2011), a researcher at the National Centre for Social Research (NatCen), and one of the authors of the SETF report, provided a short response to such claims:

> Are these the families that house the kind of young people involved in last week's riots? Unfortunately, we don't have data to test such a hypothesis. However, we do know from this research that children aged 11–15 who grow up in multiply-disadvantaged families are more likely to have multiple problems themselves – and by problems I mean things like not doing well in core subjects at school, being suspended or even excluded from school, and running away from home. However, it's important to point out that not all children in multiply-disadvantaged families have these problems. For example, 10% of 11–15 years olds from these families had been in trouble with the police – so 90% had not (this compares to 1% of 11–15 year olds who had been in trouble with the police from families with none of the aforementioned disadvantages).

Ruth Levitas was the most incisive critic of the misrepresentation of the SETF research and the conflation of poor families with poorly behaved families. She noted that because the 120,000 figure was taken from a survey carried out with a very small number of families 'anyone with any statistical sophistication will recognise it as spuriously accurate' (Levitas, 2012a: 5). She argued that if a sampling error of around plus or minus 3 per cent was taken into account, the actual figure of such families could be minus 60,000 (which she accepted was nonsense) or as high as 300,000. Levitas then turned to the label 'troubled families', which she argued 'discursively collapses "families with troubles" and "troublesome families"', while simultaneously implying that they are dysfunctional as families – a 'discursive strategy [that] is successful in feeding vindictive attitudes to the poor' (Levitas, 2012a: 8). She suggested that the original research was not the problem, but the representation of it by the government was problematic and misleading:

> ... if we interrogate the research behind the imputed existence of 120,000 troubled families, this turns out to be a factoid – something that takes the form of a fact, but is not. It is used to support policies that in no way follow from the research on which the figure is based. The problem is not the research itself, but its misuse. (Levitas, 2012a: 4)

Levitas also pointed out that the data was around seven years out of date and its use implied that the numbers of families experiencing multiple disadvantages had not changed over time. Another report that was published shortly after Levitas' critique drew on the same FACS data to highlight that the number of families experiencing multiple disadvantages had, in fact, fluctuated over time (Reed, 2012). In addition, and as a result of tax and benefit changes introduced by the coalition government, the report suggested that the number of such families was predicted to increase in the future.

The report, *In the Eye of the Storm*, published by three children's charities, highlighted that, between 2003 and 2008 (when the FACS ran) 'the number of families vulnerable under five or more measures reached a peak at around 160,000 in 2004 and then fell to just over 130,000 in 2008'. The report also noted that the threshold of meeting five or more criteria to be classed as experiencing multiple disadvantages or labelled as 'at risk' was an entirely arbitrary one. For example, the number of families experiencing four or more disadvantages was around 500,000 in 2004 and the number of families experiencing three or more disadvantages was over 1,000,000 (Reed, 2012: 23).

The government's response to such criticisms was, and has remained, dismissive. In an interview with the *Guardian* (Gentleman, 2013), Louise Casey sought to minimise the issue, suggesting that it was a trivial matter that was largely irrelevant:

> I think a lot is made of this, in retrospect, which needn't be. The most important thing when I got here in 2011 was if we take that 120,000 figure, give it to local authorities, give them the criteria behind troubled families, and they can populate it, which they have done, with real names, real addresses, real people – then I am getting on with the job.
>
> I could have said, let's get a university to spend the next three years studying, who is criminal, not in work, with kids not in school. I tell you what they will show – probably that a lot come from disadvantaged backgrounds.

In 2016, when DCLG published an overview of the first phase of the TFP, the government attempted to defend the use of the 120,000 figure and argued that 'those who have sustained a critical focus on the derivation of the 120,000 figure … risk missing the wider and more important point' (DCLG, 2016a: 12). This wider and more important point, according to the government, was that the figure 'served as a realistic estimate', based on 'the best estimate available at the time', acting as 'a launch-pad' for the programme. In maintaining this stance, the government continues, in official documents, to claim that it is legitimate to use an estimation of the number of severely disadvantaged families to develop a policy targeting criminal and anti-social families.

Casey herself has an ambivalent relationship with research. In her infamous after-dinner speech in 2005 she was reported to have rhetorically asked 'Topic for the evening. Research: help or hindrance?' before answering 'Hindrance, thanks very much' and one of the most widely publicised comments of the evening was 'there is an obsession with evidence-based policy … If No 10 says bloody "evidence-based policy" to me once more I'll deck them one and probably get unemployed' (*Guardian*, 2005). At other times, however, she has drawn on research evidence to support her argument, arguing for example, that there was confidence surrounding the family intervention approach because 'we know it works because we've already looked at studies that show that this works, basically, and also I've met countless families that have been turned around' (BBC, 2013).

Casey has dabbled in research and analysis herself and has attempted to fill gaps that she identifies in the academic literature. In 2008, Casey wrote a report called *Engaging Communities in Fighting Crime*, which she argued was:

> an analysis of what I have found by looking at the evidence, talking to the powers that be, the frontline workers and above all, the public. It's a common-sense view on what further changes need to be made to build confidence and trust, and some suggestions on how those changes should happen (Casey, 2008: 3).

A lengthy list of organisations were quoted in an appendix to the report setting out the data collection approaches. Richard Garside (2012), the Director of the Centre for Crime and Justice Studies, remarked of his meeting with Casey that 'She sat politely. Smiled at the appropriate moments. Paid no attention to anything I said and wrote a report short on evidence and long on ideology and gut prejudice'.

In 2012, DCLG published Casey's report *Listening to Troubled Families*, which highlighted the problems faced and caused by 16 families that Casey had interviewed. Again, academics were concerned enough to highlight flaws in the report, with one calling it a 'shoddy exercise', full of 'spurious generalisations and dubious conclusions' that amounted to an 'almost worthless piece of research' (Talbot, 2012). Casey was quick to dismiss such criticism and suggested that the reason she had written the report was because it had not been done before, telling a journalist 'I've looked very hard to find a similar research report that has actually spent that amount of time directly with families and written it up in the way that we did. I felt it was worth doing, otherwise I wouldn't have bothered doing it' (Hollander, 2012).

It was established, following Freedom of Information (FOI) requests by Nick Bailey, a University of Glasgow social policy academic, that no ethical approval procedure had preceded Casey's interviews with the families. Bailey suggested that it was unclear how the families that were involved had been recruited, how they gave their consent, and to what extent that consent was free and informed. DCLG responded that no ethical procedures were necessary because the report was not considered 'as being within the definition of Government social research' and instead 'falls more properly within the description "dipstick/informal information gathering"' (Bailey, 2012). Bailey pointed out that, for a 'dipstick/informal information gathering' exercise, the report had received significant promotion by DCLG, which resulted in extensive press coverage, and that, regardless of its status in the eyes of the government, certain, basic ethical standards had not been met:

> No matter what label the government wishes to give it, the report clearly involved research activities carried out on human subjects. If these activities do not require ethical approval, there is something seriously wrong with the government's guidelines. The guidelines exist to protect the public, in particular more vulnerable individuals, from harm or exploitation by those with power. It should not be possible for the powerful to simply by-pass such safeguards.

The government response was to highlight that it was 'focussed on the task of turning around the lives of 120,000 troubled families by 2015 ... not engaging in academic debate' (Ramesh, 2012b). Casey also had an answer, albeit one that appeared to contradict her view that she had been unable to find a 'similar research report'. In giving evidence to the Communities and Local Government Committee in Westminster, Casey said:

> I put my hands up: I interviewed 16. I never pretended that that was research with a capital "R". I said it was policy, and I am very clear about that. We have an academic institution; we have got the evaluation; we have let it. We will be doing that in all of those ways. (Communities and Local Government Committee, 2013: 5)

While being clear, at times, that *Listening to Troubled Families* was 'policy' and not research, Casey has separately drawn on the results of a survey carried out in the North East of England to make the case for 'radical reform'. During two separate speeches (Casey, 2013a, 2013b) she made at high profile conferences (for local authority chief executives and Directors of Children's Services), Casey offered up her own evidence as to why the TFP was needed:

> Forgive me if you've heard this example before but I think it encapsulates the problem in one story. One survey looked at 3,000 children in one area of the north east – an area that has been through every deprivation programme going, from city challenge, single regeneration budgets, through to new deal for communities and neighbourhood renewal – and more recently had the pupil premium spent on them. A survey showed that not one of those 3,000 children had been for a routine dental check-up – for free – but 300 of them had been to A&E for emergency dental treatment. It is time for radical reform. (Casey, 2013b)

In suggesting that her audience was probably aware of the statistic, Casey implied that it was well-known, and had stood the test of time. In highlighting the use of a 'survey', she suggested that the statistic was obtained via a detailed investigation and a systematic and methodical gathering of information. The survey findings thus appeared to be robust and reliable. The one obvious flaw in the survey that Casey refers to, however, is that it does not exist.

An FOI request to the DCLG asking for the name of the survey and any information relating to it, brought the response that 'following an extensive search' of the department's paper and electronic records, it was established that this information was not held by the DCLG. The 'information' had apparently been shared during a meeting held in the department. A subsequent FOI request for all relevant information pertaining to the 'survey' established that the figure was shared by a local authority in the north east at a meeting in October 2013. Correspondence from the local authority involved to the DCLG showed that their recollection of the 'discussion' that took place that day is that the pre-cursor to the figure was the phrase 'anecdotal information' (Crossley, 2013b). In effect, the source of the figure denied that it came from a survey and was, from their memory (as opposed to any written records or minutes), an anecdote. Not content with bypassing ethical obligations while collecting her own data, it appears that Casey, and indeed any member of her team, was unable or unwilling to carry out even a cursory check on a statistic they once heard in a meeting, that was subsequently held up as 'encapsulating the problem [of troubled families] in one story'. Once again, the case for working with 'troubled families' was built on what was, at best, a factoid.

Casey has also written two articles for academic journals. Displaying a remarkable lack of awareness of the long-running disputes surrounding the idea of an 'underclass', Casey (2013c: 459) suggested that idea of 'troubled families' was 'familiar to frontline workers, policy makers and academics alike'. She took aim at critics of the programme again, this time suggesting that concerns about the stigmatising nature of the label 'troubled families' was 'naïve' and that 'a debate about that the programme is called rather than whether it works seems to miss the point' (2013c: 460). In a second article published in 2014, Casey drew on information collected from families that had been worked with under the TFP. Neglecting to mention that no information on income levels or material deprivation had been collected, Casey (2014b: 58–9) stated that 'the data reveal multiple problems but, interestingly, there is no single stand-out issue that might be described as the underlying problem or root cause'. Casey did not mention the concerns relating to the misrepresentation of the SETF research at the outset of the programme in either of these journal articles.

Misunderstanding 'troubled families'

The original aim of the TFP to 'turn around' 120,000 families was expanded into a second phase to cover 400,000 extra families. Initially, these families were called 'high-risk families' but when the detail of the expansion was announced, they became known as just more 'troubled families', despite experiencing potentially very different problems from those identified under the first phase of the programme. When the detail of the expansion was announced, it was accompanied by a DCLG publication, *Understanding Troubled Families* (DCLG, 2014b), and an interim report from the independent evaluation of the programme.

A document setting out the methodology for identifying the extra 400,000 'troubled families' was subsequently published in December 2014 (DCLG, 2014g). The *Understanding Troubled Families* report, according to Louise Casey, 'paints a picture of families sinking under the weight of multiple problems', which can then 'spiral out of control' if they remain unchecked. The report claimed that, on average, nine serious problems exist in any one family at any one time and Casey reported that she did not expect the problems faced by families in the first phase to be as bad as they were (in Hellen, 2014) and that these were the 'worst families' in Britain. The front page of *The Sunday Times* claimed that the expansion of the programme was evidence of a 'new underclass' in the UK and that 'One chief constable told Casey: "I could park a police officer on the settees of some of your families 24 hours a day, they are that demanding of our services."'

The data from the official evaluation that accompanied the *Understanding Troubled Families* report has a number of very obvious weaknesses, including no standardised sampling procedure, an over-reliance on practitioner views and large amounts of missing data on families. However, of greater concern than the quality of the data is the interpretation and representation of that data by the government in making the case for a new phase of the programme to target 400,000 newly discovered 'troubled families'. The *Understanding Troubled Families* report paints a particularly negative picture of these families when, if a different, perhaps less judgemental approach was adopted, a very different picture can begin to emerge. In contrast to the workless 'neighbours from hell' and the 'worst families' who are 'off the barometer' in terms of the problems they have, we can find, for example, the following from the data on 'troubled families' in the interim national evaluation report:

- 84% of families had children who were not permanently excluded from school
- 26% of families had at least one adult in work
- 77% of families did not have any young people classified as 'NEET'
- 78% were not at risk of eviction for any reason
- 88% of families had no children on a Child Protection Plan
- 77% of families did not have any children identified as being children in need

- 85% of families had no adults with a proven criminal offence in the previous 6 months
- 97% of families had children with either one or no criminal offences in the previous 6 months
- 58% of families had no police callouts in the previous 6 months
- 95% of families had no family members identified as being Prolific and Priority Offenders (PPO)
- 89% of families had no adult subject to an ASB intervention
- 93% of families had no identified gang members in the family
- 93% of families had no adults clinically diagnosed as being dependent on alcohol
- 93% of families had no adults clinically diagnosed as being dependent on non-prescription drugs.

While these figures show that there are undoubtedly some problems within 'troubled families', they also show that the reality of the families might be somewhat different to the stereotypical, stigmatising image of them put forward by politicians, civil servants and certain sections of the media. The portrayal of these families in this way has consequences, both for the families themselves and for the services working with families identified as being 'troubled'. In promoting the publication, Casey gave interviews with a number of national newspapers, including *The Sunday Times* (Hellen, 2014), who highlighted an example that Casey had given them:

> One family triggered 90 police call-outs to their home over six months – an average of one every two days. Overall, the families were on average responsible for one police call-out a month.
>
> A mother of ten was so badly beaten by her violent partner that her children removed all the internal doors in the house and dumped them in the back garden so they would have advance warning of his attacks. Officials found out the truth only because of a complaint about the state of her garden.

The use of such case studies in the 'troubled families' agenda is particularly problematic as these case studies focus on the most extreme family circumstances. The examples of the family with multiple police callouts or the 'mother of 10' who experiences domestic violence are provided to national newspapers to highlight the problems faced by 'troubled families' and the need for a new phase of the programme.

Data was collected on over 9,300 families for the interim evaluation report. Of those 9,300 families, only one family had ten children, and only one family had 90 police callouts. These families were outliers, anomalies, exceptions to the rule that 'troubled families' aren't actually that 'troubled' or 'troublesome'. The example of a police officer stationed on a family's settee being a cheaper option than responding to all of the callouts associated with them is a familiar trope in the 'troubled families' rhetoric, but the data shows that it is also an entirely inappropriate one to illustrate the experience of the majority of the families being talked about.

An alternative reading of the data could therefore suggest that the majority of these 'troubled families' have children who are not excluded from school, are able to care for and bring up their children without statutory intervention of any kind, are not in rent arrears or at risk of eviction and are involved in no – or very low levels of – crime and ASB. Over a quarter of the families were in work within 6 months of the time of entry to the programme despite Casey previously stating that 'We have known that there is a group of families who didn't work in the boom times and won't work in the bust times. They're unemployed; they're dependent on benefits'. As the data suggests, many of them do not match this description and because of the way the data has been collected and reported, we do not know (or are not told) how many of the families had an adult in work in the 7, 8, 9, 12 or 24 months prior to entering the programme.

The reasons for individuals being out of work were not reported by DCLG during the first phase of the programme. Given the health problems and other issues faced by some 'troubled families', it is not surprising that a large number of families had nobody in work because of limiting illness, disability or caring responsibilities but this, again, does not sit particularly easy with the portrayal of families as being feckless, criminal and unwilling to work. The profile of families entering the TFP, it will be noted, was very similar to the allegedly 'problem families' who were worked with by the FIPs under New Labour.

'No impact': the official evaluation of the first phase

The evaluation of the first phase of the TFP was announced in March 2013. At the time, DCLG (2013c) issued a press release highlighting how the contract had been awarded to 'a consortium of experienced, independent research groups' and the then Secretary of State Eric Pickles said:

it is important we learn the lessons of this work for the future and leave a legacy beyond the lifetime of this programme in 2015. This study will help do that by looking at what works most effectively with troubled families and how we best spend public money on turning them around.

These positive views and high hopes for the evaluation were echoed by Casey. In giving evidence to a Public Accounts Committee (2014: 41) inquiry into the programme in 2014, Casey was confident that the scope of the evaluation and the quality of the research consortium would provide a comprehensive overview of the impact of the programme:

We have let a huge, in my view, evaluation contract to a consortium called Ecorys. Within that, there will be a cost-benefit analysis done by – I can't remember who they are, but they are terribly good at their job. There are other people, but we have got the best. We have MORI doing some stuff and whatever-they-are-called doing the finances.

Casey went on to say that:

the programme has to prove itself, it has to prove its worth, otherwise we need to find a different way to work with these families', and she hoped 'that the evaluation will show us whether we are getting it right, and if we are not, where we can improve it.

Little more was heard about the evaluation until August 2016, when it was announced that the publication of evaluation reports had been suppressed because they did not provide the government with the evidence it wanted regarding the impact of the programme. A *BBC Newsnight* report claimed that the evaluation had found '"no discernible" effect on unemployment, truancy or criminality' and that the report was 'embarrassing' for ministers who had trumpeted the scheme's success and expanded it before the findings of the evaluation were reported (Cook, 2016). The government had received the various reports from the research consortium delivering the evaluation during August and September 2015 and had originally intended to publish the evaluation by the end of 2015, or shortly afterwards. The government denied that the evaluation had been suppressed, but the allegation was enough to reignite the interest of the Public Accounts Committee

(PAC), which announced that it would be revisiting the TFP in a new inquiry in the autumn of 2016.

The government finally published the evaluation on 17 October 2016, two days before the PAC hearing, despite requests from the PAC for advance copies of the evaluation to be circulated to committee members. There were a number of different streams to the evaluation, and a number of different reports published including: a report published on data from a family survey; a report using 'family monitoring data' collected by local authorities; a report on families experiences and outcomes; a report on the 'process' of implementing the TFP drawing on interviews and discussions with local authority staff; and a report on the impact of the programme. Much of the press coverage that followed the publication of the evaluation focused on the findings from the national impact study, and one paragraph in particular:

> The key finding is that across a wide range of outcomes, covering the key headline objectives of the programme – employment, benefit receipt, school attendance, safeguarding and child welfare – we were unable to find consistent evidence that the Troubled Families programme had any significant or systematic impact. That is to say, our analysis found no impact on these outcomes attributable to the programme. The vast majority of impact estimates were statistically insignificant, with a very small number of positive or negative results. These results are consistent with those found by the separate and independent impact analysis using survey data, which also found no significant or systemic impact on outcomes related to employment, job seeking, school attendance, or anti-social behaviour. This gives us further confidence in the reliability of our results. (Bewley, 2016b: 20)

The publication of the evaluation was not accompanied by a press release from DCLG, which was unusual given that press releases extolling the success of the programme were a feature of its first phase. Instead, the government published a bizarre 'op-ed' piece by the Communities Minister Lord Bourne the day before the evaluation was published. This online editorial espoused the alleged qualities of the programme and suggested that, while the government 'never expected to get everything right and have never claimed to have done so', they did 'believe this programme has transformed the lives of thousands of families' (DCLG, 2016c). The government also published an *Overview* document on the same day that it published the evaluation reports that marginalised the key finding from the impact study into two paragraphs on pages 8 and 9 (DCLG, 2016a). The *Overview* document instead highlighted how the evaluation had 'found widespread evidence of service transformation' and trotted out platitudinous evaluation comments such as noting that the programme had 'enabled local authorities to scale-up their family intervention provision', 'driven innovation in working with families', and 'stimulated multi-agency working'. The phrase 'turned around', a key concept of the first phase of the programme, featured just twice in the document.

During the PAC hearing, a number of questions again focused on the key finding from the national impact study that the evaluation could find no impact attributable to the programme. The government's response was to criticise the evaluation team and call its professionalism into doubt, to the point where the Chair of the Committee asked if it had asked for a refund of the fee the team had been paid. Melanie Dawes, the Permanent Secretary, stated that the evaluation team 'did not deal with the data as well as they could have done' that it was necessary to 'bring in experts to look at' some of the data issues, and that 'there were some judgement calls ... that needed to be challenged'. Louise Casey had changed her opinion on the quality of the evaluation team and suggested that they 'had put through data that was inaccurate and flawed' and that the researchers had accepted this while DCLG had not. Casey also named Jonathan Portes, an outspoken critic of numerous elements of the programme and a member of the National Institute of Economic and Social Research (NIESR) team, despite insisting that she did not want to make it a personal issue. She suggested that Portes' comments in the press had been 'unedifying', and incredibly accused him and NIESR of 'misrepresenting their own research'. Casey stated that 'after a lot of correction and sorting out, I accept the findings of the research'. To be clear, then, before some of the independent organisations − and individuals − involved in the evaluation expressed some concerns about the worth of the programme, Casey stated that they were 'terribly good at their job' and 'the best', but when they offered their opinions, after the publication of the evaluation, they were accused of 'misrepresenting their own research' and being 'unedifying'.

The government narrative during the inquiry, then, was that one element of the evaluation was unable to prove the impact of the programme and that the team involved in that evaluation stream had mismanaged the data, casting doubt on their competence and professionalism. This public performance was not mirrored in the discussions that took place away from the public eye. An e-mail from the Head of Research in the Troubled Families Team at DCLG to the evaluation team highlighted that the expert called in – Professor Anna Vignoles from Cambridge University – 'concluded that the underlying data was clearly very messy (*through no fault of the evaluators*)' (emphasis added). Vignoles did not recommend any changes to the data analysis that had been carried out and was 'of the view that NIESR have done a good job in attempting to conduct an impact study with poor data'. Instead, she suggested that the writing up of the report needed to include more emphasis on the problems with and limitations of the data. The e-mail stated that 'Professor Vignoles views the report as acceptable for publication' if the appropriate caveats were added. There were no 'corrections' needed or made and the report did not need 'sorting out', as Casey had suggested (see NIESR, 2016 for a comprehensive refutation of many of the criticisms made by the DCLG representatives at the PAC hearing).

This focus on one aspect of the evaluation meant that other aspects did not receive as much scrutiny as they arguably deserved. The process evaluation report, for example, noted that in some local authorities the programme had led to services being reconfigured differently, although there is a concomitant argument that cuts to local authorities are achieving this even without factoring in the influence of the TFP. This report also noted that some local authorities had implemented the TFP without re-designing services and had 'embedded' 'troubled families' work into existing services and structures. The Family Monitoring Data report showed, mirroring the data behind the *Understanding Troubled Families* report, that the clear majority of 'troubled families' that local authorities worked with were not actually that troublesome or anti-social. The report on family experiences and outcomes was based on interviews with just 22 families, following the FIP evaluation trend of relying on qualitative data from very small numbers of families. Of those 22 families, only eight were interviewed at both the beginning and the end of their intervention. Reasons for disengagement included a case that was referred to children's social care and another where a family member entered custody in the period following the initial research visit, neither of which sound like families whose lives might have been 'turned around' by the TFP.

The Family Survey Data report (Purdon and Bryson, 2016) is perhaps the report that provides the most interesting reading, partly because it collects data from the families themselves, and partly because it provides some form of support to the national impact study findings that no impact could be attributable to the programme. It has, however, received much less publicity. The report, based on responses from 495 families who had been on the programme for 9 months and a comparison group of 314 families who had just started on the programme, was unable to find any impact attributable from the programme, based on responses from families:

> We found very little evidence that the Troubled Families Programme significantly affected the outcomes of families around nine months after starting the programme. The statistically significant improvements we did identify relate to the perceptions of main carer respondents in the Troubled Families group about how they were coping financially, and more generally about how they felt they were faring, and their expectations for the future. There were no positive (or negative) impacts identified for housing, employment and jobseeking, anti-social behaviour and crime, school behaviour and attendance, health, drug or alcohol use, family dynamics or well-being. (Purdon and Bryson, 2016: 24)

While the report was keen to state that improvements may have occurred after the 9-month survey, these findings are harder for the government to ignore and/or attempt to discredit. Similarly, qualitative research examining families experiences and outcomes reported the ambiguous finding that 'almost all of the families reported some degree of improvement in their circumstances' (Blades et al, 2016: 4), primarily around confidence issues, when they exited the programme. These are families whose lives had been, or were in the process of being, 'turned around' or 'transformed' by the government and yet they were seemingly unaware of this fact. They were oblivious to any alleged improvement in their children's attendance at school, to any reduction in crime or anti-social behaviour associated with their household, and to any progress towards finding employment. This, of course, does not fit with the government's claims about the 99% success of the first phase of the programme in 'turning around' the lives of England's 'most troubled families'.

Conclusion

The relationship between the TFP and research evidence is strained, to say the least. The original figure of 120,000 'troubled families' was arrived at through the misrepresentation of research examining families that experienced multiple disadvantages. The case for a family intervention model to 'turn around' the lives of these families was based on research that has seen its findings consistently over-stated, leading Gregg (2010) to argue that the presentation of the research amounted to 'policy-based evidence'. Louise Casey's own attempts at 'research' or 'evidence gathering' have also proven problematic, lacking ethical approval procedures and raising concerns about the informed consent of participating families. Vignettes of extreme and atypical families have been presented as 'case studies' of families, portraying a distorted picture of the types of problems faced by the vast majority of the families on the programme. Data collected by workers on the programme has been misappropriated to portray disadvantaged and marginalised families as 'the worst families' in Britain. Where researchers have highlighted concerns about the use of research in the programme, or the lack of evidence to support the claims associated with Phase 1, their concerns have been trivialised and their professionalism called into question. At the start of the programme, it was argued that no more research was necessary because the family intervention approach had been shown to work, but by the end of Phase 1, the government was stating that more research was necessary to prove the efficacy of the TFP.

The situation in regards to Phase 2 of the programme has improved, but not dramatically. The government published a report setting out the methodology for the second phase of the TFP, but no explanation was given about how the six new indicators were arrived at. In announcing the 'next phase' of the TFP in April 2017, the focus shifted to 'workless families' and an 'evidence pack' was published by the DWP. Once again, however, research evidence was used in a highly selective, often disingenuous way. On the BBC Radio 4 'Today' programme on 4 April 2017, Damian Green, the Minister for Work and Pensions, echoing Casey four years earlier, used the fact that he had 'met some' 'troubled families' who had been 'turned around' as evidence that the TFP had worked and as justification for the 'next phase' of the programme. The issue of poverty, generally ignored by the 'troubled families' publications, was also at last included in the DWP evidence pack, but presented as an issue that can best be addressed by changing family circumstances, rather than structural conditions.

Examining the research that has been presented and collected in support of the TFP only tells us part of the story, however. There is a huge amount of social scientific research stretching back over 100 years that has not been mobilised in attempting to understand the causes of the types of challenges and barriers faced by 'troubled families'. Tom Slater has previously highlighted how the 'independent' thinktank the

Centre for Social Justice (CSJ) has been involved in the production of ignorance in relation to the causes of poverty (Slater, 2014). Slater's agnotological approach – the study of ignorance-making – highlights how the CSJ marginalised existing research on poverty in favour of conducting their own half-baked investigations. The UK government has also attempted to re-define poverty and find 'better measures' for poverty, which focus on educational attainment and the number of 'workless households' (see Bradshaw, 2013, for a good critique of such attempts).

Similar approaches can be found in the 'troubled families' agenda, which has systematically ignored historical evidence surrounding previous constructions of the 'underclass'. Research into the causes and consequences of poverty, including that of Rowntree who highlighted the structural causes of poverty and many more recent publications, has been overlooked. Contemporary research examining the importance of money to children's health and wellbeing has not been drawn upon (Cooper and Stewart, 2013). Evidence surrounding specialist approaches that work with many of the individual problems faced by 'troubled families', and which might be more appropriate than 'whole family' approaches, has remained unused. The impact of government welfare reforms and austerity measures on families involved with the TFP has not been presented, despite good evidence highlighting that it is poor families with children that are the biggest losers from the government's attempts to 'reform' welfare (Beatty and Fothergill, 2016). Research evidence about the efficacy of the TFP itself has been derided, ignored or marginalised when it does not support the government narrative of 'success' and 'transformation'.

None of this critique denies that many 'troubled families' experience multiple disadvantages, or are dealing with lots of different issues, or that some families do cause trouble for other people. Nor does it seek to suggest that government should not step in and help to address some of the issues that families face. When a programme specifically and deliberately targets some of the poorest and most disadvantaged families, we should not be surprised when issues such as unemployment, domestic violence, crime, lone parenthood, educational problems and mental health issues can be found. After all, these issues occur across all cross-sections of society. What should, perhaps, be more noteworthy, given the difficulties these families face and the conditions and stresses under which many of them live, is the fact that many of them appear to function reasonably well without succumbing to the 'Shameless' stereotype often associated with them. And it is highly questionable that a family intervention approach that prioritises changes within the family through persistent and assertive challenge, at the expense of any changes to structural conditions, is the most appropriate way to help such families. Ruth Levitas (2012b) noted in relation to Casey's *Listening to Troubled Families* report that 'doubtless families with backgrounds and circumstances as difficult as Casey documents exist – although there might be quite other ways of telling their stories'.

NINE

'Nothing to hide': the structural duplicity of the Troubled Families Programme

… political discourses have a sort of structural duplicity
(Bourdieu, 1985: 738)

Introduction

The TFP has been likened to a 'policy fiasco' (Lambert, 2016) and a 'policy disaster' (Portes, 2016) and it would not be stretching it too far to call it an 'omnishambles' with mistakes made at almost every turn. While there has been a degree of public and academic scrutiny of many of the overblown claims of the programme, there has been less written of the deceit, underhandedness and political chicanery that has been evident throughout the programme. From the misrepresentation of research surrounding 120,000 disadvantaged families at the outset of the programme, to claims of a near perfect success rate and the criticism of researchers who challenged official claims, the TFP has been built on a sort of structural duplicity that requires closer attention. Louise Casey has argued that 'people like me and others … believe we have nothing to hide and nothing to be worried about' (Public Accounts Committee, 2016a: 8) in relation to scrutiny of the TFP. Casey used the same turn of phrase, stating she had 'nothing to hide' (BBC, 2001), when she was accused of involvement with homelessness figures being fiddled. Some light-touch muckraking research, however, suggests that the government not only has plenty to hide in its representation of 'troubled families', but that it has also managed to marginalise and deflect attention away from important determinants of the lives of disadvantaged families.

A wide variety of dirty data is raked into a heap in the following section, providing a summary of some of the deceptions associated with the TFP that are widely known or have already been discussed in this book. This summary includes misrepresentations of the kinds of 'troubles' faced or caused by families involved with the programme, the invented survey that 'proved' the need for radical reform, attempts to pressure local authorities into claiming for more 'turned around' families, the suppression of the official evaluation, and attempts to undermine critics of the programmes claims of success. The attention then turns to three fundamental aspects of the 'troubled families' story that have not yet been discussed in as much detail: the importance of 'family workers'; the power of the relationship between these family workers and members of 'troubled families'; and the idea that families' lives have been 'turned around' or that they are seeing 'significant and sustained progress' from their involvement with the TFP. A concluding discussion identifies the focus on families as the problem and the role of local services in the solution to this problem as the fundamental deceit of the TFP. This familial focus helps to keep structural issues on the periphery of 'troubled families' debates and marginalises the role of central government in both creating and resolving family troubles.

Obfuscation and evasion: a summary

The TFP has, from the very start of the programme, relied on deceit and duplicity to justify its existence and its subsequent development. Shortly after the 2011 riots, David Cameron (2011a) announced that structural issues such as poverty, government cuts, youth unemployment and police racism did not act as catalysts for the riots. Before any inquiry or investigation had been announced, Cameron confidently asserted:

> Let's be clear. These riots were not about race: the perpetrators and the victims were white, black and Asian. These riots were not about government cuts: they were directed at high street stores, not parliament. And these riots were not about poverty: that insults the millions of people who, whatever the hardship, would never dream of making others suffer like this.
>
> No, this was about behaviour. People showing indifference to right and wrong. People with a twisted moral code. People with a complete absence of self-restraint.

Ignoring a long and problematic history of black men dying at the hands of the police in the UK (and particularly in London), Cameron (2011a) instead argued that poor parenting or absent parents had been a key driver of the riots. The prime minister also laid the blame at the door of a welfare state that 'encourages the worst in people – that incites laziness, that excuses bad behaviour, that erodes self-discipline, that discourages hard work'. Subsequent research into the motivations of those involved in the riots highlighted a complex picture, with researchers noting that '[r]ioters identified a number of other motivating grievances, from the increase in tuition fees, to the closure of youth services and the scrapping of the education maintenance allowance' and that '[m]any complained about perceived social and economic injustices' (Lewis et al, 2011: 5). Further research (Lightowlers, 2015: 12) exploring the link between those involved in the riots and deprivation statistics argued that:

> a backdrop of deprivation, inequality and tautological over-policing of communities using stop and search procedures has been a feature of previous riots. Indeed, social–structural inequality also played a role in shaping the decisions of some to engage in rioting in the summer of 2011, as voiced in many of the underlying grievances rioters themselves expressed.

Lightowlers (2015: 12–13) went on to note that such evidence is 'continually downplayed in policy responses', with politicians preferring 'narratives that attribute blame to "pathological" individuals, their parents and even entire communities, rather than highlighting flaws in their own economic and/or social policy'. At the launch of the TFP a few months later, the government misused research that showed the number of families experiencing multiple disadvantages in the mid-2000s as 'evidence' of 120,000 'troubled families' who were the 'source of a large proportion of the problems in society' (Cameron, 2011b). This misuse has been defended and trivialised at various points throughout the lifetime of the TFP, with no admission from the government that it represents an error of judgement.

The misuse or misrepresentation of research has continued throughout the development of the TFP, as discussed in detail in the previous chapter. A survey was invented that enabled Louise Casey to make the case for radical reform of public services. 'Dipstick information gathering', undertaken without any ethical procedures being followed, was published in an official government document and was promoted by Casey in numerous interviews to national newspapers (Ramesh, 2012b). There were reports that the evaluation of the programme had been 'suppressed' because the findings did not support the government narrative of unequivocal success (Cook, 2016). The sound analytic approach to problematic data by researchers involved in the evaluation of the first phase of the programme was characterised as sloppiness by senior civil servants from DCLG during a PAC inquiry, even though independent experts suggested no changes needed to be made to the analysis that had been undertaken. Data from the evaluation that related to families' perspectives on the lack of impact of the programme in many key areas has been largely ignored, with Casey highlighting that there was only 'one element of a 700-page report that essentially says that the Troubled Families programme has no impact' (House of Commons Committee of Public Accounts, 2016a: 9), when, in fact, there were other strands of the evaluation that arrived at similar conclusions. The PAC inquiry concluded that DCLG had been 'evasive' in addressing its queries about the delayed publication of the evaluation, and that 'these delays and obfuscation have given a bad impression about the Department's willingness to be open' (House of Commons Committee of Public Accounts, 2016b: 5).

Data that highlighted that the majority of the 'troubled families' worked with in the early stages of the first phase of the programme were not involved with significant amounts of crime or anti-social behaviour was reported as proving that they were 'the worst families' (in Hellen, 2014) with greater problems than originally anticipated. This data was used as partial justification for the expansion of the programme, despite DCLG relaxing the initial criteria for identifying 'troubled families' in Phase 1 to help local authorities who were struggling to find the requisite numbers families in their area. The announcement of the 'next phase' of the TFP in 2017 was accompanied by a renewed focus on 'workless families', despite the fact that the majority of 'troubled families' in Phase 2 were in work and, of those that were not, many were not expected to be looking for work. Caring commitments for poorly or disabled family members of young children or health problems among adult carers in 'troubled families' remained largely undiscussed.

The family intervention approach employed by the TFP has shifted considerably from the 'Dundee model' it is reputedly based on. Although this is not necessarily a bad thing, it is unfortunate that the rhetoric surrounding the programme continues to highlight the importance of 'family intervention' and ignore the continuing importance of universal and/or specialist services in working with 'troubled families'. Family intervention is not a 'pioneering' approach, supported by a robust evidence base. In fact, family intervention has come to be such a diluted term that it can cover a wide range of approaches with families engaging with local services. The evidence base regarding the model, in its various forms, has, as Gregg (2010: 11) noted, been 'sexed up' at times, and there is undoubtedly a gap between the success of the approach as told by the government and the reality reported by researchers. The announcement that the programme will work with 400,000 more families in its second phase, identified using new and, at times, quite different criteria, and a different methodology, while retaining the same official, stigmatising label of 'troubled families' from the first phase, is also problematic and duplicitous.

The reporting of the success of the first phase of the TFP was particularly troubling. The government reported that the programme had 'turned around' 99 per cent of the 'troubled families' it set out to work with. This claim was despite the widespread practice of data matching during the first phase of the TFP and the fact that local authorities had worked with far more families than reported in government spreadsheets. The political capital invested in the TFP meant that the programme was never going to be allowed to 'fail'. One senior police officer remarked, at the first national 'troubled families' conference for police officers in Durham in 2015, that the programme was 'doomed to succeed' from the moment Cameron launched it and declared it was his ambition to 'turn around' the lives of all 120,000 'troubled families' before the next general election. The government tolerated, if not encouraged, the playing of the PbR system in order to realise this ambition. Officers in Northton, Westingham and Southborough spoke of DCLG officials ringing up senior officers in local authorities in the early stages of the programme, 'demanding' to know why progress had not been as swift as it could have been:

> 'It's not always been administered in the best way, you know, it's got under a number of people's skins. You know, [DCLG] ringing Chief Executives and stuff like that, kind of demanding where the people are at, in terms of results and stuff like that, in some local authorities.' (Sam, CSM, Southborough)

Despite the widespread criticism of the 99 per cent success figure, members of the government remained unrepentant. During the PAC inquiry in 2016, Casey told the committee that 'we know that 116,654 families basically *had their lives changed by the programme* according to the payment-by-results system' (Public Accounts Committee, 2016a: 27, emphasis added) even though substantial data, published by the government or provided by local authorities or families, contradicts that assertion. Melanie Dawes, the Permanent Secretary at DCLG, told the same hearing that her department had 'never said' (2016a: 17) they had a near 100 per cent success record, perhaps forgetting that in June 2015 DCLG issued a press release relaying the news that the prime minister had 'announced that the programme had succeeded in turning around 99% of the actual number of families targeted' (DCLG, 2015a). Cameron (2015a) himself claimed that 'almost all of the 117,000 families which the programme started working with have now been turned around'.

Extraordinary workers

If 'troubled families' represent an *official social problem*, created, sustained and nourished by the government, then family workers arguably represent the *official solution* to the alleged problem. The TFP has been positioned as a necessary response to not only the problems caused by 'troubled families' themselves, but by the inability of the state and the services it has traditionally delivered to 'get to grips' with them. If 'troubled families' are the perpetrators of a long list of offences and 'problems', 'failing' local services have been cast by the government as their longstanding accomplices. The TFP was supposed to 'change completely the way government interacts with' 'troubled families', fundamentally altering 'the way the state intervenes in their lives' (Cameron, 2011b). At the centre of this change was a cadre of family workers who were, in Casey's eyes, unlike other public sector workers.

Stereotypes of officious and overly-bureaucratic workers were mobilised in order to highlight the alleged difference between the TFP and previous government approaches. Social workers were castigated as arriving at family homes 'with clipboards', 'assessing the hell out of them', but without making any real lasting difference (in Bennett, 2012). Youth work and diversionary activities for young people were deemed unnecessary if young people were in mainstream education (in Winnett and Kirkup, 2012). Specialist and neighbourhood services were characterised as operating in silos, unable or unwilling to speak to partner agencies who might have been working with the same family member or other members of the same family. It was as though multi-agency or partnership working had never been invented. Not only did these services not communicate with each other, they were portrayed as simply 'failing' to address the issues that families faced and, in some cases, the problems that they caused. The best family workers were different, according to Casey, and had 'been around the block themselves, they won't take no for an answer' and often 'don't look and feel like officials' (in Hellen, 2014).

Family workers were portrayed as being 'dedicated to families', as if other workers were engaged in similar work simply for the money. They were willing and able to tell it like it is to families and 'walk in the shoes' (DCLG, 2012a: 5) of the families, and 'seen to be standing alongside the families' (DCLG, 2012a: 18). Yet no clue was given as to where these workers had been during previous government interventions or support work with 'troubled families', or what they had been doing prior to the launch of the TFP. There was no indication that the new breed of family workers would be recruited from similar services such as education welfare, youth offending teams and children's centres. There was no explanation as to how the simple adoption of a 'family intervention' approach would see such a radical change in the alleged 'performance' of street-level bureaucrats. Details and contradictions such as these were largely absent from the government's pronouncements about the successes of family workers.

As the TFP has expanded, and the range of problems faced by 'troubled families' has grown, the putative solution has remained the same. When the focus shifted from allegedly troublemaking families in the first phase, through more vulnerable families in Phase 2 and onto 'workless families' from 2017, the family intervention model has been held up as the best, if not the only, way of tackling numerous different issues. Whatever the questions posed of public services by 'troubled families' at various stages of the TFP, family intervention has remained the answer to all of them. Even when issues that might not lend themselves to a 'whole family' approach, such as domestic violence, addictive behaviour, and health issues have moved centre stage, a form of intensive family intervention has been promoted by the government as the best way to address these issues.

The views and practices of the workers themselves, many of whom have attempted to distance themselves from the stigmatising rhetoric surrounding the families they work with and the muscular rhetoric of the approach they adopt, have not troubled the government narrative. The local day-to-day practice of the TFP has relied as much on workers' ability to work with (not 'grip') partner agencies as it has on their 'rolling up their sleeves' and 'donning the marigolds' (DCLG, 2012a: 21). Some workers were either unaware that they were working on the TFP (Hayden and Jenkins, 2014: 642), or made no distinction between work with 'troubled families' and work with other families that did not meet the TFP entry criteria. The process evaluation of the first phase of the programme found 'wide variations in local practice' (White and Day, 2016: 5), 'variable levels of motivation (and competency profiles) amongst staff' (White and Day, 2016: 49) and also reported resistance to the FIP model among practitioners:

> Alongside the challenge of scaling-up the workforce, local teams sometimes encountered some resistance

where practitioners felt certain that they were already delivering effective practice in their work with families. This sometimes meant that they did not recognise a need to adapt their practice to the family intervention approach. (White and Day, 2016: 50)

The simplistic portrayal of family intervention is thus accompanied by a simplistic portrayal of family workers. The discovery of a small group of universally effective and efficient workers, able to 'turn around' the lives of some of the most marginalised families in the country regardless of their apparent lack of success in previous roles, has occurred at precisely the moment that many of their colleagues are being made redundant and partner services they rely on in their work are being cut. All this 'miraculous success' (Butler, 2015), Casey has argued, 'turns on something very simple: the relationship between the worker and the family' (in Aitkenhead, 2013).

The relationship between family and worker

It is not that family intervention workers are 'jacks of all trades', they are masters of one – the relationship. (Casey, 2014c)

Central to the family intervention model is the supposedly different relationship that exists between the worker and the families they work with. In *Working with Troubled Families*, DCLG (2012a) set out just how important this relationship is to the success of the approach in helping families:

The evidence suggests that much of the success of family intervention work is due to the skills of individual workers, both in building an honest and productive relationship with a family and influencing the actions of other agencies around that family. (DCLG, 2012a: 17)

The family will always know who their worker is and evidence shows the relationship they build with this individual is central to progress being made. (DCLG, 2012a: 19)

Families can feel that the relationship with a case worker is very different to other agencies. (DCLG, 2012a: 20)

These relationships are built and developed over time, according to the government, and often have their roots in a worker's willingness to 'get stuck in' and get their hands dirty in order to help the families:

> An initial focus on practical help, such as overdue repairs, cleaning projects, rubbish clearance or obtaining crucial items such as beds for children or a functioning washing machine is important in starting to build the relationship with families needed to bring about change. Seeing some practical and quick results can signal to families that the worker intends to keep their promises and is there to help. This may be the point where families begin to see their worker as different to other agencies in their lives (who may assess and tell families what they are doing wrong – but do not always offer assistance to make things right) and begin to trust them and become more willing to work with them. (DCLG, 2012a: 21)

Any specialist knowledge or previous experience of workers was therefore not valued as much as the ability to develop relationships with families in the TFP narrative. The emphasis on the importance of the relationship between 'the state' and citizens also fits in with some wider, progressively-tinged discussions about a need to develop 'relational welfare' (see Cottam, 2011; Muir and Parker, 2014). Personal characteristics trump professional skills. The ability to build relationships with different family members and work with 'the family from the inside out, to understand its dynamics as a whole' (DCLG, 2012a: 4) is afforded primacy. Once the surface is scratched, or raked, a little, the idea of a supposedly special relationship that is central to the successful outcomes often associated with the family intervention approach begins to look like it is built on poor foundations. First, as has already been discussed, the idea that the family intervention approach produces better outcomes than other approaches is contested to say the least, and several strands of the evaluation of the first phase of the TFP suggested that the programme had no impact at all across a number of key outcomes. If the relationship between worker and family was that important, then one would expect to see more impact and better outcomes for the family. It is, however, not just the impact of such relationships that should be scrutinised. The truth, or otherwise, of this putatively strong relationship, one that is apparently built on trust and a 'whole family' approach, also deserves closer inspection.

Interviews with 15 families in Phase 1 of the TFP suggest that they did indeed value certain aspects of the relationship with their worker. These included 'consistency; honesty and establishing trust; responsiveness; and positive reinforcement of families' strengths and achievements' (Blades et al, 2016: 5). These families, it should be noted, were identified by local authorities as being 'suitable' for interview (Blades et al, 2016: 8). A slightly different picture emerges, however, from some of the data collected from the family survey, which included responses from 495 families. The section of the evaluation report that discusses families' relationships with their worker was forced to omit 71 families (14 per cent) because they could not remember or did not know the name of their 'keyworker' (Purdon and Bryson, 2016: 51). Around 78 per cent of families saw their worker once a week or less, with around 20 per cent of families seeing their worker once a month or less often. Main carers reported that workers were not 'in contact' with the children in over 40 per cent of families and were in contact with fewer than one in ten (9 per cent) resident partners and only one in 50 (2 per cent) non-resident partners. Workers themselves, as discussed in Chapter Seven, highlighted the importance of their relationships with other services and agencies and the amount of time they spent working with a variety of other professionals on 'troubled families' cases.

These findings suggest that the relationship between worker and family might not be that strong and that a 'whole family' approach might not be that central to the type of work that is being undertaken in the TFP. It should be acknowledged that families were positive about their workers, and often valued their input over and above the support they had sometimes received from other services. It should also be accepted that it is not necessarily surprising when a new social policy programme with substantial political support and a PbR framework receives better feedback than services under severe pressure and undergoing restructuring and retrenchment as a result of cuts to public services. Despite these pressures, many families in Phase 2 of the TFP (78 per cent), reported that they were 'very satisfied' or 'fairly satisfied' with the staff they had been supported by *prior* to entry to the TFP.

One aspect where there was substantially less satisfaction (61 per cent) was in the ease of access to that support, although cuts to local authorities have had significant implications for when, where and how public services are delivered. Hastings et al (2015) have highlighted how even very small cuts can have significant impacts on the accessibility of services for disadvantaged and vulnerable groups, such as those labelled as 'troubled families'. The evidence they collected suggested that the consequences of changes to local services were 'greater for those on lower incomes' (Hastings et al, 2015: 105). Changes to timings, frequency and/or locations of services or sessions, coupled with increased costs for public transport or for accessing such services, often meant that people stopped accessing services that had previously been an important part of their lives. The cumulative impact of such changes, the researchers argue, has been to 'narrow the social realm of children and families' (Hastings et al, 2015: 106), cutting off access to support, social networks and friendship groups.

In a discussion of the effects of public sector cuts on services to children and young people, Hastings et al (2015: 52–6) highlight a number of participants' views about the increased difficulty they had in accessing both universal and specialist services. Speaking about children centres, they highlighted the overwhelmingly positive views of research participants towards the centres, including the 'intensive level of support' (Hastings et al, 2015: 54) that some parents received, before expounding the impacts of some of the changes that had been observed:

> While some service users had not noticed significant changes to services within centres, others had. As one from a less disadvantaged neighbourhood indicated: "They're good, but I think their budgets are far too stretched". Reductions in the childcare element of provision in one centre meant that users were unable to access other services. Cancelled sessions because of staff shortages were also noted, while one participant described how the toddler sessions she attends had become more crowded, with parents competing to arrive early to ensure entry. Staff turnover appeared to be an issue in one centre.

The structural duplicity of the TFP means that it is necessary for family workers and other local practitioners involved in the delivery of the programme to engage in practices that make them feel uncomfortable, or attempt to resist those practices. Almost all local authorities called their local 'troubled families' work by another name in an attempt to soften the stigmatising tone of the programme. Most authorities came up with more positive monikers such as Stronger Families, Families First or Thriving Families. In the same vein, family workers in such authorities did not routinely tell the families that they were working with that they had been identified as 'troubled', or that the support they were receiving was via the TFP. Many families were not informed of the PbR mechanism, which has the potential to skew practice towards priorities identified by the state, rather than those identified by families themselves, despite a 'veneer of empowerment' (Bond–Taylor, 2015: 378) that attaches itself to family intervention work.

The issue of informed consent and the sharing of data concerned a number of workers and managers in local authorities. The data collection requirements of the TFP increased in Phase 2 and local authorities were required to share data on families with central government to support the impact study element of the evaluation. The expanded programme also anticipated and expected greater data sharing among local practitioners from different agencies. A new 'legal gateway' was created, which allowed staff in DWP to share benefits information with colleagues in local government, and a publication was produced providing health practitioners with guidance on how to navigate data protection issues within the TFP (DCLG, 2014e).

All of these issues cast doubt on the nature of the relationship between workers and families that is supposed to be the cornerstone of the family intervention approach, and indeed the whole TFP. According to evidence collected from both workers and families, this relationship does not appear to be the central part of the work, and it certainly cannot be used to explain any successes of the TFP. Numerous issues such as the relative lack of time spent with many families, data matching processes, the importance of other services and the duplicitous nature of many interactions between workers and families, not to mention the lack of evidence about the success of the programme, undermine government claims that the relationship built on trust, and forged in shared domestic chores, is a key element of the 'troubled families' work.

Turning families around

When David Cameron (2011b) launched the TFP he stated that the government were 'committing £448 million to turning around the lives of 120,000 troubled families by the end of this Parliament' and that the funding available to local authorities would be dependent upon the results they achieved. Cameron informed the audience that the PbR mechanism would involve:

> Simple tests such as are the children going to school? How many people have they got back into work? Have they stopped – and I mean completely stopped – anti-social behaviour? How many crimes have been prevented?

By the time that the details of the PbR system was announced a 'complete stop' to anti-social behaviour was no longer required. Instead, the financial framework for the first phase of the TFP stated that only a 60 per cent reduction in anti-social behaviour associated with the household was required in order to qualify as a success (DCLG, 2012c: 9). Families could also be on the road to meeting the criteria for being 'turned around' if there was a 33 per cent reduction in criminal offences by minors living in the household.

When questions about these issues were put to the Communities Secretary Eric Pickles in the House of Commons in early 2014 (Hansard, 2014), he denied that families could be classed as 'turned around' if they were still committing crimes or involved in anti-social behaviour, suggesting there was not 'a scintilla of truth' in such assertions:

> Nic Dakin (Scunthorpe) (Lab): Will the Secretary of State clarify whether a family can be considered "turned around" if they are still committing crimes or engaging in antisocial behaviour?

> Mr Pickles: The short answer is no. We went about it in a very straightforward way and so have some very straightforward criteria. Basically, the kids must be in school, and for three terms, which is why there is a bit of a lag, and somebody must be on the road to work, in the same way that they will be within a programme, and the incidence of antisocial behaviour on the estate must have been reduced measurably.

> ...

> Lyn Brown (West Ham) (Lab): I fear that the Secretary of State is in denial, because his programme actually causes a reduction, not a cessation, in the problems for which the families have been put on the programme. Is it not the truth that many of the families that he says have been turned around are still truanting and engaging in antisocial behaviour? How on earth does he justify the fact that many local authorities are failing to monitor those families after they come off the programme? Is it not the truth that he is scared of real scrutiny of the claims he makes?

Mr Pickles: I invite the hon. Lady to come to my office and talk with Louise Casey. I do not think there is a scintilla of truth in anything the hon. Lady said, and I greatly regret the breach in bipartisanship towards the programme. Our books are open, so she should come in to see them. I have to tell her, in the nicest possible way, that she should put up or shut up.

There were, then, a number of obvious contradictions between the phrase 'turned around' and the operation of the PbR mechanism under the first phase of the TFP, and the experiences of families involved with the programme. Families could be deemed to be 'turned around' if they were still committing crime and involved in anti-social behaviour, as long as they had reduced the frequency of these offences. The severity of any offences could increase and a family could meet the PbR criteria and be deemed as 'turned around' as long as the frequency had reduced. Adults in 'troubled families' could *become involved* in crime and it would potentially have no bearing on whether or not the family could be classed as 'turned around'. Other issues in the household such as domestic violence, drug or alcohol abuse, health conditions, illnesses or material deprivation could either emerge, continue or even escalate without any impact on the likelihood of a family being classed as 'turned around'. Entire families could be classed as 'turned around' by a single child simply leaving school. Families that had been 'turned around' in Phase 1 could still meet the criteria for being a 'troubled family' in Phase 2.

The centrality of work and, more specifically, moving people off out-of-work benefits is one of the most important aspects of the PbR system under both phases of the programme. Getting an adult from a 'troubled family' into work 'trumped' all other changes in the family circumstances. It is symbolically prioritised in the PbR mechanism by it being worth £800 to local authorities in the first phase – equivalent to both of the other possible payments combined. This was despite the issue noted above that other issues or troubles associated with the household could continue or even escalate and this would not affect a local authority from claiming a success in 'turning around' an entire 'troubled family' if a single adult moved off out-of-work benefits and into 'continuous employment'. 'Continuous employment' was measured in two ways, both of which suggest some elasticity in the use of the term 'continuous'. For adults claiming JSA, continuous employment was classed as being in work for 26 out of 30 weeks. It is unclear why four weeks of unemployment in a period of around seven months can be officially classed as 'continuous employment'. For individuals claiming other benefits such as Incapacity Benefit, Income Support, Employment and Support Allowance, 13 consecutive weeks counts as 'continuous employment'. Thus somebody entering work on a three month temporary contract, who might not find any work following that contract, can meet the definition of having found 'continuous employment', depending on the type of benefits they previously claimed.

The 'continuous employment' aspect of the PbR mechanism needed, according to the government, to 'be self-certified by the local authority, using locally determined verification systems, as Jobcentre Plus do not collect this information' (DCLG, 2012c: 23). In effect, Jobcentre Plus and the DWP do not know how many people who 'sign off' benefits are in employment, or remain in employment at later dates. This casts doubt on the validity of government claims about the number of people 'in work' as a result of the TFP, with many local authorities relying on the same DWP systems to locally verify 'continuous employment'. As Tina, a Troubled Families Employment Advisor from Westingham, noted in a discussion about tracking the employment status of adults in 'troubled families':

> Well no because all we can do is verify that they've told us they've started work today for Fred Blogs. And that status, so they've signed off benefit today, started work today, sent their card in, rang up, whatever, said, I'm starting work today. So six months down the line, I would still monitor and if that little Billy hasn't signed back on again in six months, then we can put a claim in. You don't know he's still in employment. All that you can do is say, he's never reclaimed.
>
> And that was a bit of a bone of contention because there's nobody, other than the employer, who can ever confirm that, you know what I mean? The customer themselves can tell you whatever you, whatever it was. He could be in prison, he could be out of the country, he could be anywhere. But the fact that he hasn't reclaimed, you don't know a hundred percent, other than speaking to that employer, how you can a hundred percent know that ... because from a benefit point of view, they're not really interested. They're just interested that he's closing his claim down and they'll pay him to the day before he starts work ... But no, you don't know that they've been in that same

job for six months. All you know is they've been off benefit
for a period of time.

Many people will also have found work themselves, with or without the
intervention of a family intervention worker. The data matching process
used by local authorities highlighted that a number of 'troubled families'
managed to 'turn themselves around' without any input associated with
the TFP (Bawden, 2015). The importance of moving into work of
any kind, however, marginalises some of the problems associated with
the quality and security of work that is often on offer in the UK at
the current time, especially for people who may lack work experience
and/or skills and qualifications. Any job in the 'gig economy', or on
a zero-hours contract, or with unscrupulous employers on, or even
below, the national minimum wage, never mind the Living Wage is
enough for local authorities and the government to claim that a family
has been successfully 'turned around'. The Deputy Chief Executive of
Manchester City Council told parliament that only 19 per cent of the
'troubled families' who found work in Phase 1 of the programme, and
were thus identified as being 'turned around' sustained that employment
for 12 months (Hansard, 2015).

In a similar vein, a child's experience of school is completely
inconsequential to the idea of their life being 'turned around', as can
be seen by the education element becoming neutral upon a child
leaving school. In Phase 1 a child needed only to walk through the
school gates and be registered as being in 85 per cent of the time in
order for the education element of the PbR process to be considered a
'success'. It matters not, to the government at least, if the child is being
bullied in school, what their achievement prospects are, of whether
they are segregated from other pupils. We know that our education
systematically fails disadvantaged children, and Val Gillies (2016:
182), in highlighting the systems of exclusion and marginalisation
that exist within schools, notes that 'in many cases "inclusion" merely
exacerbated existing problems, ensuring pupils fell further behind their
classmates … [marking] them out for close surveillance and increased
harassment in the mainstream school'.

Practitioners involved with the TFP largely rejected the idea that
families' lives had been 'turned around' by the programme or when
they met the PbR criteria. Some suggested that the idea that families
were 'turned around' was 'a load of bloody rubbish' while another
also highlighted that the PbR claim for 'turning around' a family was
'very, very different' to ensuring that all of a family's needs had been
met and addressed:

'I think that's a load of bloody rubbish and I think it's political rhetoric. I think there are some families who we can make a difference to, usually at lower level, usually if we get in early enough. But by the time you come to the families that were initially targeted by the Government, erm, it's chronic, it's entrenched, it's multi-generational. I think if we can get them to a point where they're functioning good enough, for the next six months, and the kids get to school for the next six months and the house is clean for the next six months, erm… Well come on, it's ridiculous. It's political rhetoric.' (Emma, CSM, Westingham)

'How is it that work is top trumps? You can still be beating nine bells out of your wife and children, and your children may not be achieving anything at school because they don't attend because they're busy mopping the blood up off the floor. But actually, you went out and you got a job in a betting office or whatever you got. And that's top trumps and that hurts.' (Janet, Commissioning Manager, Northton)

'[C]laim and closure are two different things. Erm, you know, you can say, you know, mum has just secured a job in Dorothy Perkins – it's a claim but there is whole range of unmet needs which mean that you need to continue [working with] that family for months. And I think sometimes for people outside the troubled families agenda, they, they, they blur that, they say 'well, you've claimed for the family, ergo, you've turned them around'. Well, actually no, we've followed some very specific guidance on something that's claimable but the needs of that family are still unmet, so the closure is months away but the claim can be generated for, you know, for, for Jimmy can get back to school, claimable, but the housing conditions are appalling and the youngest child hasn't had an immunisation and, and mum has a severe mental health problem, but they've been claimed for, so you know, I think those two things are very, very different.' (Ben, CSM, Northton)

Families involved with the TFP have not suggested that their lives had been 'turned around' by the programme. Neither the family survey (Purdon and Bryson, 2016) nor the report on families experiences and outcomes (Blades et al, 2016) featured the phrase 'turn around' (or derivatives or variations of the phrase) outside a standard section on the aims of the TFP. This suggests that the families involved in the evaluation may never have been asked for their views on whether their lives had been 'turned around'. As reported in the previous chapter, the family survey found no statistically significant better outcomes for 'troubled families' who had been on the TFP for around 9 months when compared to families with similar problems who had yet to start on the programme. Similarly, the findings from the qualitative interviews with families reported the very ambiguous finding that '[b]y the time they were approaching the exit point of their intervention, *almost all* of the families reported *some degree of improvement* in their circumstances' (Blades et al, 2016: 4, emphasis added). While some families reported some significant improvements, often around their confidence in dealing with the issues they faced as opposed to any improvements in or resolutions of those issues, there were also families who were concerned about their ability to sustain any perceived improvements.

The government changed the phrase 'turned around' to 'significant and sustained progress' for Phase 2 of the TFP, perhaps recognising and anticipating some of the criticisms of the phrase. During the 2016 PAC inquiry into the programme, Melanie Dawes and Louise Casey responded to a question about whether it would be better if the phrase was dropped (Public Accounts Committee, 2016a: 34). Casey suggested that it was 'right for the time' and 'it worked at the time' but she would not use it in future, without explaining what had changed. Dawes attempted to claim that a 17 percentage point improvement in families who were confident that their worst problems were behind them was 'striking' and 'quite interesting', as if this could justify the government's claim that 99 per cent of families lives had been 'turned around' by the programme. The evidence that the first phase of the programme had no impact, never mind not 'turning around' the lives of 'troubled families', calls into question the government's desire to transform local services around the family intervention approach.

The 'structural duplicity' of the Troubled Families Programme

This concluding chapter has examined the 'structural duplicity' (Bourdieu, 1985: 738) of the TFP and how the programme, from start to finish and from top to bottom, has relied on dirty data, deceitful practices and dubious claims throughout. The government, in the words of Parliament's own website (Parliament, 2016), 'over-claimed' the success of the first phase of the programme, and was evasive and guilty of obfuscation in its responses to the PAC inquiry in 2016. Previous chapters have highlighted problems with the misuse and abuse of research in the TFP, with claims made about the effectiveness of the family intervention approach, and with the depiction of 'troubled families' as 'neighbours from hell'. This chapter has focused primarily on three key aspects of the 'troubled families' narrative: the distinctive qualities of family workers; the strength of the relationship between family workers and families; and the idea that families lives have been 'turned around' by their involvement with the TFP.

It should be noted that the government appears to have accepted some of these criticisms, although it is reluctant to acknowledge others. It quietly accepted all of the PAC recommendations and has stopped using the term 'turned around'. The PbR mechanism was amended for the second phase of the programme and a subsequent review of the method of funding the programme has been announced. Three 'pillars' of the TFP remain, however. The government has not yet acknowledged that the misuse of research around 120,000 disadvantaged families at the outset of the programme was problematic. The myth of the family intervention approach, transforming local services, also remains, as does the damaging and stigmatising portrayal of families involved with the TFP, despite evidence that many families with relatively minor issues are engaged with the TFP. These three issues remain at the core of the 'troubled families' agenda. In essence, the narrative of 'troubled families' has, despite the putative 'evolution' of the programme and the 'lessons learnt' from Phase 1, remained the same: poor families are troublesome and costly, and the best way of changing this is to work with family members to change their behaviour.

This is the real fundamental deceit behind the TFP, the insurmountable ideological barrier that policy tweaks can never overcome. The identification of poor, vulnerable and disadvantaged families as a costly 'problem' to 'the taxpayer' that can only be solved by intensive work by local services with the families themselves has remained at the heart of the 'troubled families' tale since Cameron first launched the programme back in 2011. Cameron was, of course, merely building on decades, if not centuries, of concerns about the dangers presented by the 'undeserving poor'.

Highlighting the central tenets of the political construction of 'troubled families' can only tell us a certain amount, however. Governments and their representatives not only have the power to create official problems such as 'troubled families' and identify their preferred solutions to such problems, they also have the ability to largely close off discussions about alternative courses of action. Politicians not only decide what goes on the agenda and which decisions are made, they also have the power to keep things off the political agenda and thus engage in 'non-decision making' (Bachrach and Baratz, 1970: 44). In a book called *The Un-politics of Air Pollution*, Matthew Crenson (1971: 23) highlights how 'some issues are organized into politics while others are organized out'. In suggesting that the things which are organised out of politics or suppressed are potentially key issues that need to be uncovered, he goes on to argue that 'the proper object of investigation is not political activity but political inactivity'.

The intense political focus on 'the family' as both the problem and the solution has served to keep structural issues such as such as poverty and inequality off the 'troubled families' agenda. Accompanying the 'troubled families' activity and the desire to see the transformation of local services has been a complete inactivity in addressing, or even acknowledging, structural issues. Poverty, as mentioned in previous chapters, has been systematically marginalised in the wider discourse around 'troubled families' (see Gupta, 2017, for a similar discussion in relation to the child protection system). Louise Casey, when she listened to 'troubled families' (Casey, 2012a), did not hear anything about poverty, inequality, disadvantage or marginalisation. The evaluation publications from the first phase of the TFP included just two mentions of poverty, both in relation to local authorities' acknowledgement of the issue as something that needed to be considered, in over 750 pages of analysis. The annual report published in 2017 and the other publications that accompanied it managed just a single mention of poverty – a quote from a family member – in 400 pages of analysis. Even the Public Accounts Committee report (2016b), which was critical of the government's obfuscation in other areas, did not think the omission of any consideration of poverty from the workings of TFP was worthy of mention. Housing conditions, labour market conditions, the accessibility of public services and the impacts of welfare reforms and cuts to local government are issues that are also kept off the 'troubled families' agenda.

A 'below the line' commenter (who claimed to be from a local authority) on an online story in the *Guardian* about the claims surrounding the TFP being 'too good to be true' (Bawden, 2015) highlighted the complicity that was required of local services and explained how the government managed to close off dissent from councils surrounding the programme before it surfaced:

> Troubled Families is the only new money we have available
> in drastically sinking services. It deserves criticism but we

have massive anxiety that it will just get pulled and we'll be completely screwed … The funding matrix is and always was a mess … while we all roll our eyes at the funding matrix between ourselves we daren't project this criticism to the national stage because we'll be starved of any funding at all if the Government pull it. We are a bit like abused children made to eat gruel, complaint won't lead to better food, it'll lead to less gruel.

Local government was once, according to Winifred Holtby:

in essence the first line defence thrown up by the community against our common enemies – poverty, sickness, ignorance, isolation, mental derangement and social maladjustment. The battle is not faultlessly conducted, nor are the motives of those who take part in it all righteous and disinterested. But the war is, I believe, worth fighting, and this corporate action is at least based upon recognition of one fundamental truth about human nature – we are not only single individuals, each face to face with eternity and our separate spirits; we are members one of another. (1988: xi–xii)

The use of family workers to target 'troubled families' using a family intervention model, which seeks to look at the family 'from the inside out' rather than acknowledging the impact of wider society on family life, suggests that times have changed. The abdication of central government responsibility, beyond setting the framework of the TFP, encourages a focus on micro-encounters between individuals which then 'become conceptually overburdened with expectation' (Garrett, 2013: 182). The service transformation that central government wants to see as part of local 'troubled families' work also suggests that the role of local services and the state more widely is changing, especially in relation to disadvantaged populations who are now viewed almost exclusively in terms of their alleged shortcomings, and the inconvenience they cause to their more respectable others – the hardworking and 'ordinary working' (DfE, 2017) families. Tackling 'worklessness' among 'troubled families' now trumps eradicating poverty. Local authorities and frontline workers are no longer the 'first line of defence'. Instead, as Wacquant (in Bourdieu et al, 1999: 136) has noted in relation to public services in the US, they are just as likely to be deployed as the first line of attack:

... given that their clientele has been whittled down to the most marginalized strata ... inner-city public services can be converted into instruments of surveilling and policing of a surplus population ... Far from attenuating the inequalities that weigh upon them, public institutions thus tend to accentuate the isolation and stigmatization of their users. ... Instead of serving as a weapon in the fight against poverty, public authority turns into a war machine against the poor.

This book, drawing on a wide range of sources and social scientific research, has adopted a muckraking sociological approach to the study of the Troubled Families Programme. Resisting the temptation to ratify or legitimise the social problem of 'troubled families' constructed by the government, the focus has been on the problematic and troublesome behaviour of the state in regard to this agenda, rather than that of any 'troubled' families themselves. 'Dirty data' – information that is potentially discrediting and damaging – has been uncovered in a number of key areas, which casts doubt on almost all of the government claims in relation to the TFP. The evidence set out in this book calls into question the government's desire to expand the programme and then continue with it. If evidence of malpractice and duplicity on this scale does not force a re-think, then it is unclear what will. That is unless, as Wacquant argues, the priority is the reform of the state and the quelling of social turbulence associated with increasing inequality and impoverishment, as opposed to the 'turning around' of 'troubled families' or supporting them to make 'significant and sustained progress'.

The TFP, as we have seen, is attempting to change the behaviour of some of the most marginalised populations in England, but does not officially attempt to address poverty or 'attenuating the inequalities' that weigh upon 'troubled families'. The programme itself, and the daily activities of those involved with it, help to produce and reproduce the duplicitous concept of 'troubled families', the latest in a long line of labels for a supposedly 'undeserving poor'. Localised family intervention is not, of course, the only form of action available to the government, and nor is it the only way that the government intervenes in the lives of 'troubled families'. The effects of central government reforms and policies in other areas and the role of the state in creating and resolving the troubles faced by families engaged with the programme appear to be, at best, completely benign and unimportant in discussions about the lives of 'troubled families'.

In conclusion, then, if any group of people should be the target of an intensive intervention, aimed at re-training and re-educating them in the hope that they can become more responsible, respectable and productive members of society, it is not the 'troubled families' of the government's imagination that would be the worthiest recipients of such a programme. We all have far more to gain from a programme that can 'get to grips' with and 'turn around' the attitudes, behaviour and dispositions of some of the most politically powerful and influential members of our society.

References

Aitkenhead, D. (2013) Troubled Families head Louise Casey: 'What's missing is love', *The Guardian*, 29 November, https://www.theguardian.com/society/2013/nov/29/troubled-families-louise-casey-whats-missing-love

Alden, S. (2015) Discretion on the Frontline: The Street Level Bureaucrat in English Statutory Homelessness Services, *Social Policy and Society*, 14 (1): 63–77.

Allen, G. (2011a) *Early intervention: the next steps: An Independent Report to Her Majesty's Government*, London: Cabinet Office.

Allen, G. (2011b) *Early Intervention: Smart Investment, Massive Savings: The Second Independent Report to Her Majesty's Government*, London: Cabinet Office.

Allen, G. and Smith, I.D. (2008) *Early Intervention: Good Parents, Great Kids, Better Citizens*, London: Centre for Social Justice/The Smith Institute.

Allen, K. and Taylor, Y. (2012) Placing Parenting, Locating Unrest: Failed Femininities, Troubled Mothers and Riotous Subjects, *Studies in the Maternal*, 4 (2), www.mamsie.bbk.ac.uk/articles/abstract/10.16995/sim.39/

Ashworth, A. (2004) Social control and "anti-social behaviour": the subversion of human rights? *Law Quarterly Review*, 120: 263–91.

Asthana, A. (2017) Take care of your elderly mothers and fathers, says Tory minister, *Guardian*, 31 January, www.theguardian.com/society/2017/jan/31/take-care-of-your-elderly-mothers-and-fathers-says-tory-minister

Auletta, K. (1981) The Underclass, *The New Yorker*, 16 November, p 63.

Bachrach, P. and Baratz, M.S. (1970) *Power and poverty: theory and practice*, Oxford: Oxford University Press.

Back, L. and Puwar, N. (2012) A manifesto for live methods: provocations and capacities, *The Sociological Review*, 61 (S1): 6–17.

Bagguley, P. and Mann, K. (1992) Idle Thieving Bastards? Scholarly Representations of the 'Underclass', *Work, Employment and Society*, 6 (1): 113–26.

Bailey, N. (2012) Policy based on unethical research, Poverty and Social Exclusion, 24 October, www.poverty.ac.uk/news-and-views/articles/policy-built-unethical-research

Ball, E., Batty, E. and Flint, J. (2016) Intensive family intervention and the problem of figuration of 'Troubled Families', *Social Policy and Society*, 15 (2): 263–74.

Barnes, M. (2011) UK riots: who are these 120,000 troubled families?, NatCen, 25 August, www.natcen.ac.uk/blog/uk-riots-who-are-these-120,000-troubled-families

Baumberg, B., Bell, K. and Gaffney, D. (2012) *Benefits stigma in Britain*, London: Turn2Us, https://wwwturn2us-2938.cdn.hybridcloudspan.com/T2UWebsite/media/Documents/Benefits-Stigma--in-Britain.pdf

Bawden, A. (2015) Is the success of the government's troubled families scheme too good to be true?, *Guardian*, 11 November, www.theguardian.com/society/2015/nov/11/troubled-family-programme-government-success-council-figures

BBC (2001) Homeless boss denies fiddling figures, 24 November, http://news.bbc.co.uk/1/hi/england/1674334.stm

BBC (2011) England riots: Maps and timeline, 15 August, http://www.bbc.co.uk/news/uk-14436499

BBC (2013) Former Portsmouth police officer back on ASBO beat, *BBC News*, 2 September, www.bbc.co.uk/news/uk-england-hampshire-23896776

Beatty, C. and Fothergill, S. (2016) *The uneven impact of welfare reform: The financial losses to places and people*, CRESR: Sheffield Hallam University.

Becker, H. (1963) *Outsiders: Studies in the Sociology of Deviance*, New York: The Free Press.

Becker, H. (1967) Whose side are we on?, *Social Problems*, 14 (3): 239–47.

Beer, D. (2014) *Punk Sociology*, Basingstoke: Palgrave Macmillan.

Bennett, R. (2012) Local Authority Officials "Should Scrub Floors", *The Times*, 27 April, p 21.

Berthoud, R. (1983) Transmitted deprivation: the kite that failed, *Policy Studies*, 3 (3): 151–69.

Bewley, H., George, A., Rienzo, C. and Portes, J. (2016) *National Evaluation of the Troubled Families Programme: National Impact Study Report Findings from the Analysis of National Administrative Data and local data on programme participation*, London: DCLG.

Blades, R., Day, L. and Erskine, C. (2016) *National Evaluation of the Troubled Families Programme: Families' experiences and outcomes*, London: DCLG.

Bochel, H. and Powell, M. (2016) *The coalition government and social policy: Restructuring the welfare state*, Bristol: Policy Press.

Bond-Taylor, S. (2015) Dimensions of Family Empowerment in Work with So-Called 'Troubled' Families, *Social Policy and Society*, 14 (3): 371–84.

Bond-Taylor, S. (2017) Tracing an Ethic of Care in the Policy and Practice of the Troubled Families Programme, *Social Policy and Society*, 16 (1): 131–41.

Booth, W. (1890) *In Darkest England and The Way Out*, London: The Salvation Army.

Bourdieu, P. (1985) The Social Space and the Genesis of Groups, *Theory and Society*, 14 (6): 723–44.

Bourdieu, P. (1993) *Sociology in Question*, London: Sage.

Bourdieu, P. (1996) On the family as a realized category, *Theory, Culture and Society*, 13 (1): 19–26.

Bourdieu, P. (2000) For a scholarship with commitment, *Profession*, pp 40–5.

Bourdieu, P. (2005) *The Social Structures of the Economy*, Cambridge: Polity Press.

Bourdieu, P. (2011) *On Television*, Cambridge: Polity Press.

Bourdieu, P. (2014) *On the State*, Cambridge: Polity Press.

Bourdieu, P., Accardo, A., Balazs, G., Beaud, S., Bonvin, F., Bourdieu, E., Bourgois, P., Broccolochi, S., Champagne, P., Christin, R., Faguer, J. P., Garcia, S., Lenoir, R., Œuvrard, F., Pialoux, M., Pinto, L., Podalydès, D., Sayad, A., Soulié, C. and Wacquant, L. (1999) *The weight of the world: Social suffering in contemporary society*, Stanford: Stanford University Press.

Bourdieu, P. and Wacquant, L. (1992) *An Invitation to Reflexive Sociology*, Cambridge: Polity Press.

Bourdieu, P. and Wacquant, L. (2001) NewLiberalSpeak: Notes on the new planetary vulgate, *Radical Philosophy*, 105: 2–5.

Bourdieu, P., Wacquant, L. and Farage, S. (1994) Rethinking the State: Genesis and Structure of the Bureaucratic Field, *Sociological Theory*, 12 (1): 1–18.

Bradshaw, J. (2013) *Consultation on child poverty measurement*, PSE policy response working paper, No. 8, www.poverty.ac.uk/sites/default/files/attachments/PSE%20policy%20working%20paper%20No.%208,%20Bradshaw,%20CONSULTATION%20ON%20CHILD%20POVERTY%20MEASUREMENT.pdf

Bright, M. (1999) Sweep the homeless off streets, *Observer*, 14 November, www.theguardian.com/uk/1999/nov/14/martinbright.theobserver

Bristol City Council (2014) *Troubled Families – One Year On*, Edition 1.

Brodkin, E. (2011) Putting Street-Level Organizations First: New Directions for Social Policy and Management Research, *Journal of Public Administration Research and Theory* 21 (Suppl 2): i199-i201.

Brown, G. (2009) Speech to Labour Party Conference, www.ukpol. co.uk/gordon-brown-2009-speech-to-labour-party-conference/

Brown, M. and Madge, N. (1982) *Despite the Welfare State: A Report on the SSRC/DHSS Programme of Research into Transmitted Deprivation*, London: Heinemann.

Building Blocks Study Team (2015) *The Building Blocks Trial: Executive Summary*, Department of Health Policy Research Programme Project, http://medicine.cardiff.ac.uk/media/filer_public/f5/db/f5db1bcc-a280-4f08-a34e-14a54d861c14/bb_exec_summary.pdf

Bunting, L., Webb, M.A. and Shannon, M. (2015) Looking again at troubled families: parents' perspectives on multiple adversities, *Child and Family Social Work*, 22 (S3): 31–40.

Burawoy, M. (2005) 2004 Presidential address: For Public Sociology, *American Sociological Review*, 70 (1): 4–28.

Burney, E. (2005) *Making People Behave: Anti-social Behaviour, Politics and Policy*, Cullompton: Willan.

Burney, E. (2009) Respect and the politics of behaviour, in A. Millie (ed) *Securing Respect: Behavioural expectations and anti-social behaviour in the UK*, Bristol: Policy Press, pp 23–40.

Butler, P. (2013) Councils fear for services in £2.1bn cut to budgets, *Guardian*, 26 June, www.theguardian.com/politics/2013/jun/26/councils-fear-services-cut-budgets

Butler, P. (2015) *Troubled families scheme outcomes: miraculous success or pure fiction?*, *Guardian*, 22 June, www.theguardian.com/politics/2015/jun/22/troubled-families-scheme-outcomes-miraculous-success-or-pure-fiction

Byrne, D. (1999) *Social Exclusion*, Buckingham: Open University Press.

Bywaters, P., Brady, G., Sparks, T. and Bos, E. (2014) Inequalities in child welfare intervention rates: the intersection of deprivation and identity, *Child and Family Social Work*, 21 (4): 452–63, doi:10.1111/cfs.12161.

Bywaters, P., Brady, G., Sparks, T., Bos, E., Bunting, L. Daniel, B. Featherstone, B. Morris, K. and Scourfield, J. (2015) Exploring inequities in child welfare and child protection services: Explaining the 'inverse intervention law', *Child and Youth Services Review*, 57: 98–105.

Cadwalladr, C. (2016) The man accused of starting the 2011 riots – and what he did next, *Observer*, 26 June, www.theguardian.com/society/2016/jun/26/man-accused-of-starting-2011-london-riots-mark-duggan

Cameron, D. (2009) Full text of David Cameron's speech: Conservative conference, *Guardian*, 8 October, www.theguardian.com/politics/2009/oct/08/david-cameron-speech-in-full

Cameron, D. (2010) Speech on families and relationships, 10 December, www.gov.uk/government/speeches/speech-on-families-and-relationships

Cameron, D. (2011a) PM's speech on the fightback after the riots, 15 August, www.gov.uk/government/speeches/pms-speech-on-the-fightback-after-the-riots

Cameron, D. (2011b) Troubled families speech, 15 December, www.gov.uk/government/speeches/troubled-families-speech

Cameron, D. (2011c) Statement to Parliament, Hansard, 11 August: cols 1051–1055, www.publications.parliament.uk/pa/cm201011/cmhansrd/cm110811/debtext/110811-0001.htm

Cameron, D. (2014) Speech at the Relationships Alliance Summit, 18 August, www.gov.uk/government/speeches/david-cameron-on-families

Cameron, D. (2015a) PM speech on opportunity, 22 June, www.gov.uk/government/speeches/pm-speech-on-opportunity

Cameron, D. (2015b) Prime Minister: My vision for a smarter state, 11 September, www.gov.uk/government/speeches/prime-minister-my-vision-for-a-smarter-state

Cameron, D. (2016) Prime Minister's speech on life chances, 11 January, www.gov.uk/government/speeches/prime-ministers-speech-on-life-chances

Casey, L. (2008) *Engaging Communities in Fighting Crime: A review by Louise Casey*, London: Cabinet Office.

Casey, L. (2012a) *Listening to Troubled Families*, London: DCLG.

Casey, L. (2012b) Re: The British government's Troubled Families Programme, *BMJ* Editorial, 16 May, www.bmj.com/content/344/bmj.e3403/rr/586466

Casey, L. (2013a) Local Government Association annual conference, 16 July, www.gov.uk/government/speeches/local-government-association-annual-conference

Casey, L. (2013b) Troubled Families Programme, 4 July, www.gov.uk/government/speeches/troubled-families-programme

Casey, L. (2013c) Working with troubled families, *Families, Relationships and Societies* 2 (3): 459–61.

Casey, L. (2014a) Letter from Director General Louise Casey to Chief Executives of Local Authorities, Received via FOI: 1239015.

Casey, L. (2014b) The National Troubled Families Programme, *Social Work and Social Sciences Review*, 17 (2): 57–62.

Casey, L. (2014c) Speech to Women's Aid Conference, 26 November, www.ukpol.co.uk/louise-casey-2014-speech-to-womens-aid-conference/

Casey, L. (2016) Lessons from Rotherham and my work with troubled families, in E. Solomon (ed) *Rethinking Children's Services: Fit for the Future?*, London: NCB/Catch 22, pp 42–6.

Chambers, J. (2012) Interview: Louise Casey, *Civil Service World*, 27 July, www.civilserviceworld.com/interview-louise-casey

Chorley, M. (2012) Problem families told – 'Stop blaming others', *Independent on Sunday*, 9 June, www.independent.co.uk/news/uk/politics/ios-exclusive-problem-families-told-stop-blaming-others-7834235.html

Churchill, H. and Fawcett, B. (2016) Refocusing on Early Intervention and Family Support: A Review of Child Welfare Reforms in New South Wales, Australia, *Social Policy and Society*, 15 (2): 303–16.

Clarke, J. and Newman, J. (2012) The alchemy of austerity, *Critical Social Policy*, 32 (3): 299–319.

Clarke, K. (2011) Punish the feral rioters, but address our social deficit too, *Guardian*, 5 September, www.theguardian.com/commentisfree/2011/sep/05/punishment-rioters-help

Cohen, S. (1985) *Visions of social control*, Cambridge: Polity Press.

Cohen, S. (2002) *Folk Devils and Moral Panics* (3rd edition), London: MacGibbon and Kee.

Communities and Local Government Committee (2013) *Uncorrected Transcript of Oral Evidence: Community Budgets*, HC 163-IV.

Conservative Party (2010) *Invitation to Join the Government of Britain: The Conservative Manifesto 2010*, http://conservativehome.blogs.com/files/conservative-manifesto-2010.pdf

Cook, C. (2016) Troubled Families report 'suppressed', *BBC News*, 8 August, www.bbc.co.uk/news/uk-politics-37010486

Cooper, K. and Stewart, K. (2013) *Does money affect children's outcomes? A systematic review*, York: Joseph Rowntree Foundation, www.jrf.org.uk/sites/default/files/jrf/migrated/files/money-children-outcomes-full.pdf

Cornford, J., Baines, S. and Wilson, R. (2013) Representing the family: how does the state 'think family'?, *Policy and Politics*, 41 (1): 1–18.

Cottam, H. (2011) Relational welfare, *Soundings*, 48: 134–44.

CPAG (2011) *Complacent Budget puts child poverty promise at risk*, 23 March, Child Poverty Action Group, www.cpag.org.uk/content/complacent-budget-puts-child-poverty-promise-risk-1

Crenson, M.A. (1971) *The Un-politics of Air Pollution: A Study of Non-decisionmaking in the Cities*, Baltimore: Johns Hopkins University Press.

Crossley, S. (2013a) 400,000 'high risk' families – policy making by 'estimate', 3 December, https://akindoftrouble.wordpress.com/2013/12/03/400000-high-risk-families-policy-making-by-estimate/

Crossley, S. (2013b) *Moral entrepreneurs, 'radical reform' and factoids*, ESRC Moral Panic Seminar Series, 2012–2014, 9 December, https://moralpanicseminarseries.wordpress.com/2013/12/09/moral-entrepreneurs-radical-reform-and-factoids/

Crossley, S. (2015) *The Troubled Families Programme: the perfect social policy?*, Centre for Crime and Justice Studies, Briefing 13, www.crimeandjustice.org.uk/sites/crimeandjustice.org.uk/files/The%20Troubled%20Families%20Programme%2C%20Nov%202015.pdf

Crossley, S. (2016) The Troubled Families Programme: in, for and against the state?, in M. Fenger, J. Hudson and C. Needham (eds), *Social Policy Review 28: Analysis and Debate in Social Policy*, Bristol: Policy Press, pp 127–46.

Crossley, S. (2017a) *In their place: The imagined geographies of poverty*, London: Pluto Press.

Crossley, S. (2017b) 'Making trouble': a Bourdieusian analysis of the UK Government's Troubled Families Programme, PhD thesis, Durham University, http://etheses.dur.ac.uk/12271/

CSJ (2006) *Breakdown Britain: Interim report on the state of the nation*, London: Social Justice Policy Group.

CSJ (2007) *Breakthrough Britain: Ending the costs of social breakdown*, London: Social Justice Policy Group.

Davis, A. (1952) *Social class influences upon learning*, Cambridge: Harvard.

Day, L., Bryson, C., White, C., Purdon, S., Bewley, H., Kirchner Sala, L. and Portes, J. (2016) *National Evaluation of the Troubled Families Programme: Final Synthesis Report*, London: DCLG.

DCLG (2010) 16 areas get 'community budgets' to help the vulnerable, 22 October, www.gov.uk/government/news/16-areas-get-community-budgets-to-help-the-vulnerable

DCLG (2011a) A letter from Sir Bob Kerslake to all local authority chief about community budgets, 28 July, www.gov.uk/government/publications/community-budgets-letter-from-the-permenant-secretary-dclg

DCLG (2011b) *Troubled Family Estimates Explanatory Note*, 15 December, http://webarchive.nationalarchives.gov.uk/20120919132719/http://www.communities.gov.uk/documents/newsroom/pdf/2053538.pdf

DCLG (2012a) *Working with Troubled Families,* London: DCLG.

DCLG (2012b) Eric Pickles hails 100% troubled families take-up, 11 June, www.gov.uk/government/news/eric-pickles-hails-100-troubled-families-take-up

DCLG (2012c) Louise Casey call for family intervention approach, 15 December, www.gov.uk/government/news/louise-casey-calls-for-family-intervention-approach

DCLG (2013a) *Troubled Families Programme: frequently asked questions*, 28 October, www.gateshead.gov.uk/DocumentLibrary/ChildrensTrust-FamiliesGateshead/Frequently-asked-questions-about-the-Troubled-Families-Programme-oct13.pdf

DCLG (2013b) Massive expansion of Troubled Families programme announced, 24 June, www.gov.uk/government/news/massive-expansion-of-troubled-families-programme-announced

DCLG (2013c) Study to assess impact of troubled families work, 14 March, www.gov.uk/government/news/study-to-assess-impact-of-troubled-families-work

DCLG (2014a) Troubled Families programme expanded to help younger children, 19 August, www.gov.uk/government/news/troubled-families-programme-expanded-to-help-younger-children

DCLG (2014b) *Understanding Troubled Families,* London: DCLG.

DCLG (2014c) *Troubled Families Leadership Statement 2014*, London: DCLG.

DCLG (2014d) *Troubled Families Programme – Health Skills and training*, London: DCLG.

DCLG (2014e) *Interim guidance for troubled families programme early starter areas: sharing health information about patients and service users with troubled families*, London: DCLG.

DCLG (2014f) Troubled families case studies, 1 May, www.gov.uk/government/collections/troubled-families-case-studies

DCLG (2014g) *Estimating the number of families eligible for the expanded Troubled Families Programme*, London: DCLG.

DCLG (2015a) PM praises Troubled Families programme success, 22 June, www.gov.uk/government/news/pm-praises-troubled-families-programme-success

DCLG (2015b) *Financial Framework for the Expanded Troubled Families Programme*, London: DCLG.

DCLG (2016a) *The first Troubled Families Programme 2012 to 2015: An overview*, London: DCLG.

DCLG (2016b) Troubled Families Programme: transforming the lives of thousands of families, 15 October, www.gov.uk/government/news/troubled-familes-programme-transforming-the-lives-of-thousands-of-families

DCLG (2017a) *Supporting disadvantaged families Troubled Families Programme 2015 to 2020: progress so far*, London: DCLG.

DCLG (2017b) Dame Louise Casey to leave government, 21 April, www.gov.uk/government/news/dame-louise-casey-to-leave-government

DCLG (2017c) *National evaluation of the Troubled Families Programme 2015 to 2020: family outcomes – national and local datasets: part 1*, London: DCLG.

DCLG (2017d) *National evaluation of the Troubled Families Programme 2015 to 2020: service transformation – case study research: part 1*, London: DCLG.

DCLG (2017e) *National evaluation of the Troubled Families Programme 2015 to 2020: service transformation – staff survey: part 1,* London: DCLG.

DCLG (2017f) *National evaluation of the Troubled Families Programme 2015 to 2020: family outcomes – family survey: part 1*, London: DCLG.

DCLG (2017g) *Early help service transformation maturity model*, London: DCLG.

De Agostini, P., Hills, J. and Sutherland, S. (2014) *Were we really all in it together? The distributional effects of the UK coalition government's tax-benefit policy changes*, Social Policy in a Cold Climate Working Paper 10, Centre for Analysis of Social Exclusion, http://sticerd.lse.ac.uk/dps/case/spcc/wp10.pdf

De Benedictis, S. (2012) 'Feral' parents: austerity parenting under neoliberalism, *Studies in the Maternal*, 4 (2), www.mamsie.bbk.ac.uk/articles/abstract/10.16995/sim.40/

De Schweinitz, K. (1961) *England's Road to Social Security*, London: Perpetua Books.

Deacon, A. (1976) *In Search of the Scrounger: The administration of Unemployment Insurance in Britain, 1920–1931*, London: G. Bell & Sons.

Dean, H. (1991) Underclassed or undermined? Young people and social citizenship, in R. Macdonald (ed) *Youth, the Underclass and Social Exclusion*, Abingdon: Routledge, pp 55–69.

Demianyk, G. (2015) Jeremy Hunt Signals 'Draconian' Plan To Tackle 'National Disgrace' Of Childhood Obesity, *Huffington Post*, 5 October, www.huffingtonpost.co.uk/2015/10/05/jeremy-hunt-childhood-obesity-protests-conservative-conference_n_8244550.html

DfE (2016) *Children's social care reform: A vision for change*, London: Department for Education (DfE).

DfE (2017) *Analysing family circumstances and education Increasing our understanding of ordinary working families*, London: DfE.

Dillane, J., Hill, M., Bannister, J. and Scott, S. (2001) *Evaluation of the Dundee Families Project,* Edinburgh: Stationery Office.

Dixon, J., Schneider, V., Lloyd, C., Reeves, A., White, C., Tomaszewski, W., Green, R. and Ireland, E. (2010) *Monitoring and evaluation of family interventions (information on families supported to March 2010)*, London: DfE.

Drass, K.A. and Spencer, W.J. (1987) Accounting for Pre-Sentencing Recommendations: Typologies and Probation Officers' Theory of Office, *Social Problems*, 34 (3): 277–93.

Driscoll, M. (2011) I dare you to find jobs for feckless families; Emma Harrison; The problem teenager turned self-made tycoon who is trying to get Britain back to work wants us all to adopt a family. To show us how, she has taken on four, *The Sunday Times*, 21 August.

DuBois, V. (2014) The State, Legal Rigor and the Poor: The Daily Practice of Welfare Control, *Social Analysis*, 58 (3): 38–55.

DWP (2015) *Troubled Families: Benefits and employment, Apr 2012 to Jul 2015 (experimental)*, London: DWP.

DWP (2017a) New support to help workless families and improve children's lives, 4 April, https://www.gov.uk/government/news/new-support-to-help-workless-families-and-improve-childrens-lives

DWP (2017b) *Income-Related Benefits: Estimates of Take-up: Data for financial year 2014/15*, London: DWP.

Edwards, A. and Hughes, G. (2008) Resilient fabians? Anti-social behaviour and community safety work in Wales, in P. Squires (ed), *ASBO Nation: The Criminalisation of Nuisance*, Bristol: Policy Press, pp 57–72.

Edwards, R., Gillies, V. and Ribbens-McCarthy, J. (2012) The politics of concepts: family and its (putative) replacements, *British Journal of Sociology*, 63 (4): 730–46.

Fairclough N. (2000) *New Labour, New Language*, Abingdon: Routledge.

Featherstone, B., White, S. and Morris, K. (2014a) *Re-imagining Child Protection: Towards humane social work with families*, Bristol: Policy Press.

Featherstone, B., Morris, K. and White, S. (2014b) A Marriage Made in Hell: Early Intervention Meets Child Protection, *British Journal of Social Work*, 44 (7): 1735–49.

Field, F. (2010) *The Foundation Years: Preventing poor children becoming poor adults: The report of the Independent Review on Poverty and Life Chances*, London: Cabinet Office.

Fletcher, D. (2011) Welfare Reform, Jobcentre Plus and the Street-Level Bureaucracy: Towards Inconsistent and Discriminatory Welfare for Severely Disadvantaged Groups? *Social Policy and Society* 10 (4): 445–58.

FNP (no date) About us, http://fnp.nhs.uk/about-us

Gans, H. (1970) Poverty and Culture: Some Basic Questions about Methods of Studying Life-Styles of the Poor, in P. Townsend (ed) *The Concept of Poverty: Working Papers on Methods of Investigation and Life-Styles of the Poor in Different Countries*, London: Heinemann, pp 146–64.

Gans, H. (1995) *The War Against the Poor: The Underclass and Antipoverty Policy*, New York: Basic Books.

Garland, D. (2001) *The Culture of Control: Crime and Social Order in Contemporary Society*, Oxford: Oxford University Press.

Garrett, P.M. (2007) "Sinbin" solutions: the "pioneer" projects for "problem families" and the forgetfulness of social policy research, *Critical Social Policy*, 27 (2): 203–30.

Garrett, P.M. (2013). *Social work and social theory*, Bristol: Policy Press.

Garside, R. (2012) Let them scrub floors, Centre for Crime and Justice Studies, 2 May, www.crimeandjustice.org.uk/resources/let-them-scrub-floors

Gentleman, A. (2013) Troubled families tsar: intervention programme will free up resources, *Guardian*, 7 April, www.theguardian.com/society/2013/apr/07/troubled-families-tsar-intervention-resources

Gillies, V. (2011) From Function to Competence: Engaging with the New Politics of Family, *Sociological Research Online*, 16 (4) 11, www.socresonline.org.uk/16/4/11.html

Gillies, V. (2014) Troubling Families: Parenting and the Politics of Early Intervention, in S. Wagg and J. Picher (eds) *Thatcher's Grandchildren? Politics and Childhood in the Twenty-First Century*, London: Palgrave, pp 204–24.

Gillies, V. (2016) *Pushed to the Edge: Inclusion and behaviour support in schools*, Bristol: Policy Press.

Gillies, V., Edwards, R. and Horsley, N. (2017) *Challenging the politics of early intervention: Who's 'saving' children and why*, Bristol: Policy Press.

Gold, T. (2011) 'Problem families' do not need an army of Hyacinth Buckets shouting at them, *Guardian*, 26 August, www.theguardian.com/commentisfree/2011/aug/26/working-families-everything-scheme-tanya-gold

Golding, P and Middleton, S. (1982) *Images of Welfare: Press and Public Attitudes to Poverty*, Oxford: Martin Robertson.

Gordon, D. (2011) *Consultation Response; Social Mobility & Child Poverty Review*, Policy Response Series No.2, www.poverty.ac.uk/system/files/WP%20Policy%20Response%20No.%202%20Consultation%20Resp%20Social%20Mobility%20&%20Child%20Poverty%20(Gordon%20Oct%202011).pdf

Gregg, D. (2010) Family *intervention projects: a classic case of policy-based evidence*, Centre for Crime and Justice Studies, www.crimeandjustice.org.uk/sites/crimeandjustice.org.uk/files/family%20intervention.pdf

Guardian (2005) An evening with Louise Casey, 7 July, www.theguardian.com/politics/2005/jul/07/ukcrime.whitehall

Gupta, A. (2017) Poverty and child neglect – the elephant in the room?, *Families, Relationships and Societies*, 6 (1): 21–36.

Gupta, A., Featherstone, Thoburn, J., Morris, K. and White, S. (2015) By rushing to speed up forced adoptions we are letting children down, *The Conversation*, 9 December, https://theconversation.com/by-rushing-to-speed-up-forced-adoptions-we-are-letting-children-down-51609

Hall, S., Critcher, C., Jefferson, T., Clarke, J. and Roberts, B. (1978) *Policing the crisis: mugging, the state and law and order*, Basingstoke: Palgrave Macmillan.

Hancock, L. and Mooney, G. (2012) "Welfare Ghettos" and the "Broken Society": Territorial Stigmatization in the Contemporary UK, *Housing, Theory and Society*, 30 (1): 46–64.

Hansard (2014) *Oral Answers to Questions*, 20 January, www.publications.parliament.uk/pa/cm201314/cmhansrd/cm140120/debtext/140120-0001.htm#140120-0001.htm_wqn14

Hansard (2015) *Welfare Reform and Work Bill (First Sitting)*, 10 September, Available at https://hansard.parliament.uk/Commons/2015-09-10/debates/ac862a78-3f21-4363-8200-64b42dffd2ca/WelfareReformAndWorkBill(FirstSitting)

Harrington, M. (1962) *The Other America: Poverty in the United States*, Harmondsworth: Penguin.

Harrison, E. (2010) *Working Families Everywhere is announced*, 10 December, https://web.archive.org/web/20110818180930/http://www.workingfamilieseverywhere.com/news/10/12/2010/working-families-everywhere-is-announced/

Hastings, A., Bailey, N., Bramley, G., Gannon, M. and Watkins, D. (2015) *The cost of the cuts: the impact on local government and poorer communities*, York: Joseph Rowntree Foundation

Hayden, C. and Jenkins, C. (2013) Children taken into care and custody and the 'troubled families' agenda in England, *Child & Family Social Work,* 20 (4): 459–69.

Hayden, C. and Jenkins, D. (2014) 'Troubled Families' Programme in England: 'wicked problems' and policy-based evidence, *Policy Studies*, 35 (6): 631–49.

Hellen, N. (2014) Rise of new underclass costs £30bn, *The Sunday Times*, 17 August, p 1.

Hencke, D. Wintour, P. and Mulholland, H. (2008) Cameron launches Tory 'broken society byelection' campaign, *Guardian*, 7 July, www.theguardian.com/politics/2008/jul/07/davidcameron.conservatives

Himmelfarb, G. (1984) *The idea of poverty: England in the early Industrial Age*, New York: Knopf.

Hirsch, D. (2010) Benefit uprating: a return to human decency?, *Poverty*, 141: 6–9.

HM Government (2010) *The Coalition: our programme for government*, London: Cabinet Office.

HM Government (2011) *A New Approach to Child Poverty: Tackling the Causes of Disadvantage and Transforming Families' Lives*, London: The Stationery Office.

HM Treasury (2013) *Spending Round 2013*, Cm 8639, London: HM Treasury.

HM Treasury (2014) *Budget 2014*, London: HM Treasury.

Hollander, G. (2012) On the Casey, *Inside Housing*, 28 September, www.insidehousing.co.uk/home/home/on-the-casey-33141

Holmes, D. (2015) Delivering Phase 1 of the Troubled Families Programme: A Provider's Perspective, in K. Davies (ed) *Social Work with Troubled Families: A critical introduction*, London: Jessica Kingsley, pp 30–52.

Holtby, W. (1988) *South Riding: An English Landscape*, London: Virago Press.

Home Office (2007) Innovative new help to tackle 'neighbours from hell', 11 April, http://webarchive.nationalarchives.gov.uk/20100405140447/http:/asb.homeoffice.gov.uk/members/news/article.aspx?id=10316

Hughes, G. (2007) *The Politics of Crime and Community*, Basingstoke: Palgrave.

Jensen, T. (2013) Welfare Commonsense, Poverty Porn and Doxosophy, *Sociological Research Online*, 19 (3) 3.

Jensen, T. (2014) A Summer of Television Poverty Porn, *The Sociological Imagination*, http://sociologicalimagination.org/archives/14013

Join-Lambert, H. (2016) Parental Involvement and Multi-Agency Support Services for High-Need Families in France, *Social Policy and Society*, 15 (2): 317–29.

Jones, H. (2015) Sociology as 'progress' and 'passion': a debate, Discover Society, 1 December, http://discoversociety.org/2015/12/01/focus-sociology-as-progress-and-passion-a-debate/

Jordan, B. (1974) *Poor Parents: Social Policy and the 'Cycle of Deprivation'*, London: Routledge and Kegan Paul.

Katz, M.B. (1989) *The Undeserving Poor: America's Enduring Confrontation With Poverty*, Oxford: Oxford University Press.

Kingdon, J.W. (1995) *Agendas, Alternatives and Public Policies* (2nd edition), New York: Longman.

Kirkup, J. (2008) James Purnell defends welfare reform after accusations of 'stigmatising' benefits claimants, *Telegraph*, 10 December, www.telegraph.co.uk/news/politics/labour/3700176/James-Purnell-defends-welfare-reform-after-accusations-of-stigmatising-benefits-claimants.html

Knijn, T. and Hopman, M. (2015) Parenting Support in the Dutch 'Participation Society', *Social Policy and Society*, 14 (4): 645–56.

Koven, S. (2004) *Slumming: Sexual and Social Politics in Victorian London*, Princeton, NJ: Princeton University Press.

Lambert, M. (2016) The Troubled Families fiasco should be a warning to children's services, *Community Care*, 21 October, www.communitycare.co.uk/2016/10/21/failure-troubled-families-programme-warning-childrens-services/

Lambert, M. (2017) 'Problem families' and the post-war welfare state in the North West of England, 1943-74, PhD, Lancaster University. DOI: 10.17635/lancaster/thesis/29

Leacock, E. (1971) *The culture of poverty: A critique*, New York: Simon & Schuster.

Lemert, E. (1951) *Social pathology; A systematic approach to the theory of sociopathic behaviour*, New York: McGraw-Hill.

Levitas, R. (1998) *The Inclusive Society? Social Exclusion and New Labour*, Houndmills: Macmillan.

Levitas, R. (2012a) There may be trouble ahead: What we know about those 120,000 'troubled families', Poverty and Social Exclusion, www.poverty.ac.uk/policy-response-working-papers-families-social-policy-life-chances-children-parenting-uk-government

Levitas, R. (2012b) Still not listening, Poverty and Social Exclusion, 17 July, www.poverty.ac.uk/articles-families/still-not-listening

Lewis, O. (1959) *Five families: Mexican case studies in the culture of poverty*, New York: Basic Books.

Lewis, O. (1961) *The children of Sanchez*, New York: Random House.

Lewis, O. (1965) *La Vida: A Puerto Rican family in the culture of poverty – San Juan and New York*, New York: Random House.

Lewis, P., Newburn, T., Taylor, M., Mcgillivray, C., Greenhill, A., Frayman, H. and Proctor, R. (2011) *Reading the Riots: Investigating England's summer of disorder*, LSE and the Guardian: London, http://eprints.lse.ac.uk/46297/1/Reading%20the%20riots(published).pdf

Lightowlers, C. (2015) Let's get real about the 'riots': Exploring the relationship between deprivation and the English summer disturbances of 2011, *Critical Social Policy*, 35 (1): 89–109.

Lipsky, M. (1980) *Street-level Bureaucracy; Dilemmas of the Individual in Public Services*, New York: Russell Sage Foundation.

Lister, R. (ed) (1996) *Charles Murray and the Underclass: The Developing Debate*, London: Institute for Economic Affairs (IEA).

Lister, R. and Bennett, F. (2010) The new 'champion of progressive ideals'? Cameron's Conservative Party: poverty, family policy and welfare reform, *Renewal*, 18 (1–2): 84–109.

Little, A. (2014) Welfare squads to target problem families costing UK £30bn, *Daily Express*, 18 August, p 1

Lloyd, C., Wollny, Y., White, C., Gowland, S. and Purdon, S. (2011) *Monitoring and evaluation of family intervention services and projects between February 2007 and March 2011*, London: DfE, www.education.gov.uk/publications/RSG/AllPublications/Page1/DFE-RR174

London Councils (2014) *Troubled Families Programme: Lessons for future public service reform*, London: London Councils.

London Edinburgh Weekend Return Group (1980) *In and Against the State*, London: Pluto Press.

Low, C.M., Grey-Thompson, T. and Meacher, M. (2015) *Halving The Gap? A Review into the Government's proposed reduction to Employment and Support Allowance and its impact on halving the disability employment gap*, London: Mencap, www.mencap.org.uk/sites/default/files/2016-08/esa-review-december-2015.pdf

Lowe, T. and Wilson, R. (2015) Playing the game of Outcomes-Based Performance Management. Is gamesmanship inevitable? Evidence from theory and practice, *Social Policy and Administration*, DOI: 10.1111/spol.12205

Lury, C. (2012) Going live: towards an amphibious sociology, *The Sociological Review*, 60 (S1): 184–97.

Macnicol, J. (1987) In pursuit of the underclass, *Journal of Social Policy*, 16 (3): 293–318.

Macnicol, J. (1999) From 'problem family' to 'underclass' 1945–95, in H. Fawcett and R. Lowe (eds) *Welfare policy in Britain: The road from 1945*, Basingstoke: Macmillan, pp 69–93.

Macnicol, J. (2017) Reconstructing the Underclass, *Social Policy and Society*, 16 (1): 99–108.

Mann, K. (1994) Watching the defectives: Observers of the underclass in the USA, Britain and Austialia, *Critical Social Policy*, 14 (41): 79–99.

Mann, K. and Roseneil, S. (1994) "Some Mothers Do 'Ave 'Em": backlash and the gender politics of the underclass debate, *Journal of Gender Studies* 3 (3): 317–31.

Martin, C. (2015) Parenting Support in France: Policy in an Ideological Battlefield, *Social Policy and Society*, 14 (4): 609–20.

Marx, G.T. (1972) (ed) *Muckraking Sociology: Research as Social Criticism*, New Brunswick, NJ: Transaction Books.

Marx, G.T. (1984) Notes On The Discovery, Collection, And Assessment Of Hidden And Dirty Data, in J. Schneider and J. Kitsuse (eds), *Studies in the Sociology of Social Problems*, Norwood, NJ: Ablex, pp 78–114.

Matthews, R. and Briggs, D. (2008) Lost in translation: interpreting and implementing anti-social behaviour policies, in P. Squires (ed) *ASBO Nation: The criminalisation of nuisance*, Bristol: Policy Press, pp 87–100.

May, T. (2011) Riots: Theresa May's speech on 11 August 2011, www.gov.uk/government/speeches/riots-theresa-mays-speech-on-11-august-2011

McGlone, F. (1990) Away from the Dependency Culture? Social Security Policy, in S.P. Savage and L. Robins (eds) *Public Policy under Thatcher*, Basingstoke: Palgrave Macmillan, pp 159–71.

McKibbin, R. (2002) *The Ideologies of Class: Social Relations in Britain 1880-1950*, Oxford: Clarendon.

McNeil, C. and Hunter, J. (2015) *Breaking Boundaries: Towards a 'Troubled Lives' programme for people facing multiple and complex needs*, London: IPPR.

McNeill, F., Burns, N., Halliday, S., Hutton, N. and Tata, C. (2009) Risk, responsibility and Reconfiguration: Penal adaptation and misadaptation, *Punishment and Society*, 11 (4): 419–42.

Miller W. B. (1958) Lower class culture as a generating milieu of gang delinquency, *Journal of Social Issues*, 14: 5–19.

Millie, A. (ed) (2009) *Securing Respect: Behavioural Expectations and Anti-Social Behaviour in the UK*, Bristol: Policy Press.

Millie, A., Jacobson, J., McDonald, E. and Hough, M. (2005) *Anti-social behaviour strategies: Finding a balance*, Bristol: Policy Press.

Mooney, G. (2009) The 'broken society' election: class hatred and the politics of poverty and place in Glasgow East, *Social Policy and Society*, 8 (4): 437–50.

Morris, L. (1994) *Dangerous Classes: The underclass and social citizenship*, London: Routledge

Morrison, J. and Symenliyska, E. (2001) Rough sleepers unit 'fiddled the figures', *Independent*, 23 December, www.independent.co.uk/news/uk/home-news/rough-sleepers-unit-fiddled-the-figures-5363227.html

Muir, R. and Parker, I. (2014) *Many to many: How the relational state will transform public services*, London: IPPR.

Murray, C. (1984) *Losing Ground: American Social Policy, 1950–1980*, New York: Basic Books.

Murray, C. (1990) *The Emerging British Underclass*, London: Institute of Economic Affairs.

Murray, C. (1994) *The Underclass: The Crisis Deepens*, London: Institute of Economic Affairs

Nader, L. (1972) Up the anthropologist: perspectives gained from studying up, in D.H. Hymes (ed) *Reinventing Anthropology*, New York: Pantheon Books, pp 284–311.

NatCen (2010) *ASB Family Intervention Projects: Monitoring and Evaluation*, Research Report DCSF-RR215, London: DCSF.

Neal, S. Mohan, G., Cochrane, A. and Bennett, K. (2016) 'You can't move in Hackney without bumping into an anthropologist': why certain places attract research attention, *Qualitative Research*, 16, (5): 491–507.

Newcastle City Council (2015) Cabinet Update, July 2015.

Nicolaus, M. (1968) Fat-cat Sociology: remarks at the American Sociological Association Convention, www.colorado.edu/Sociology/gimenez/fatcat.html

NIESR (2016) Written evidence from the National Institute of Economic and Social Research, 31 October, http://data.parliament.uk/writtenevidence/committeeevidence.svc/evidencedocument/public-accounts-committee/troubled-families/written/42437.html

Nixon, J., Parr, S., Hunter, C., Myers, S., Sanderson, D. and Whittle, S. (2006) *Anti-social Behaviour Intensive Family Support Projects: An evaluation of six pioneering projects*, London: DCLG.

Nixon, J., Parr, S., Hunter, C., Sanderson, D. and Whittle, S. (2008) *The longer term outcomes for families who had worked with Intensive Family Support Projects*, London: DCLG.

Nixon, J., Pawson, H. and Sosenko, P. (2010) Rolling out Anti-social Behaviour Families Projects in England and Scotland: Analysing the Rhetoric and Practice of Policy Transfer, *Social Policy and Administration*, 44 (3): 305–25.

North Tyneside Council (2014) Troubled Families Tsar visits North Tyneside, 27 February, www.northtyneside.gov.uk/browse-display.shtml?p_ID=551360&p_subjectCategory=23

Nunn, A. and Tepe-Belfrage, D. (2017) Disciplinary Social Policy and the Failing Promise of the New Middle Classes: The Troubled Families Programme, *Social Policy and Society*, 16 (1): 119–29.

Owen, J. (2013) Austerity is being exploited and children denied basic rights – report, *Independent*, 20 November, www.independent.co.uk/news/uk/home-news/austerity-is-being-exploited-and-children-denied-basic-rights-report-8950143.html

Parliament (2016) Government 'over-claimed' on performance of families programme, 20 December, https://www.parliament.uk/business/committees/committees-a-z/commons-select/public-accounts-committee/news-parliament-2015/troubled-families-report-published-16-17/

Parr, S. (2009) Family Intervention Projects: A Site of Social Work Practice, *British Journal of Social Work*, 39: 1256–73, doi:10.1093/bjsw/bcn057

Parr, S. and Nixon, J. (2008) Rationalising family intervention projects, in Squires, P. (ed) *ASBO nation: The criminalisation of nuisance*, Bristol: Policy Press, pp 161–79.

Parr, S. and Nixon, J. (2009) Family Intervention Projects: sites of subversion and resilience, in M. Barnes and D. Prior (eds) *Subversive Citizens: Power, agency and resistance in public services*, Bristol: Policy Press, pp 101–19.

Pascoe-Watson, G. (2008) Cam: I'll mend broken Britain, *The Sun*, 30 January.

Paton, K. (2015) The Future Imagination: Going Live, Getting Real, DIY, *The Sociological Review*, 24 November, www.thesociologicalreview.com/blog/the-future-imagination-going-live-getting-real-diy-1.html

Pearson, G. (1975) *The Deviant Imagination: Psychiatry, Social Work and Social Change*, Basingstoke: Macmillan Press.

Peckover, S. (2013) From 'public health' to 'safeguarding children': British health visiting in policy, practice and research, *Children and Society*, 27 (2): 116–26.

Phillips, M. (2011) Britain's liberal intelligentsia has smashed virtually every social value, *Daily Mail*, 11 August, www.dailymail.co.uk/debate/article-2024690/UK-riots-2011-Britains-liberal-intelligentsia-smashed-virtually-social-value.html#ixzz4h3Wr0UbW

Philp, A.F. and Timms, N. (1957) *The problem of 'the problem family': a critical review of the literature concerning the 'problem family' and its treatment*, London: Family Service Units.

Pickles, C. (2010) Repairing the Broken Society: The Way Forward, *Journal of Poverty and Social Justice*, 18 (2): 161–6.

Pickles, E. (2011) Action on problem families, 17 October, www.gov.uk/government/speeches/action-on-problem-families

Pine, L. (1995) Hashude: The imprisonment of 'Asocial' Families in the Third Reich, *German History*, 13 (2): 182–97.

Piven, F.F. and Cloward, R. (1971) *Regulating the Poor: The Functions of Public Welfare*, New York: Vintage Books.

Portes, J. (2015) A troubling attitude to statistics, 15 March, www.niesr.ac.uk/blog/troubling-attitude-statistics#.VuA8GPmLSM8

Portes, J. (2016) Troubled Families – anatomy of a policy disaster, 17 October, Available at http://notthetreasuryview.blogspot.co.uk/2016/10/troubled-families-anatomy-of-policy.html

Pressman, J.L. and Wildavsky, A. (1984) *How Great Expectations in Washington Are Dashed in Oakland; Or, Why It's Amazing that Federal Programs Work at All, This Being a Saga of the Economic Development Administration as Told by Two Sympathetic Observers Who Seek to Build Morals on a Foundation*, Berkeley: University of California Press.

Prior, D. (2009) Policy, power and the potential for counter-agency, in M. Barnes and D. Prior (eds) *Subversive Citizens: Power, agency and resistance in public services*, Bristol: Policy Press, pp 17–32.

Public Accounts Committee (2014) *Programmes to help families facing multiple challenges: Fifty-first Report of Session 2013–14* (HC 668), House of Commons Committee of Public Accounts, London: The Stationery Office.

Public Accounts Committee (2016a) *Public Accounts Committee Oral evidence: Troubled Families*, HC 711, 19 October, House of Commons Committee of Public Accounts, http://data.parliament.uk/writtenevidence/committeeevidence.svc/evidencedocument/public-accounts-committee/troubled-families/oral/41442.pdf

Public Accounts Committee (2016b) *Troubled families: progress review: Thirty-third Report of Session 2016–17*, HC 711, House of Commons Committee of Public Accounts, www.publications.parliament.uk/pa/cm201617/cmselect/cmpubacc/711/711.pdf

Purdon, S. and Bryson, C. (2016) *Evaluation of the Troubled Families Programme Technical report: impact evaluation using survey data*, London: DCLG.

Ramesh, R. (2012a) The civil servant who thinks she can fix troubled families, *Guardian*, 17 July, www.theguardian.com/society/2012/jul/17/louise-casey-troubled-families

Ramesh, R. (2012b) Troubled families tsar Louise Casey criticised over research, *Guardian*, 24 October, www.theguardian.com/society/2012/oct/24/families-tsar-louise-casey-criticised

Reed, H. (2012) *In the eye of the storm: Britain's forgotten children and families*, London: Action for Children/The Children's Society/ NSPCC, www.actionforchildren.org.uk/media/3212/in_the_eye_ of_the_storm.pdf

Rigdon, S. (1988) *The Culture Façade: Art, Science and Politics in the Work of Oscar Lewis*, Chicago: UIP.

Roach, J.L. and Gursslin, O.R. (1967) An Evaluation of the Concept 'Culture of Poverty', *Social Forces*, 45 (3): 383–92.

Robinson, F. and Gregson, N. (1992) The 'Underclass': a class apart?, *Critical Social Policy*, 12 (34): 38–51.

RTF (2006a) *Respect Action Plan*, London: Home Office.

RTF (2006b) *Family Intervention Projects*, London: Home Office.

Rutter, J. and Harris, J. (2014) *The Special Ones: How to make central government units work*, London: Institute for Government.

Rutter, M. and Madge, N. (1976) *Cycles of Disadvantage: A Review of Research*, London: Heinemann.Ryan, F. (2017) Painting disabled people as 'workshy': that's what benefits cuts are all about, *Guardian*, 30 March, www.theguardian.com/commentisfree/2017/mar/30/ disability-benefit-jobseekers-allowance-sick-workshy

Ryan, W. (1971) *Blaming the victim*, New York: Vintage Books.

Savage, M. (2017) Failed troubled families scheme gets a reboot, *The Times*, 17 February, www.thetimes.co.uk/article/failed-troubled- families-scheme-gets-a-reboot-zwswqw95n

Selwyn, R. (2016) *Pillars & Foundations: Next practice in children's Services*, Manchester: ADCS.

SESL (2013) *Implementing the Troubled Families Programme in the South East of England*, South East Strategic Leaders (SESL), http://documents. hants.gov.uk/sesl ImplementingTroubledFamiliesintheSouthEast 27SeptemberFinalVersion240913pdf.pdf

SETF (2007a) *Families At Risk: Background on families with multiple disadvantages*, London: Cabinet Office.

SETF (2007b) *Reaching Out: Think Family: Analysis and themes from the Families At Risk Review*, London: Cabinet Office.

SEU (2000) *Report of Policy Action Team 8: Anti-social behaviour*, London: Home Office.

Sherman, J., Ford, R. and Asthana, A. (2011) The big crackdown: Convicted rioters face loss of benefits: Cameron launches big crackdown, *The Times*, 16 August, p 1.

Sherraden, M.W. (1984) Working over the 'Underclass', *Social Work*, 29 (4): 391–2.

Shildrick, T., Macdonald, R., Furlong, A., Roden, J. and Crow, R. (2012) *Are cultures of worklessness passed down the generations?*, York: JRF.

Shildrick, T. and Macdonald, R. (2013) Poverty talk: how people experiencing poverty deny their poverty and why they blame 'the poor', *The Sociological Review*, 61 (2): 285–303.

Skeggs, B. (1997) *Formations of Class and Gender: Becoming Respectable*, London: Sage

Slater, T. (2014) The Myth of "Broken Britain": Welfare Reform and the Production of Ignorance, *Antipode*, 46 (4): 948–69.

Sparrow, A. (2008) James Purnell accused of introducing US 'workfare' with benefits reform, *Guardian*, 10 September, www.theguardian.com/politics/2008/dec/10/jamespurnell-welfare

Spector, M. and Kitsuse, J. (1977) *Constructing Social Problems*, New York: Aldine de Gruyter.

Spicker, P. (2013) Troubled Families: What is an 'official statistic'?, *Radical Statistics*, 108: 47–52.

Starkey, P. (2000) The feckless mother: women, poverty and social workers in wartime and post-war England, *Women's History Review*, 9 (3): 539–57.

Stabile, C.A. and Morooka, J. (2010) Between Two Evils, I Refuse To Choose The Lesser, *Cultural Studies*, 17 (3–4): 326–48.

Stedman Jones, G. (1971) *Outcast London: A Study in the Relationship Between Classes in Victorian Society*, London: Oxford University Press.

Stratton, A. (2013) Plan to divert benefits of troubled families scrapped, BBC News, 26 September, www.bbc.co.uk/news/uk-politics-24286726

Squires, P. (ed) (2008) *ASBO Nation: The criminalisation of nuisance*, Bristol: Policy Press.

Squires, P. and Stephen, D.E. (2005) *Rougher justice: Anti-social behaviour and young people*, Cullompton: Willan Publishing.

Swinford, S. (2013) Mothers in problem families should be given contraception, government adviser says, *Telegraph*, 10 September, www.telegraph.co.uk/news/10297486/Mothers-in-problem-families-should-be-given-contraception-government-adviser-says.html

Talbot, C. (2012) Louise Casey and "Listening to Troubled Families": an (almost) worthless piece of 'research' leading to dangerous policy prescriptions, Manchester Policy Blogs: Whitehall Watch, 28 July, http://blog.policy.manchester.ac.uk/whitehallwatch/2012/07/louise-casey-and-listening-to-troubled-families-an-almost-worthless-piece-of-research-leading-to-dangerous-policy-prescriptions-2

Taylor-Gooby, P. (2013) *The Double Crisis of the Welfare State and What We Can Do About It*, Basingstoke: Palgrave Macmillan.

Taylor-Gooby, P. and Dean, H. (1992) *Dependency Culture: The Explosion of a Myth*, Abingdon: Routledge.

Thane, P. (2010) *Happy Families? History and Family Policy*, London: The British Academy.

Tuke, J. (2014) Letter from Director Joe Tuke to Chief Executives of Local Authorities, Received via FOI: 1239015.

Tyler, I. (2013) The riots of the underclass? Stigmatisation, mediation and the government of poverty and disadvantage in neoliberal Britain, *Sociological Research Online*, 18 (4) 6, www.socresonline.org.uk/18/4/6.html

UNCRPD (United Nations Committee on the Rights of Persons with Disabilities) (2016) Inquiry concerning the United Kingdom of Great Britain and Northern Ireland carried out by the Committee under article 6 of the Optional Protocol to the Convention: Report of the Committee, United Nations Committee on the Rights of Persons with Disabilities, www.ohchr.org/EN/HRBodies/CRPD/Pages/InquiryProcedure.aspx

Valentine, C. (1968) *Culture and Poverty*, London: UCP.

Van Wel, F. (1992) A century of families under supervision in the Netherlands, *British Journal of Social Work*, 22 (2): 147–66.

Wacquant, L. (2009a) *Punishing the Poor: The Neoliberal Government of Social Insecurity*, Durham, NC: Duke University Press.

Wacquant, L. (2009b) *Prisons of Poverty*, Minneapolis: University of Minnesota Press.

Walker, D. (2003) Civil servant squares up to anti-social behaviour, *Guardian*, 2 January, www.theguardian.com/uk/2003/jan/02/ukcrime.whitehall

Wastell, D. and White, S. (2012) Blinded by neuroscience: social policy, the family and the infant brain, *Families, Relationships and Societies*, 1 (3): 397–414.

Watt, N. and Wintour, P. (2008) Our next prime minister?, *Guardian*, 16 July, www.theguardian.com/politics/2008/jul/16/davidcameron.conservatives

Waxman, C.I. (1983) *The Stigma of Poverty: A Critique of Poverty Theories and Policies*, Oxford: Pergamon Press.

Webster, D. (2015) *Benefit sanctions: Britain's secret penal system*, 26 January, www.crimeandjustice.org.uk/resources/benefit-sanctions-britains-secret-penal-system

Welshman, J. (2012a) *From transmitted deprivation to social exclusion: Policy, poverty and parenting*, Bristol: Policy Press.

Welshman, J. (2012b) History graduate Louise Casey, Head of the Government's #Troubled Families Unit, doesn't seem very aware of history, 8 November, https://twitter.com/johnwelshman1/status/266600347198435328

Welshman, J. (2013) *Underclass: A History of the Excluded* (2nd edition), London: Hambledon/Continuum.

Welshman, J. (2017) Troubles and the Family: Changes and Continuities Since 1943, *Social Policy and Society*, 16 (1): 109–18.

Wenham, A. (2017) Struggles and Silences: Young People and the 'Troubled Families Programme', *Social Policy and Society*, 16 (1): 143–53.

White, C. and Day, L. (2016) *National Evaluation of the Troubled Families Programme: Process evaluation final report*, London: DCLG.

White, C., Warrener, M., Reeves, A. and La Valle, I. (2008) *Family Intervention Projects: An Evaluation of Their Design, Setup and Early Outcomes*, DCSF-RW047, DCSF: London.

Whitley, J. (2016) *National Evaluation of the Troubled Families Programme: Final Report on the Family Monitoring Data*, London: DCLG.

Wiggins, K. (2012) Councils question troubled families numbers, *Local Government Chronicle*, 13 August, www.lgcplus.com/briefings/services/childrens-services/councils-question-troubled-families-numbers/5048165.article

Williams, Z. (2012) The real 'problem' with these families is that they're poor, *Guardian*, 18 July, www.theguardian.com/commentisfree/2012/jul/18/problem-families-poverty

Wills, R. Whittaker, A., Rickard, W. and Felix, C. (2016) Troubled, Troubling or in Trouble: The stories of 'Troubled Families', *British Journal of Social Work*, Advance Access doi:10.1093/bjsw/bcw061.

Wilson, W. (2015) *Housing cost element of Universal Credit: withdrawing entitlement from 18–21 year olds*, House of Commons Library, Briefing Paper Number 06473, 8 March.

Winnett, R. and Kirkup, J. (2012) Problem families have 'too many children', *Telegraph*, 20 July, www.telegraph.co.uk/news/politics/9416535/Problem-families-have-too-many-children.html

Women's Group on Public Welfare (1943) *Our Towns: A Close-Up*, London: Oxford University Press.

Wootton, B. (1959) Daddy Knows Best, *The Twentieth Century*, October: 248–61.

Wright Mills, C. (1959) *The Sociological Imagination*, Oxford: Oxford University Press.

Index

U

underclass 4, 16, 21, 22, 23, 30–2, 37,
    38–9
  research 141, 142–5, 161
  riots 1, 42, 49, 86
  US 11, 30
  see also troubled families
Underclass: The Crisis Deepens (Murray)
    31–2
Understanding Troubled Families (DCLG)
    18, 66, 152–4, 158
unemployables 26
unemployment *see* worklessness
United Nations Committee on the
    Rights of Persons with Disabilities
    (UNCRPD) 88
Universal Credit 87
USA
  research 143, 144
  underclass 11, 30, 144

V

van Wel, F. 101–2
Veit-Wilson, J. 33
Vignoles, Anna 158

W

Wacquant, Loïc 12
  neoliberalism 17, 55, 84, 85–6, 94,
    95, 97
  poverty 37, 184
Walker, D. 53
Waxman, C.I. 24
Webster, David 89–90
Welfare Reform and Work Act 2016
    73, 95
welfare system
  dependency culture 4–5, 23, 30, 32,
    37–8, 47, 164
  reforms 17, 84, 87–91, 94–6, 97, 161
Welshman, J. 25, 26, 27, 28, 100, 142
Wenham, A. 126
White, C. 115, 169–70
Wildavsky, A. 121
Women's Group on Public Welfare 27
Wood Committee 26–7
Wootton, Barbara 118
Work Programme 5
Working Families Everywhere (WFE)
    42, 46, 47, 50, 54, 60, 112
Working with Troubled Families (DCLG)
    114–15, 170–1
worklessness 2, 47

greater focus on 64, 75–6, 77–81,
    176–8, 183
reasons for 154
troubled families criteria 3, 4, 21, 35,
    38, 55, 66
see also employment